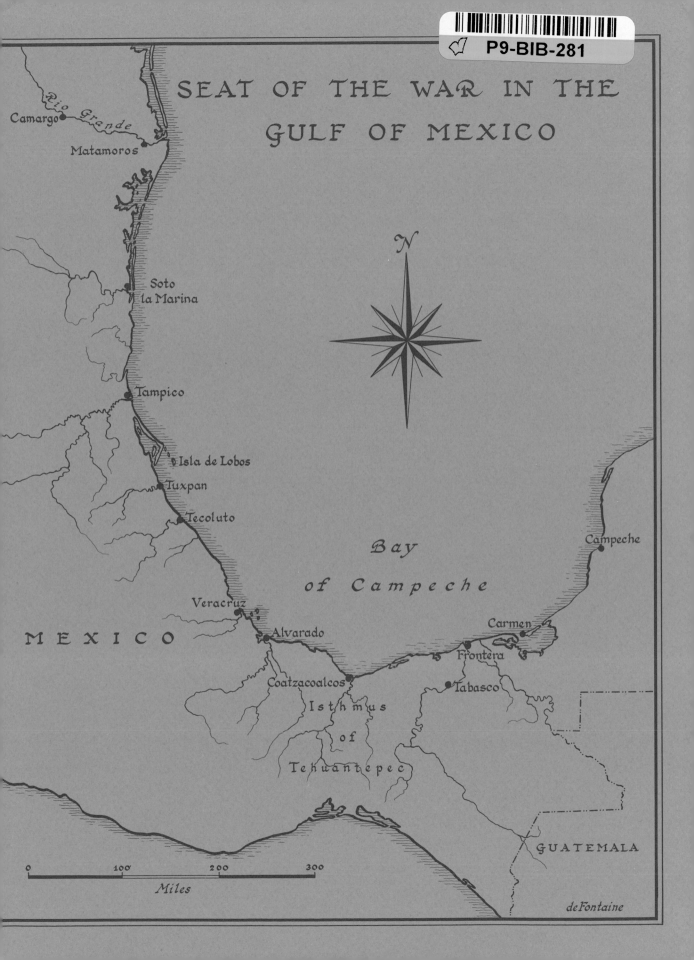

SEAT OF THE WAR IN THE GULF OF MEXICO

N

Rio Grande

Camargo

Matamoros

Soto la Marina

Tampico

Isla de Lobos

Tuxpan

Tecoluto

Bay

of Campeche

Campeche

Veracruz

Alvarado

Carmen

Frontera

MEXICO

Coatzacoalcos

Tabasco

Isthmus

of

Tehuantepec

GUATEMALA

0   100   200   300

Miles

deFontaine

SURFBOATS AND HORSE MARINES

SURFBOATS AND HORSE MARINES

U. S. Naval Operations in the Mexican War, 1846-48

K. JACK BAUER

United States Naval Institute, Annapolis, Maryland

To
the memory of
JOHN ALLEN KINNAMAN,
friend and scholar

PREFACE

Naval operations during the Mexican War have never been treated in the detail they deserve. No naval historian has devoted an entire work to them, and the attention given them by general historians has, necessarily, been limited and interspersed among other events. Few monographs have been written on specific naval operations or specific naval problems that arose in the course of the war, and the majority of them leave much to be desired. This work, then, is an attempt to present, between the covers of one book, a detailed history that deals only with the naval operations that took place during the Mexican War.

The two theatres in which the war was fought—the Gulf of Mexico in the East, and the Pacific Ocean in the West—were both a long way from Washington, and they were a long way from one another.

Communications in the mid-nineteenth century permitted the authorities in Washington to direct operations only in the most general manner. It was not unusual for a message to take a month to reach the commander in the Gulf of Mexico, or for a message to the Pacific coast to take three months to reach its destination.

Since there was little opportunity for coordination of the operations in the two theatres, it is fortunate that there was also little need for it. In effect, the war fought by the naval forces in the Gulf was distinct from the one fought in the Pacific. The lack of relationship between their operations permits me to treat the two theatres separately and, thus, to minimize interruptions in the flow of the narrative. The first part of the book will concentrate on the war in the Gulf of Mexico, and the second on the war in the Pacific.

I am indebted to the officers and staffs of the following libraries and repositories, not only for allowing me to use their collections, but also for their kindnesses and generous help: National Archives, Navy Department

Library, Historical Branch of the U.S. Marine Corps, Library of Congress, Bancroft Library of the University of California, Henry E. Huntington Library and Art Gallery, Indiana University Library, Sterling Memorial Library of Yale University, New York Public Library, Franklin D. Roosevelt Library, Massachusetts Historical Society, Los Angeles Public Library, Library of the California Historical Society, and the Library of the Society of California Pioneers.

My thanks go to Samuel Eliot Morison, who most graciously allowed me to read pertinent portions of his biography of Commodore Perry, *"Old Bruin:" Commodore Matthew Calbraith Perry*, while it was still in manuscript form, and to Robert L. Scheina, who took time from his busy schedule to prepare the appendix on the Mexican Navy.

Many other people have, by contributing their time and knowledge, aided in the preparation of this book. Space does not permit me to mention them all, but I cannot fail to record the help given by Albert L. Kohlmeier, Oscar O. Winther, William K. Shonkweiler, Robert W. Krauskopf, and William H. Russell. To all of them, named and unnamed, go my very deep appreciation and gratitude.

Special thanks go to my wife, Dorothy, who not only struggled through the preparation of this book, but typed most of the numerous drafts through which it has passed.

K. Jack Bauer

Troy, New York
April 1969

TABLE OF CONTENTS

APPENDIXES

LIST OF ILLUSTRATIONS

*One of a series of water-color sketches done by Lieutenant Henry Walke, U.S. Navy, who served on board the *Vesuvius*.

**One of a series of water-color sketches done by Gunner William H. Meyers, of Philadelphia, who served on board the *Dale*.

Unless otherwise indicated, the illustrations were provided by the U.S. Navy. Maps and plans are by Dorothy de Fontaine.

WAR IN THE GULF OF MEXICO

I

TENSION IN TEXAS

The background of the Mexican War as it was fought in the Gulf of Mexico lies in the history of the settlement and development of Texas, in Mexican-American relations, and in Manifest Destiny.

Like Mexico, Texas originally formed part of the vast Spanish empire in the New World. Unlike Mexico, however, it was not settled by the Spaniards until nearly the end of the seventeenth century, and then only as a buffer against the growing French power in Louisiana. Under the terms of the Treaty of Fontainebleau in 1762, France ceded Louisiana to Spain and, thereafter, Spanish interest in Texas waned. Although it rose again after the Louisiana Purchase in 1803, preoccupation with the Napoleonic wars and with the revolt of her American colonies prevented Spain from taking any significant steps towards further colonization.

In 1821, just prior to their exit from Mexico and their consequent loss of control over Texas, the Spanish authorities had granted Moses Austin permission to settle a few families of Americans in Texas. Before Austin could carry out his plans or even get his permission confirmed by the new government of Mexico, he died. However, in that same year, 1821, his son Stephen secured a new land grant from Mexico, and a number of Americans, attracted by Mexico's liberal land laws, followed the Austins. So many Americans went to Texas that the Mexican government grew fearful of and increasingly hostile to American immigration. In 1830 these apprehensions culminated in legislation prohibiting further American colonization of Texas and abolishing slavery there, and in threats to settle the country with convicts. Although the Mexican government never enforced the immigration laws, the threat that it might do so hung heavily over the heads of the American settlers in Texas.

Suspecting that a centralized form of government in Mexico would try to

3

exert even greater control over them, the Texans supported the proponents of Mexican federalism. Consequently, when the government of General Antonio López de Santa Anna, who had become president in 1834, framed a centralist constitution in 1835, they refused to accept it.

Under the circumstances, it was natural that there should be a clash between the Texans and the Mexican authorities—indeed, probably nothing short of the complete subjugation of Texas could have prevented it. Antagonism began to build up during 1834; irresponsible and irrepressible parties of Texans took the offensive in October 1835 and, by December, had captured Goliad and San Antonio. In November a provisional government of Texas was established and, the following month, Santa Anna countered by leading an army against the insurgents.

On 2 March 1836, while Santa Anna was besieging the Alamo, the Texans proclaimed their independence: David G. Burnet was elected provisional president, Sam Houston was made commander of the Army, and the rudiments of a navy were acquired. Shortly afterwards, on 21 April, the Texans captured Santa Anna at the Battle of San Jacinto and the Texas Revolution was over.

Throughout the Revolution, there was U.S. sympathy for the Texans and many Americans, influenced by the prospect of cheap land, by a love of adventure, or by a sense of mission, went to help them. They did so in spite of the U.S. neutrality laws—laws whose enforcement was haphazard, at best. Considering the conditions prevailing at the time, it would have been nearly impossible for any government effectively to prevent assistance going from the United States to Texas: transportation facilities were poor, there were no means of rapid communication, and the sentiments of the population living along the Texas border were strongly pro-Texan. Nevertheless, the official attitude of the government of the United States was one of neutrality and, even if sympathies lay with the Texans, attempts were made to enforce the letter of the law.

Overland communications between Mexico and Texas were virtually non-existent, and the Mexican army used against the Texans had to be supplied by sea. Consequently, the policy pursued by the U.S. Navy was very important, and orders issued to naval officers during the Texas Revolution show that the United States refused to intervene, even surreptitiously, to the advantage of the Texans. In fact, much of the logistic support for the Mexican army in Texas came from New Orleans, and the United States could have cut off that source of supplies without using naval force. The mere presence of a Mexican army in Texas required the sufferance of the United States and especially of its Navy.

During the fighting between Texas and Mexico, vessels of the U.S. West

DAVID CONNER

India Squadron cruised the Gulf of Mexico in order to see that blockades were real, not paper, ones and that no American vessel was taken illegally. Both Mexican and Texan warships were seized for making illegal captures, and both Mexican and Texan paper blockades were raised. Commodore Alexander J. Dallas, U.S. Navy, even instituted convoys for vessels bound for Mexico and Texas, much to the dissatisfaction of the Texans.

Although the two belligerents kept up a desultory war at sea for some time, the active war in Texas had ceased by the spring of 1837, and the pressure on Commodore Dallas' squadron had eased. Except for a short-lived Texan blockade of Mexico in 1842, nothing that occurred on the seas required the full attention of the West India Squadron, or, as it became in 1841, the Home Squadron.

With the appointment on 30 December 1843 of Commodore David Conner to command of the Home Squadron, there appeared on the scene the man who was to direct the squadron during the three trying years that followed. A former Navy Commissioner, he had just completed a short tour as the first chief of the Navy's Bureau of Construction, Equipment and Repair. Conner was an admirable choice, for he was an able and brave officer and an accomplished linguist who spoke both French and Spanish. Something of a dandy, he was reputedly the best-dressed officer in the service, and he enjoyed music and had a reputation as a good dancer. He was also considered to be one of the best seamen in the Navy. His thoughtfulness, prudence, judgment, and fidelity left nothing to be desired but, having served through the thirty-year stagnation that followed the War of 1812, he lacked the capacity for making quick decisions, and this unfortunately strengthened his natural overcautiousness. A wound he received during the War of 1812 left him with facial neuralgia which at times incapacitated him.

During 1844 President John Tyler and his Secretaries of State, Abel P. Upshur and his successor John C. Calhoun, negotiated a treaty of annexation with Texas. Tyler feared that Mexico, which had yet to recognize Texan independence, might attempt an invasion prior to the ratification of the treaty. Sam Houston, at that time President of Texas, had the same fear and had agreed to the annexation treaty on the condition that, during the period between its signing and its ratification, the United States would provide Texas with military and naval protection along its southwestern border and along its coast. Accordingly, the Secretary of the Navy, John Y. Mason, on 15 April ordered Commodore Conner to concentrate his force in Mexican waters and to proceed as follows, in the event of a Mexican invasion:

> You will remonstrate with the commanding officer, and you will accompany your remonstrance with the assurance that, the President of the United States will regard the execution of such a hostile purpose towards Texas, under such circumstances, as evincing a most unfriendly spirit towards the United States, and which, in the event of the Treaty's ratification, must lead to actual hostilities with this country.

Conner's orders to protect Texas during the interim period were hardly extraordinary. It was natural and proper that a country acquiring new territory should protect that territory against invasion during the period of acquisition. That the territory under consideration was a sovereign state technically at war with a third state did not change the case. However, the treaty of annexation was rejected by the U.S. Senate on 8 June 1844, and Conner received orders to return his vessels to their normal cruising stations.

Following the victory of the expansionist James K. Polk in the presidential election of 1844, President Tyler recommended that Texas be annexed to the United States by a joint resolution of both houses of Congress. Such a resolution was passed, and was signed by President Tyler on 1 March 1845. Before the annexation could be completed, however, the Texans had to accept the terms of the joint resolution, and it again appeared possible that Mexico might invade Texas or declare war on the United States on the grounds that the latter was attempting to annex what Mexico still considered part of her own territory. When the Mexican Minister to Washington demanded his passport on 6 March, it appeared that one or both of those possibilities would become reality, and on 20 March Commodore Conner's

GEORGE BANCROFT
Library of Congress

squadron was ordered back to Mexican waters. On the last day of March, Mexico broke off diplomatic relations with the United States.

Commodore Robert F. Stockton was in Philadelphia preparing to sail for Europe with a special squadron consisting of his own vessel, the steamer *Princeton*, the sloops of war *St. Mary's* (Commander John L. Saunders) and *Saratoga* (Commander Irvine Shubrick), and the brig *Porpoise* (Lieutenant William E. Hunt). In order to strengthen Conner's force in Mexican waters, the new Secretary of the Navy, George Bancroft, directed Stockton to report instead to Conner at Veracruz and to remain with Conner as long as the threat of hostilities existed.

Conner in his flagship, the frigate *Potomac* (Captain John Gwinn), along with the sloop of war *Falmouth* (Commander Joseph R. Jarvis), and the brigs *Lawrence* (Commander Samuel Mercer) and *Somers* (Commander Duncan N. Ingraham), anchored in the roadstead of Antón Lizardo, the anchorage for Veracruz, on 18 April. Midshipman William H. Parker, who was serving in the squadron, described the visit as somber, with shore leave being replaced by gunnery exercises and the crews on half-rations of water.

On 22 April Stockton was ordered to take his squadron to Galveston before joining Conner at Veracruz; to consider Texas a part of the United States as soon as she accepted the joint resolution; and, when that moment arrived, to consider an invasion of Texas an invasion of the United States.

Although relations between the United States and Mexico were deteriorating, Conner took a singularly optimistic view of them. On 10 May he reported that peace between Texas and Mexico might quite possibly be maintained and that a declaration of war against the United States was not imminent. Two weeks later, he qualified his report by noting that, should the government of General José Joaquín Herrera fall, war might develop. General Herrera opposed going to war with the United States.

A month later, on 23 June, the Commodore advised that in his opinion the Mexicans would not begin hostilities until after their elections in August. At the same time, he reported that the Castle of San Juan de Ulloa, commanding Veracruz and its small harbor, had been rebuilt and considerably strengthened, and he listed the vessels of the Mexican Navy, noting that all of them were shorthanded and most of them in need of repair.

On 3 July Secretary Bancroft advised Conner that the *St. Mary's*, the *Saratoga*, and the *Porpoise* were being withdrawn from Stockton's force and placed under his direct command, and that the steamer *Mississippi* (Captain Andrew Fitzhugh) and the sloop *John Adams* (Commander William J. McCluney) would soon sail from the United States for the Gulf. Commodore Stockton in the *Princeton* was ordered to return to Philadelphia.

Major General Zachary Taylor had been chosen to command the U.S. Army at the Texas border, and orders for his operations following the annexation of Texas were issued before those for Conner were written on 11 July. Conner was directed:

"When you ascertain, satisfactorily, that the Texas convention . . . has also acceded to annexation, You will regard Texas as a part of your country. . . . You are charged to commit no act of aggression; and, at the same time, you are invested with the command of a force sufficient to take from others a disposition to hostile acts. . . . That you may precisely understand what is meant by the aggression which you are instructed to avoid, I will add that while the annexation of Texas extends our boundary to the Del Norte [Rio Grande], the President reserves the vindication of our boundary, if possible, to methods of peace. You will, therefore, not employ force to dislodge Mexican troops from any post east of the Del Norte which was in the actual possession of the Mexicans at the time of annexation. While the action of Mexico is uncertain, you will employ the force under your command, with a just regard to the health of the officers and men at this season of the year, in such a manner as will be most likely to disincline Mexico to acts of hostility, and will keep you fully informed of the movements of that power. Should Mexico declare war, you will at once dislodge her troops from any post she may have east of the mouth of the Del Norte; take possession of Tampico; and *if your force is sufficient*, will take the castle of San Juan d'Ulloa . . ."

To carry out these orders, Conner had at hand the frigate *Potomac*, the sloops *Falmouth*, *Saratoga*, and *St. Mary's*, and the brigs *Somers*, *Porpoise*, and *Lawrence*. He was awaiting the arrival of the sloop *John Adams* and of the steamers *Mississippi* and *Princeton* (Commander Frederick Engle), the latter steamer being scheduled to return from Philadelphia.

A Texan convention accepted the terms of the annexation on 4 July, and General Taylor prepared to move into Texas by water. He wrote Conner requesting a convoy for his transports from New Orleans to Corpus Christi. Conner complied by dispatching the *St. Mary's* with orders to escort the transports; to assist the troops in landing; and then to cruise in the vicinity of Corpus Christi. Taylor's force embarked at New Orleans during 22 and 23 July and, on 25 July, set up a temporary camp on St. Joseph's Island in Aransas Bay, near Corpus Christi.

On 11 August Conner reported that persistent rumors to the effect that Mexico had decided on war were nothing more than talk for Mexican consumption and should be discounted. Even so, on 16 August, Bancroft directed him to keep part of his squadron positioned so that it could intercept supplies destined for the Mexican Army on the Rio Grande, in case war should break out. Also, while reminding Conner that the "policy of the government is the preservation of peace, if possible," he requested an estimate of the force that would be necessary to take San Juan de Ulloa.

The Cabinet in Washington decided on 29 August to order Conner to blockade the Mexican ports on the Gulf of Mexico—exclusive of Tabasco and those in Yucatán—as soon as he learned that war had broken out. The day after that decision was made, Secretary Bancroft wrote to Conner to advise him that he should consider that war had begun if a sizable Mexican force crossed the Rio Grande or if the Mexicans attacked an American vessel. Another decision relating to naval operations in the event of war with Mexico was reached by the Cabinet on 2 September: to follow French practice and treat as pirates any foreigners caught operating under Mexican letters of marque.

Replying to an earlier inquiry from Bancroft about the needs of the squadron in case of war, Conner reported on 3 September that his force was sufficient to protect American commerce and to blockade the Mexican ports, but he suggested that, because most Mexican ports lie up rivers that have shallow bars at their mouths, some vessels drawing not more than eight or ten feet of water be sent out to him. In response to the question about the force needed to capture the Castle of San Juan de Ulloa, he estimated that two ships-of-the-line, three large frigates, and a pair of bomb vessels mounting 13-inch mortars would be needed. Three days later, Conner amended his estimate to include a steamer, because the calms prevalent in the Gulf of Mexico during the autumn hampered the movement of his sailing craft.

In the hopes of avoiding the war that seemed inevitable, the Cabinet decided in mid-September to take the initiative in reopening diplomatic relations with Mexico by appointing John Slidell, a former congressman from Louisiana, minister to Mexico. In order to be prepared to back up Slidell's mission, Conner assembled his squadron at Veracruz. However, on 17 October, John Black, U.S. Consul at Mexico City, advised Secretary of State James Buchanan that the Mexicans were willing to receive a new American minister on the condition that Conner withdraw his squadron from Veracruz. Without waiting for orders, Conner acceded to the Mexican condition and withdrew his ships on 31 October.

The *Potomac*, the *Princeton*, and the small dispatch schooner *On-ka-hy-e* (Lieutenant Arthur Sinclair), which had come down from Texas, were in need of repairs which the primitive Navy Yard at Pensacola could not handle, so Conner took advantage of the lull to send them to Norfolk. After the departure of the *Potomac*, he wore his pennant in the *Falmouth*. In December, on orders from the Navy Department, he detached the *Saratoga* to the Brazil Squadron.

With instructions to settle the dispute over the boundary of Texas and, if possible, to negotiate the U.S. purchase of California and New Mexico, John Slidell disembarked from the *St. Mary's* at Veracruz on 30 November. After a courteous reception there, he made his way to Mexico City, only to learn that General Herrera's tottering government was certain to fall if it showed any willingness to negotiate with the Americans and, consequently, did not dare receive him. Although Herrera made his refusal to receive Slidell final on 21 December, his government fell on the 31st, two days after President Polk had signed the joint resolution admitting Texas into the Union. The new government of Mexico, headed by General Mariano Paredes y Arrillaga, was intensely anti-American, and his persistent attempts to reopen negotiations having been rebuffed, Slidell abandoned his mission and sailed from Veracruz for New Orleans in the steamer *Mississippi* on 30 March 1846.

While Slidell was in Mexico, the vessels of Conner's squadron carried the minister-designate's reports to his government and the latter's instructions to him. On 17 January 1846, acting on a Cabinet decision, Secretary Bancroft ordered Conner to leave the *Mississippi* and a sailing vessel at Pensacola to continue that dispatch service but once again to assemble the rest of his squadron at Veracruz. He informed Conner that on 13 January General Taylor had been ordered to move his forces to the Rio Grande, instructed the Commodore to send a sailing vessel to cooperate with Taylor, and promised to send reinforcements to Conner. This policy, a reversal of that in effect during the negotiations when the squadron had been withdrawn from Mexican waters, was intended to pressure the Mexican government into reopening negotiations with the United States.

The Frigate *Cumberland*

The *Falmouth*, with the Commodore aboard, and the *John Adams* left Pensacola on 6 February and, eleven days later, joined the *Lawrence* and the *Porpoise* at the anchorage behind Sacrificios Island, off Veracruz. The *St. Mary's*, carrying a letter from Conner to General Taylor, telling him that the squadron was returning to Veracruz and asking him how the Navy could best cooperate with the Army, sailed from Pensacola for Texas four days after the Commodore left.

General Taylor asked the authorities in Washington for a shallow-draft naval vessel to cover his left flank as he marched his force down the Texas coast and to convoy his transports. Secretary Bancroft responded by ordering the *Somers* to be sent to his aid: her draft was not shallow enough to answer fully Taylor's needs, but no other available vessel was any better. However, as things turned out, it was the *Lawrence* that answered Taylor's appeal, and she was joined by the *Porpoise*, which Commodore Conner ordered into Texas waters on 2 March.

General Taylor began his march south from Corpus Christi on 8 March, before the promised naval support had arrived. He partially solved his problem by borrowing the revenue cutter *Woodbury* to convoy his transports, and on 11 March the *Porpoise* arrived off Aransas Bay, in time to assist the *Woodbury*. Taylor chose as his base Point Isabel, on Brazos Santiago, a shallow arm of the sea just north of the mouth of the Rio Grande, and arrived there with a cavalry escort on 23 March. Within a half-hour of his arrival, the transports came in. Over the bar of Brazos Santiago, the water was only eight and one-half feet deep, and was still shallower inside the bar, so the *Porpoise*, the *Woodbury*, and the *Lawrence*—the last-named having joined the escort just before it arrived at the Brazos—had to anchor outside, five miles from the post. They remained there while Taylor's army moved into its encampment opposite Matamoros on the Rio Grande. When that operation had been completed, Taylor released the *Porpoise*, which left for Pensacola on 26 March, and he sent the *Woodbury* back to her regular station at Galveston.

Meanwhile, some of the reinforcements promised Conner had arrived and, on 5 April, the Home Squadron consisted of the frigates *Cumberland* (Captain Bladen Dulany) and *Potomac*, the latter having returned from Norfolk on 1 April, and the sloops *Falmouth*, *John Adams*, and *St. Mary's* at Sacrificios; the steamer *Mississippi*, having dropped Slidell at South West Pass, was going on to Pensacola; the brig *Lawrence* off Brazos Santiago; and the brigs *Porpoise* and *Somers* at Pensacola.

On 19 March, from aboard his new flagship, the frigate *Cumberland*, at Veracruz, Conner had reported that Mexico was in too exhausted a condition to declare war and had repeated his belief that she would not fight. Still of that opinion on 9 April, he requested permission to withdraw part of the squadron from Veracruz during the yellow-fever season. The request was granted, but hostilities began before the move could be made.

Apparently believing that an exchange of notes between himself and General Pedro de Ampudia, the Mexican commander at Matamoros, concerning the American advance to the Rio Grande foreshadowed an early outbreak of hostilities and that he would be negligent if he allowed any more supplies to reach the Mexican Army, General Taylor proclaimed a blockade of the Rio Grande. Consequently, on 17 April when the *Lawrence* and the newly arrived revenue cutter *Santa Anna* sighted the schooners *Equity* and *Floridian* bound from New Orleans to Matamoros with supplies for the Mexican Army, they stopped them and warned them off. Five days after that incident, Ampudia protested the blockade and, indeed, it is hard to find any justification for it, since the war had not begun and the United States did not claim jurisdiction over the south bank of the river. Nevertheless, the Rio Grande remained closed to Mexican shipping.

While the probability of war on the Rio Grande increased, Conner was attempting to solve the problem of his dwindling water supply at Veracruz and, at the same time, to keep his squadron at maximum strength, by sending his vessels, one by one, to Pensacola to refill their water tanks. The first to go was the *St. Mary's* on 18 April, but her departure was more than offset by the arrival five days later of the frigate *Raritan* (Captain Francis H. Gregory) from the Brazil Squadron, and of the brig *Somers* from Pensacola on the last day of the month.

II

WAR STARTS IN THE GULF

On 3 May 1846 Commodore David Conner was at Veracruz with the frigates *Cumberland*, *Raritan*, and *Potomac*, the sloops of war *John Adams* and *Falmouth*, and the brig *Somers*. That day he received a copy of a manifesto by Mexican President Paredes (apparently one dated 23 April, in which he declared a defensive war) from which he deduced that, given an opportunity, the Mexicans would attack General Taylor's army. The Commodore decided to take his squadron to the Rio Grande, in the hope that its presence would deter them.

The following morning Conner in the *Cumberland* left Veracruz for the Brazos with the *Raritan*, the *Potomac*, the *John Adams*, and the *Somers*. He left the dull-sailing *Falmouth* at Veracruz to watch over American interests and, in case of hostilities, to blockade, and ordered the sloop of war *St. Mary's* to join him at the Brazos as soon as she had completed watering at Pensacola.

The Commodore had kept his fear of a Mexican attack to himself, and both officers and men were taken by surprise when the squadron suddenly put to sea. However, they realized that "something was in the wind" when extensive small-arms drills were ordered. Late on the morning of 8 May the squadron reached Brazos Santiago but, because of the bar at the mouth of the bay, anchored outside, about five miles from Point Isabel. Shortly after noon, the sound of firing to the west announced that Conner had arrived too late to prevent the attack he feared.

During the afternoon, Major John Monroe, commander of Fort Polk, the Army's supply base at Point Isabel, became concerned over the safety of the fort and asked Conner for help. Conner responded by sending to his assistance the commander of the *Raritan*, Captain Gregory, with 500 sailors and Marines in the Army steamer *Monmouth*. Gregory's men took up positions

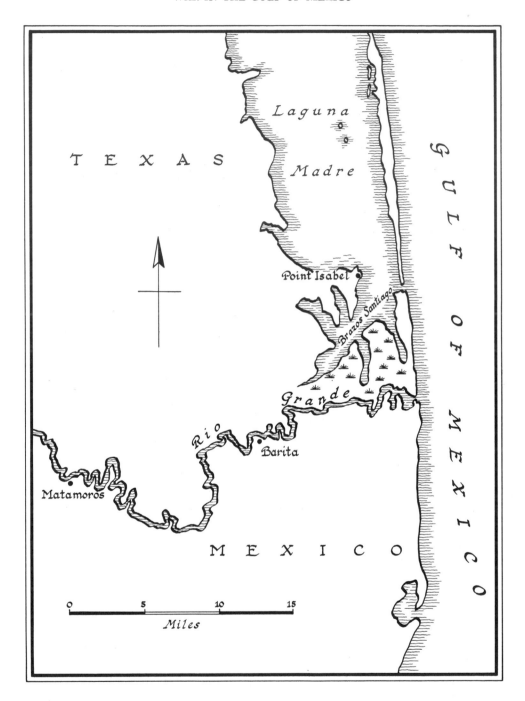

MOUTH OF THE RIO GRANDE

within the fort, with First Lieutenant William Lang's Marines holding the exposed center section. The men, having expected to march to the relief of General Taylor, found their assignment to a passive role irksome and, as the firing seemed to approach ever closer to the fort, became increasingly apprehensive about the safety of the Army and increasingly impatient to join in the fight. About midnight, a Negro camp follower arrived at the fort with the frightening news that the Army had been defeated, that there had been great loss of life, and that General Taylor himself had barely escaped. Upon receipt of this news, Captain Gregory asked Conner for permission to take his force to the rescue of the Army. Pointing out that the men with Gregory were not trained for land fighting and that a regiment of cavalry could cut them to pieces and cripple the squadron at the very outset of the war, Conner turned down the request.

With the morning came word that the noise Gregory and his men had heard came from a battle at Palo Alto, in which Taylor was the victor. Although the need for the Navy relief column had passed, the possibility of a raid kept the sailors and Marines ashore until 13 May, by which time the Mexican withdrawal across the Rio Grande had eliminated the threat to Taylor's base.

It was General Taylor's plan to pursue the enemy, and on 15 May Commodore Conner's squadron organized an expedition to assist the Army in crossing the Rio Grande. Captain John H. Aulick, the new skipper of the *Potomac*, was in charge of the expedition, which originally was to consist of 500 men but in fact consisted of 155. However, high seas off the river mouth and rough water on the bar made it impossible for the naval boats to get into the river until 18 May, by which time the Army, using small boats, had crossed some miles upstream and was established at Barita.

When Conner arrived at Brazos Santiago on 8 May, he advised Secretary Bancroft that the squadron would stay there only as long as necessary because the *Cumberland*, the *Potomac*, and the *John Adams*—three of the five ships he had there—would have to go to Pensacola to refill their water tanks before returning to their blockade stations along the coast of Mexico. He assured the Secretary that he would not wait for those vessels to return, but would begin a blockade with the vessels he had left, and, reminding Bancroft of the shallow water on the bars at the entrances to most Mexican ports and rivers, repeated his request for vessels drawing less than eight feet of water.

By 9 May it was obvious in Washington that fighting would break out momentarily and President Polk called his Cabinet together to consider asking Congress for a declaration of war. Bancroft was the only member of the Cabinet not in favor of doing so. He wanted to await word of a Mexican attack. That same evening, the White House received General Taylor's report that on 25 April a reconnaissance patrol under Captain Seth Thornton, U.S. Army, had been attacked by Mexicans north of the Rio Grande, and the Cabinet was unanimous in recommending a declaration of war.

The first set of wartime orders for the Gulf of Mexico, signed by Bancroft on 10 May, instructed Conner to distribute his vessels "to meet in the best possible manner the new position of affairs" and to assist the Army when possible—instructions that had been carried out before they were written. They also countermanded earlier orders for the return of the *Raritan* and the *Potomac*.

On 11 May, the President formally asked Congress to declare war on the grounds that American blood had been shed on American soil, and on the afternoon of 13 May he signed the declaration. That same day, he signed "An Act providing for the Prosecution of the existing War between the United States and the Republic of Mexico" which, among other things, provided for vessels already on the ways to be completed and for the purchase of others. In spite of that Act, the only vessels whose completion was pushed were the sloops of war *Germantown* and *Albany*, which were almost finished at the time. The Navy already had more large vessels than it could man, and the small vessels under construction drew too much water to satisfy its need in that respect. Consequently, the small steamers, schooners, brigs, and storeships which the Act allowed the Navy to acquire had to be purchased.

As Commodore Conner had discovered and reported the previous autumn, the nature of the war facing the squadron in the Gulf of Mexico required a large number of shallow-draft vessels. Also needed would be a smaller number of sloops of war that could keep the sea during the stormy winter months and enforce the blockade, and seagoing steamers to act as dispatch vessels and to tow the smaller craft. Although the crews of the deep-draft frigates and big, awkward ships-of-the-line could and did furnish manpower for naval landing parties, the vessels themselves were virtually useless on the blockade. They would be needed only if the Navy were to undertake the reduction of the fortress of San Juan de Ulloa without assistance from land forces. As American strategy unfolded, however, it never became necessary for the Navy to be given that assignment, and the Home Squadron in the Gulf fought the war with small vessels, sloops of war, steamers, and frigates.

Three days after signing his first wartime orders, Bancroft notified Conner that war had been declared and that he should "exercise all the rights that belong to you as commander-in-chief of a belligerent squadron." In his letter of notification, he directed the Commodore to blockade Mexican ports, to seize Mexican vessels, to capture any Mexican coastal towns he could, and to render all possible assistance to General Taylor. The conditions of the blockade were spelled out: it must be strict and absolute with only neutral warships permitted to pass; neutral vessels caught in port by the blockade

GULF OF MEXICO

Blanquilla Reef

Gallega Reef

Isla Verde

Veracruz

Isla de Sacrificios

Chopas Reef

Salmedina I.

Antón Lizardo
Anchorage

VERACRUZ AND THE ANCHORAGES

were to be given twenty days to load and leave; and, following French practice, the English mail steamers to Veracruz and Tampico were to be allowed through the blockade.

Then, after dwelling at some length on the possibility of detaching some of the Mexican states from their allegiance to the central government, the scholarly Secretary concluded: "Your own intimate acquaintance with the condition of Mexico, will instruct you best what measures to pursue in the conduct of hostilities. . . ."

In the same letter, the Commodore was informed that the *Princeton* had already sailed from Boston bound for the Gulf, and that the brigs *Perry* (Lieutenant George S. Blake), *Truxtun* (Commander Edward W. Carpender), and *Porpoise* would soon follow. Even with the arrival of these vessels the squadron would consist of no more than three frigates, the *Potomac*, the *Raritan*, and the *Cumberland*; three sloops, the *John Adams*, the *Falmouth*, and the *St. Mary*'s; two steamers, the *Princeton* and the *Mississippi*; five brigs, the *Perry*, the *Truxtun*, the *Porpoise*, the *Somers*, and the *Lawrence*; and the schooner *Flirt*—a very small force with which to blockade the entire eastern coast of Mexico. Yet Bancroft exhorted his commander: "The country relies on you to make such a use of this force as will most effectually blockade the Principal Mexican ports; protect our commerce from the depredations of privateers, assist the operations of our army, and lead to the earliest adjustment of our difficulties with Mexico."

These instructions set forth with clarity the aims of American naval operations in the Gulf of Mexico, and pointed out the only positive contributions it would be possible for the Navy to make. The Mexican Navy was too small to engage in a struggle for control of the sea. Mexico's best hope of disrupting the American supply lines lay in using privateers, but that threat never became a reality. Indeed, at no time during the war did the Mexican Navy send a vessel to sea in the Gulf. The U.S. Navy's principal objective, to keep the seas clear for the passage of troops and supplies, was accomplished even before the fighting began. Except for supporting Major General Winfield Scott's expedition to Veracruz, the Navy could not even give the Army much direct support. Therefore, its main operation became the establishment of a tight blockade, and nearly all the operations of Conner's squadron were directed to that end.

On 13 May, the same day as Bancroft wrote his instructions to Conner, the latter was advising the Secretary that he intended to begin the blockade of Mexican ports, that the *Lawrence* would remain off the Rio Grande to protect the Army's supply vessels, and that he would not be able to attack the Castle of San Juan de Ulloa in Veracruz Harbor with the forces he had. He announced his intention of making Antón Lizardo his base and, stressing

The Iron Steam Frigate *Guadaloupe*
The National Maritime Museum, Greenwich, England

the need for a plentiful supply of water, asked that storeships be stationed at that anchorage.

The following day, 14 May, he issued a proclamation placing Veracruz, Alvarado, Tampico, and Matamoros under blockade and warning that the blockade would be extended as soon as circumstances permitted. That same evening the *Mississippi* sailed for Veracruz with orders to blockade that port, the *John Adams* sailed for Pensacola to take on water and provisions preparatory to moving to Veracruz, and the *St. Mary's*, back from replenishing water and stores at Pensacola, got under way to blockade Tampico. Four days later, Captain Gregory in the *Raritan* left to take command of the forces at Veracruz. The blockade of Alvarado was to be handled by the vessels at Veracruz, and an Army detachment that interdicted traffic on the Rio Grande, in fact, enforced the blockade of Matamoros. The Navy's active participation in operations on the Rio Grande was ended.

Upon the return of the expedition that had gone up the Rio Grande to help General Taylor get his army across the river, Conner dispatched the *Cumberland* and the *Potomac* to Pensacola for water, and sent Commander Ingraham in the *Somers* to Campeche, Yucatán, to "conciliate" that state and to discover whether it would hold aloof from the war—which it did. When those three vessels left, Conner had to take the calculated risk of leaving only the *Lawrence* to protect the Army transports off Brazos Santiago. He knew that, although small and weak, the Mexican Navy did possess two large, British-built steamers, the *Montezuma* and the *Guadaloupe*, that were capable of destroying American shipping off the Brazos. Apparently, however, he believed that they were not operational and he would be able to blockade them before they could be made so. He was mistaken, for, having been repossessed by their former British owners and flying the British flag, they put to sea from Alvarado on 18 May and escaped to Havana. On the one hand, Conner was chagrined at their escape, and also regretful, because they would have made very useful additions of his squadron. On the other hand, their departure simplified his problems, since they were the only seagoing Mexican warships of any consequence on the east coast.

III

BLOCKADE ESTABLISHED

Having received from Secretary of the Navy Bancroft specific and exacting instructions covering the blockade, Conner, on 14 May, issued to his commanders instructions that were equally strict: "No neutral vessel, proceeding towards the entrance of the blockaded port, shall be captured or detained, if she shall not previously have received from one of the blockading squadron, a special notification of the blockade. This notification shall be, moreover, inserted in writing on the muster role of the neutral vessel by the cruiser which meets her, and it shall contain the announcement, together with the statements of the day, and the latitude in which it was made."

Neutral vessels that were in Mexican ports when the blockade was declared were to be allowed fifteen days in which to depart, with or without cargo, and the neutral, noncommercial mail packets running to Veracruz and Tampico were exempt from the blockade. "In all cases," Conner wrote to Captain William A. Howard, of the U.S. Revenue Marine, "you are to act upon the doctrine that 'free ships make free goods,' and except in cases of contraband, with respect to France, the Netherlands, and Sweden, upon that of 'enemy's ships, enemy's goods'."

Those instructions were in line with contemporary American doctrine that blockades must be effective to be legal and that free ships make free goods. "The policy of our government," the Secretary of the Navy wrote to Commodore Thomas ap Catesby Jones in late 1847, "has been, from the beginning of the war with Mexico, to interfere, in as small a degree as possible, with neutral commerce." So carefully did the squadron follow the law that all of its captures were sustained by the admiralty courts, and foreign governments made surprisingly few protests. In that respect, the record of the Pacific Squadron was almost the antithesis.

Blockade duty was very irksome. Vessels so engaged cruised constantly back and forth before a port, usually alone, and, apart from occasionally sighting a sail on the horizon and, less frequently, a vessel trying to slip into the port, there was little to break the monotony. As Raphael Semmes wrote: "During the parching heats of summer, and the long boisterous nights of winter, our vigilance was expected to be, and was, unremitting."

When the war started, eight major ports along the Gulf of Mexico flew the Mexican flag. Matamoros quickly fell to the Americans, and Carmen was neutralized by the revolutionary government of Yucatán, but the other six presented problems for a blockading force. Five of them—Soto la Marina, Tampico, Tuxpan, Alvarado, and Tabasco*—lay up shallow-mouthed rivers. Most ports so situated can be blockaded by a ship lying either off or inside the mouth of the river. Not so the Mexican ports: only vessels of very light draft could navigate the shallow water over the bars at the mouths of the rivers. Furthermore, these Mexican river mouths had no natural protection and, hence, no place for blockading vessels to take refuge from storms. The sixth port, Veracruz, had no real harbor: although its main anchorages were controlled by the American squadron, the Mexicans could still use the port by taking advantage of the slight protection offered by Gallega Reef, upon which squatted, as it does today, the Castle of San Juan de Ulloa. When a storm came up, the blockading vessels off Veracruz proper had to lie to so far from the harbor entrances that they could not prevent blockade running. Thus, several blockade-runners got in to the port during storms by sailing close to the shore.

In other ways, too, the weather was a handicap. Along the east coast of Mexico there are really only two seasons: the dry one, which lasts from October to April, and the wet one, which lasts from April to October. The former is the season of the northers, and the latter is the season of the "vomito," or yellow fever. Northers are very strong northerly gales which spring up with little or no warning and are among the most vicious winds known to seamen. The vessels of the period could not ride them out in open roadsteads, and even when they were in protected anchorages they had to take extreme precautions.

Equally dangerous was the yellow fever. With no known cure for it, the disease could completely immobilize a vessel or a squadron, as it did during the summer of 1847. Veracruz was particularly noted as a yellow-fever area, and in an era when Veracruzanos were believed to be immune to it, it was common practice for pregnant women to go to Veracruz to bear their children so that the children might enjoy immunity to the scourge.

---

* In the 1840s the proper name of Tabasco was San Juan Bautista, and today the town is called Villahermosa. However, since most American records refer to it as Tabasco, that name will be used herein.

In response to Conner's pleas for light-draft vessels, on 19 May Bancroft authorized the purchase of two such steamers that were being built in New York for the Mexican Navy by the shipbuilding firm of Brown and Bell. These small, side-wheel vessels, 118 feet long, 22½ feet on beam, and mounting three guns, were named the *Vixen* and the *Spitfire*. Their large paddle boxes made them easily recognizable, and these very handy and useful craft were by far the best of all the small steamers sent to the Gulf. They were, however, poor sea boats, jumping about in a short sea, and were subject to frequent engine troubles.

Six days after the above authorization had been given, the Navy bought three 59-foot schooners also building by Brown and Bell for the Mexican Navy. These vessels, which were named the *Bonita*, the *Petrel*, and the *Reefer*, mounted one 18- or 32-pounder each. Having been designed for the Mexican service they were uniquely suited for their intended tasks and did more fighting than any other vessels in the squadron. The crews of these little schooners soon developed great pride in their vessels, as Midshipman Parker found out when he made the mistake of trampling on the dignity of the *Reefer*. "I went along side her once," he later recalled, "in our barge, which was nearly as long, and not knowing any better stepped over her port quarter. The First Lieutenant immediately informed me in no very gentle tone that 'there was a *gangway* to that vessel!' Oh! there was a good deal of style kept up in these schooners, if they were little; they were gotten underweigh with the longest of speaking trumpets and the hoarsest of voices; and I once saw one of them crossing the stern of the line-of-battle-ship *Ohio*, and carefully throwing the lead. They drew about six feet of water!"

The reinforcements promised in Bancroft's letter of 13 May began reaching Conner's squadron in June. Although reported in that letter to be en route, the *Princeton* did not leave Boston until 19 May, the same day the *Perry* left Norfolk: the former arrived on 7 June, and the latter on 9 July. Within a month two more brigs arrived: the *Porpoise* on 18 July, and the *Truxtun* on 9 August.

Also on 19 May, Secretary of the Treasury Robert J. Walker ordered Captain John A. Webster, of the U.S. Revenue Marine, to the Gulf with a squadron of revenue cutters, consisting of the steamers *McLane* (Captain W. A. Howard, U.S. Revenue Marine), *Spencer* (Captain Caleb Currier, U.S. Revenue Marine), and *Legare* (Captain H. L. Caste, U.S. Revenue Marine), and the schooners *Woodbury* (Captain Winslow Foster, U.S. Revenue Marine), *Ewing* (Captain Gay Moore, U.S. Revenue Marine), *Forward* (Captain H. B. Nones, U.S. Revenue Marine), and *Van Buren* (Captain Thomas C. Randolph, U.S. Revenue Marine). Captain Webster was instructed to operate under General Taylor's direction and to assist the Navy when possible. Although the cutters seldom ventured south of Texas, the *McLane*, the *Legare*, and the *Forward* did, from time to time, serve with the Navy.

Owing to various delays, the first of the ex-Mexican schooners, the *Reefer* (Lieutenant Isaac Sterrett), did not reach Veracruz until 10 July; the *Petrel* (Lieutenant T. Darrah Shaw) followed on 21 July, and the *Bonita* (Lieutenant Timothy G. Benham) a week later. Delivery of the ex-Mexican steamers to the U.S. Navy was so long delayed that on 16 July, Bancroft, unaware that they had been delivered two days previously, threatened to cancel their purchase. The *Vixen* (Commander Joshua Sands) reached Veracruz on 23 September, and the *Spitfire* (Commander Josiah Tattnall) on 10 November, too late for Conner to make descents on the Mexican ports during good weather.

The *St. Mary's* reached Tampico on 19 May and the next day her energetic commander, John L. Saunders, proclaimed the blockade. On learning that, in violation of contemporary international practice, the Mexican authorities had prevented the American brig *Foam* from loading and departing Tampico, Saunders threatened to withdraw the privileges that custom dictated he should grant to Mexico, unless she was allowed to do so. The Mexicans relented.

Captain Fitzhugh in the *Mississippi* proclaimed the blockade at Veracruz on the same day—20 May. Four days later, when Captain Gregory arrived in the *Raritan*, the *Falmouth* was cruising off the port and the *Mississippi* was at Antón Lizardo. The day of his arrival was also the day the first two prizes of the war were taken: the *Falmouth* intercepted the Mexican schooner *Criolla* inbound from Tampico, and the *Somers*, en route to Campeche, arrived with the prize schooner *Amada* in company. However, when Captain Gregory learned that the Mexicans had permitted the departure of four American vessels caught at Veracruz by the outbreak of war, he released the *Criolla* and the *Amada*.

At the end of May, Secretary Bancroft requested the Commodore's views on the practicality of seizing the Castle of San Juan de Ulloa and again asked what force would be necessary to take it. He also asked Conner if he needed a field-grade Marine officer. This last inquiry raised the question of how Conner intended to use his squadron's Marines for, if he were to combine them into a single unit for amphibious operations, he would need an officer of field rank to command it. Implying clearly that he did not intend to use them as a single unit, Conner replied that he needed another Marine captain, because he expected to use his Marines on detached service.

In the first week of June, Conner asked for more surgeons because there were cases of dysentery in the squadron, and on 22 June he had to report that scurvy had broken out in the *Raritan*, the *Mississippi*, and the *St. Mary's*: so many men in the *Raritan* were suffering from scurvy that she could scarcely be operated. Conner could not obtain fresh fruit on the hostile coast, but he was confident that the situation would be rectified when he received the additional steamers he was expecting, because they were fast enough to deliver fresh fruit before it spoiled.

President Polk was of the opinion that if the exiled General Santa Anna could be returned to Mexico from Cuba he would help to bring about a quick end to the war and, as early as 13 May, Conner had been ordered: "If Santa Anna endeavors to enter the Mexican ports, you will allow him to pass freely."

On 6 June Commander Alexander Slidell Mackenzie, brother of John Slidell, whose mission to Mexico the previous fall had been unsuccessful, was ordered to Havana to investigate the outfitting of Mexican privateers there and, at the same time, to pursue a secret and more important mission: "to ascertain in a prudent way what Santa Anna's views were in regard to peace with the U.S., and whether, if restored to Mexico, there was a reasonable probability that he would make peace." Mackenzie, who spoke Spanish fluently, reached Havana on 5 July and met Santa Anna on the 7th. At the interview, Mackenzie suggested that if Santa Anna were to regain power and announce a willingness to treat for peace, the United States would suspend all operations, except the blockade. He then outlined the U.S. peace terms: no indemnity; settlement of the spoliation claims; purchase by the United States of the disputed territory; and purchase by the United States of New Mexico.

Santa Anna put his reply in a letter to President Polk, in which he stated his hopes for peace and said he would negotiate a settlement. Thus it appeared that if Santa Anna could recover control of Mexico, the prospects for an early peace would be bright.

Commander Saunders in the *St. Mary's*, impatient with the relatively inactive role of blockading, was convinced that Tampico could be taken by 500 men. However, Conner, apparently sharing a hope entertained in Washington that the town might revolt, warned his impetuous subordinate not to attack it, since such a move would obviously make it stay in the camp of the central government of Mexico.

In the course of his vessel's patrols back and forth off the mouth of the Pánuco River, seven miles below Tampico, Saunders learned from an English resident of the town that the Mexicans were fitting out the three gunboats in the port and were strengthening the forts on either side of the mouth of the river. A few days after he received that information, the schooner-gunboats *Union*, *Isabel*, and *Pueblano* dropped down the river and took position off the forts.

Saunders decided to impede the reinforcement of the Mexican defenses by attacking and, in the early afternoon of 8 June, the *St. Mary's* sailed north from her anchorage. When she got within range of the fort on the north side of the river mouth, she backed her main topsail and fired one shell and four round shot. Shoaling water forced her to claw off, but an hour later she circled back and came in as close as the tide would allow. This time, however, the range proved too great and she retired, having done no more than damage slightly one of the gunboats.

The return to their unexciting blockade duty dismayed the officers of the *St. Mary's*, and they proposed cutting out the Mexican gunboats. Saunders gave the plan his blessing, and during the night of 14 June the *St. Mary's* moved as close as possible to the forts. Shortly before midnight, the ship's boats cast off and pulled for the bar. Meanwhile, Saunders had his two port-side, 8-inch Paixhans shell guns shifted to starboard so that all four of his guns would bear on the forts. As the boats neared the bar, they ran into a strong current and had to inch along. Then, one of them grounded on the bar. The resulting noise and confusion alerted the Mexicans, and having lost the element of surprise, so necessary in a cutting-out expedition, the boats had no choice but to return to the *St. Mary's*. Saunders then had all his shell guns shifted to port, swung his ship, and, soon after daybreak, opened on the fort and the gunboats. The *St. Mary's* fired for half an hour, then, because her shells were falling short, she ceased, hoisted anchor, and returned to her old anchorage. Thus ended Saunders' abortive attempt to reduce the defenses of Tampico.

As Commodore Conner intended, the anchorage of Antón Lizardo, about twelve miles south of Veracruz, became the main base of the American squadron in Mexican waters. Even in the strongest northers, vessels could ride at anchor safely at Antón Lizardo, where a chain of shoals, reefs, and small barren islands about nine miles long broke the sea. Because it was only about four miles from Veracruz, a much smaller and less protected anchorage behind Sacrificios Island was also used by the squadron.

Both Conner and his successor, Matthew Calbraith Perry, were plagued by a shortage of vessels of the type needed, a lack of good charts, and a scarcity of competent pilots. Moreover, the logistic support of the squadron was haphazard: keeping supplied with water was the greatest single problem, but securing fresh fruit and coal also presented difficulties. The Navy Department was not unaware of the problems, but the slowness of communication over long distances and uncertainty about the squadron's future opera-

MATTHEW C. PERRY

tions hampered the supply bureaus in Washington. The Bureau of Provisions and Clothing, being less affected by operations than the others, was a conspicuous exception to those limitations.

Commodore Charles Morris, Chief of the Bureau of Construction, Equipment, and Repair, notified Conner on 8 June that Isla Verde, near Veracruz, had been picked as the main depot in the theatre of operations, and reminded him that "as early and as full notice of the probable wants of the squadron as practicable is always an advantage to the Bureau." Neither Conner nor Perry was as careful as he might have been about providing advance warning of the squadron's needs, and the problem was compounded by the fact that until early in 1847 the Navy did not have enough storeships to keep the squadron properly supplied. Particularly irritating to Conner was the lack of a coal hulk at the Antón Lizardo anchorage. Without one, he wrote to his wife on 24 October 1846, ships' boats had to unload the coal from the colliers onto one of the low islands in the anchorage, then, as it was needed, unload it again into the bunkers of the squadron's steamers.

The *Lawrence* was still on duty at Brazos Santiago, off the mouth of the Rio Grande, where she had been joined by the schooner *Flirt* (Lieutenant Arthur Sinclair), and on 9 June Conner ordered both vessels to run down the Mexican coast as far as Soto la Marina in search of Mexican supply ships. Their mission was fruitless.

Under date of 11 June, Conner sent Bancroft a raised estimate of the force he would need to take San Juan de Ulloa: five ships-of-the-line, four bomb vessels, three frigates, and the sloops he already had. This was a force far larger than the Navy Department had any hope of providing. The Commodore concluded his pessimistic letter with the cheering thought that if the castle were resolutely defended, it would be very hard to subdue under any conditions.

When he got back to Veracruz from a visit to Pensacola, he made another report on San Juan de Ulloa. After pointing out that it was difficult to obtain reliable information, he reported that the castle was most strongly fortified on the sides commanding the north and east entrances to the harbor, and that, while the north side was the weaker of the two, it would be harder to assault because the reef on which the castle stood would prevent vessels from approaching closer than two miles. He added that between 2,500 and 4,000 men garrisoned the castle and the town, but that they were provisioned only on a day-to-day basis. Therefore, he noted, a surprise landing which would cut off the garrison's supplies could force it to surrender before help could arrive from the interior. He concluded this letter with the caution that any land operations around Veracruz would be complicated by the climate and by the prevalence of yellow fever during the rainy season, and with the observation that Veracruz would be useful only as a depot for an advance on Mexico City, for which purpose he thought Tampico would be better suited, anyway.

It is hardly surprising that the Polk administration soon gave up any thought of seizing San Juan de Ulloa and Veracruz.

Mexico settled upon the traditional method of contesting superior sea power and, on 25 June 1846, the Mexican Congress authorized the issuance of letters of marque and reprisal. The following day, President Paredes set forth regulations governing privateering: even if the captain and crew of a privateer in the service of Mexico were foreigners, they could be considered to be Mexican subjects; commissions could be issued abroad; and prizes could be sent to neutral ports.

Whether the Mexicans expected to reap great profits from privateering is questionable. Probably, the best they hoped for was to annoy the Americans. In the fall of 1846, Mexican agents flooded the West Indies, Britain, France, and Spain with commissions. General Juan N. Almonte in Havana and J. N. Pareda in Madrid were particularly active. Apparently, only two privateers were fitted out, both with commissions issued in Madrid. Although the large American merchant marine offered lucrative targets, potential privateers were discouraged by American arrangements for the protection of its merchant vessels, by the threats to treat all foreigners serving under the

Mexican flag as pirates, and by the difficulties they would almost certainly encounter in disposing of prizes.

As soon as Conner learned that on 21 July the Mexican Congress had promulgated some new regulations on privateering and had designated Alvarado, Tecoluto, Tuxpan, and Soto la Marina as ports of entry, he prepared to include them in his blockade. So strictly did he enforce the blockade that even a rule making blockade-runners exempt from port dues and from one-quarter of the import duties, which the Mexican government passed on 11 September, seems to have done little to increase Mexico's commerce.

Most of the gold and silver mines in Mexico were foreign-owned, and their products were, therefore, in American eyes, neutral property, not contraband, and not subject to seizure. In accordance with official American policy in such matters, Conner had, towards the end of June, relaxed the blockade enough to allow neutral mail packets to carry out gold and silver and to land quicksilver, which was indispensable for refining the latter. On 8 July he instructed his squadron to make further concessions and to allow neutral vessels stopped off blockaded ports to communicate with their consignees through the Senior Officer Present, and to be provided with water and supplies, if needed. However, he revoked the latter concession on 25 July, apparently because it was working a hardship on the blockading vessels by depleting their precious stock of supplies.

During July Conner attempted to solve the problem of water shortage by getting it from the Antigua River, about twenty miles north of Veracruz. Captain Gregory in the *Raritan* got some water at the Boca Partida without difficulty, but other watering parties had to skirmish with the Mexicans. After that experience, the Americans got water only from rivers under their control. On 19 July Conner sent Commander Ingraham in the *Somers* south again with orders to gather information about the political inclination in the country around Carmen, to look in at the Tabasco and Alvarado rivers,* and to bring back fruit. Conner needed the information because of the operations he planned to undertake as soon as his light vessels arrived, and he needed the fruit to combat the outbreak of scurvy which had reached such proportions in the squadron that it was a cause for considerable concern.

At this time, the "vomito," or yellow-fever, season was in full swing and Bancroft wrote to Conner to tell him that "should disease of an epidemic character show itself in one of your vessels, it should be ordered to a different latitude without delay." Luckily, the incidence of yellow fever in the squadron was not great and none of the vessels had to be sent north.

When the brig *Perry* arrived off Veracruz on 9 July, she brought a report

---

* Now the Grijalva and Papaloapán rivers.

from Havana that there was a Mexican privateer off Cape San Antonio, the western tip of Cuba, claiming to have captured several American vessels, so Conner ordered the brig to investigate. He doubted that there was any truth in the report, and the *Perry*, one of the fastest vessels in the Navy, found nothing.

A broad bar covering the mouth of the Alvarado River made it extremely difficult for the large ships of Conner's squadron to blockade the port of Alvarado, which was twenty miles southeast of the anchorage at Antón Lizardo and was an important place of entry for war supplies. In September the season for the northers would begin and would make blockading even more difficult, for any ship caught off the bar in one of those gales would be in danger of being driven ashore by the wind and current. Consequently, although he was still short of the vessels he needed for such an operation, Conner decided to attack the Mexican warships in the Alvarado River late in July. Another reason not to delay the attack was that if any of the Mexican ships were captured, they could be put into service and Conner's shortage of small craft would be alleviated.

At this early stage in the war, the defenses of Alvarado under the command of Capitán de Fragata Pedro Diaz Miron, of the Mexican Navy, were weak. They consisted of the brig *Zempoalteca*, the gunboats *Guerrero*, *Queretana*, and *Victoria*, and a four-gun fort at the mouth of the river, and, upstream, the brigs *Mexicano* and *Veracruzano Libre*, and the schooners *Águila*, *Libertad*, and *Morelos*. However, because of the eight or ten feet of water on the bar, the only American vessels that could enter the river were the shallow-draft schooner-gunboats.

On the afternoon of 28 July, Conner ordered his force—the *Cumberland*, the *Potomac*, the *Raritan*, the *Reefer*, and the *Petrel*—to get under way from the anchorage at Antón Lizardo. As the flagship, the *Cumberland*, passed through the channel leading to the open ocean, a strong current forced her onto the northwest side of Chopas Reef, and she struck in three fathoms. All thoughts of an attack were given up, as all hands concentrated on saving her. She was lightened a foot by having water pumped out, stores and shot transferred to other vessels, and some of the guns from her spar deck landed on the reef. The following evening, with the aid of a pull from the steamer *Mississippi*, she was floated off. Her false keel was damaged, and most of her copper bottom plates were lost, but she saw more service before the Navy Department gave Conner permission to send her north for an inspection of the damage on 22 August.

A few days of settled weather in early August induced Conner to try again to seize the Mexican squadron at Alvarado. He issued his plan for the forthcoming operation on 6 August. No record of that plan has survived but,

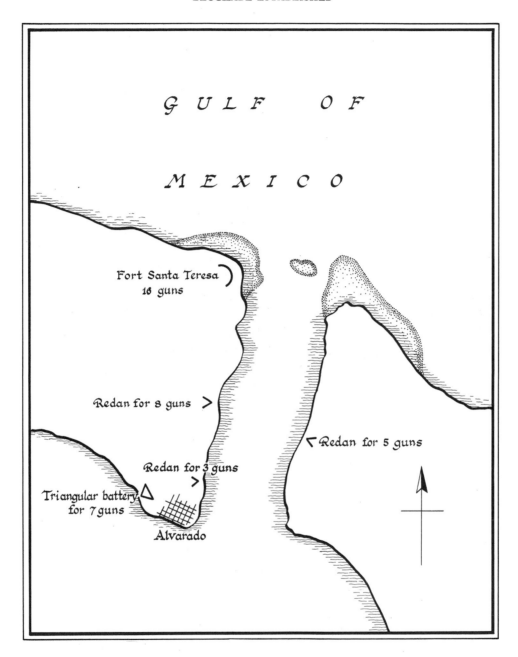

GULF OF

MEXICO

Fort Santa Teresa
16 guns

Redan for 8 guns >

< Redan for 5 guns

Redan for 3 guns
>

Triangular battery
for 7 guns

Alvarado

ALVARADO AND THE MOUTH OF ITS RIVER

The Steamer *Princeton*

The absence of her stack is explained
by the fact that early war steamers
had folding stacks.

apparently, he intended to move all available vessels to the mouth of the Alvarado River, destroy the fortifications there by bombardment, and then send his light-draft gunboats and ships' boats upstream in pursuit of the Mexican squadron.

On the afternoon of 6 August, the *Falmouth* worked out of Antón Lizardo and sailed south to join the *Somers* on blockade off the Alvarado. Early the following morning, the *Mississippi*, the *Princeton*, the *Potomac*, the *Reefer*, the *Petrel*, the *Bonita*, and a spectator, the British frigate *Endymion*, followed the flagship *Cumberland* to sea. By mid-morning the whole force had cleared Antón Lizardo, and the *Mississippi* took the *Potomac* in tow and the *Princeton* put a tow line aboard the *Cumberland*. Three hours later, the steamers cast off their tows and the vessels moved independently to their assigned positions. First to join the *Falmouth* and the *Somers* at anchor off the bar was the *Princeton*, and the last, the *Mississippi*, arrived two hours behind her. The ships of the expedition lay in a fan-shaped formation off the fort guarding the bar.

That evening, about an hour after the *Mississippi* had taken position, Conner ordered his two steamers and his gunboats to begin the bombardment. The steamers "beat to quarters," while the gunboats moved in towards the fort and anchored about half a mile from the *Princeton*. A strong current created by the water from the swollen river rushing over the bar prevented the *Mississippi* and the *Princeton* from steaming close enough to inflict significant damage. Although the *Princeton* could not even bring her whole broadside to bear on the fort, she, the *Mississippi*, the *Reefer*, and the *Bonita* opened on it. They fired slowly and drove one of the Mexican gunboats upriver out of range. The bombardment had been going on for less than one hour when, because of the falling darkness, the *Cumberland* at 6:30 signaled "Cease Firing."

The Mexicans had been unable to make any effective reply, because the American ships lay outside the range of their guns, but when the latter ceased firing, a few Mexican infantrymen moved through the chaparral opposite the gunboats, and someone in the *Reefer* fired a musket at them. Thereupon, the Mexicans directed a rattle of musketry towards the gunboats, which replied with fire from their small arms and great guns. The *Mississippi* and the *Princeton* soon joined in the cannonade, which lasted until the Mexicans ceased firing about half an hour later. In order to prevent a repetition of this episode, Conner ordered the gunboats to move out of musket range and by 7:30 they had anchored astern of the *Potomac*.

During the night, Conner organized a boat expedition, whether with the intention of seizing the fort or of capturing the Mexican vessels is not clear. It would seem that the strength of the current over the bar would have precluded any attempt to cut out the vessels lying behind it. However, his intention is of no real importance because the night brought indications that a norther was approaching and, on the recommendation of his pilots, he called off the attack, much to the chagrin of many men in the squadron.

Leaving the *Falmouth* on blockade duty, the American squadron left Alvarado at daylight and headed north. As they had done on the way south, the steamers took the two frigates in tow, and before noon the squadron dropped anchor in the familiar waters of Antón Lizardo.

Conner's failure at Alvarado was more than just a repulse for, as he found out the next time he attacked the port, the awakened Mexicans used the time gained to good advantage by strengthening the defense of the area: they brought militia from Tlacotalpán and other nearby villages to reinforce the garrison, and built a fort on the left bank of the river.

Newspapers in the United States strongly censured Conner not only for the fiasco at Alvarado, but for his squadron's lack of "accomplishments" in general, a position taken also by some politicians and junior officers. As usual, the press overlooked the importance of things that were not "newsworthy" and did not take into account such obstacles as weather, sickness, and the lack of vessels suitable for the job to be done. In fact, Conner's squadron had accomplished much: in the first six weeks of the war, its "unnewsworthy" blockade was responsible for the Mexicans losing an estimated 500,000 dollars in duties alone.

Undoubtedly, Commodore Conner's continuing belief that the Mexicans would make peace affected his operations until at least early September. On 16 July he had relayed to Washington a message from Consul Black, in Mexico City, to the effect that Mexico was ready to receive from the United States some proposal for opening peace negotiations. He sent Black's letter by the *Raritan*, which was going to Pensacola to replenish supplies, cure her crew of scurvy, and bring back more seamen for the squadron.

Immediately upon receipt of the message, President Polk responded with the suggestion that envoys of both countries meet either in Mexico City or in Washington. His reply was conveyed in a letter from Secretary of State Buchanan to the Mexican Foreign Minister, dated 27 July, and went to Mexico City via Conner. In a covering letter, Buchanan cautioned Conner against accepting any Mexican armistice offers, and instructed him to forward any answer to Washington as swiftly as possible. These instructions were carried by the revenue cutter *Legare*, and reached Conner at Veracruz on 25 August. On 6 August, the government of Mexican President Paredes had been overthrown, and Polk's message, forwarded to Mexico City through the governor of Veracruz, was delivered to Acting President José Mariano Salas. The Mexicans refused to make a decision until after the meeting of their Congress, and when Polk learned this on 19 September, he directed the Commodore to notify John Slidell at New Orleans whenever he learned that the Mexicans were willing to open negotiations. Shortly thereafter, Santa Anna returned to control in Mexico and, in spite of American hopes that such a situation would lead to early peace, he effectively put an end to proposals for negotiations.

IV

OTHER FOES TO FIGHT

On 10 August 1846 President Polk signed an act authorizing the Navy to increase its strength from 7,500 to 10,000 men for the duration of the war. However, authorizing an increase in the strength of the Navy was one thing, and finding the men to fill the additional billets was another. In the labor market, the Navy could not compete against the merchant marine, where wages were high and jobs plentiful, and at no time during the war did its strength exceed 8,000 men. In fact, so acute was the shortage of seamen that some of the vessels the Navy Department hoped to send to the war zones could not be manned.

His failure at Alvarado had convinced Conner that it was utterly foolhardy to attempt to fight both the Mexicans and the elements. He believed that he must wait for the dry season before he launched another attack, and he hoped that by then the additional small vessels promised him would have arrived. Consequently, naval operations in the Gulf had to revert to the unspectacular duties that were as much a part of naval warfare as were the thunder of cannon and the rattle of sails: the boring, fatiguing, unrewarding, and irksome blockade, the assembling and shifting of ships, and attention to a multitude of other details. To aid in his future operations against the Mexican ports, Conner decided to use the slack period to form a landing force consisting of detachments of sailors and Marines, which would be held on board the vessels and be available for landing on call. However, he could equip only 600 men and he had no field artillery for them.

On 12 August he ordered the fast-sailing *Truxtun*, which had joined the squadron three days earlier, to relieve the *John Adams* off Tampico. Shortly before dusk on 14 August, with a gale blowing, she reached the latitude of Tuxpan, 100 miles south of her destination. Commander Carpender turned his vessel towards land, so that he would be able to send

The Brig *Truxtun*

ashore for fresh provisions the following morning. As the *Truxtun* worked in under jib and spanker, she hit Tuxpan Reef where, despite all efforts to free her, she remained stuck. With a full gale blowing and the sea rolling her on the reef, her position was extremely precarious. A small fire that broke out aboard was quickly doused but did not add to her commander's peace of mind. Although he refused General Antonio Rosas' demand that he surrender, Carpender realized that he could not free the *Truxtun* without help and, when morning came, he sent Lieutenant Ortway H. Berryman in one of the brig's cutters to Antón Lizardo for help.

While Berryman was away, on 16 August, the stranded Americans sighted a sail in the offing. The gale still blew with unabated force, but Lieutenant Bushrod W. Hunter and a boat's crew took the *Truxtun*'s first cutter through the thundering surf to see who the stranger was. She proved to be a small Mexican vessel so they seized her and sailed her towards the *Truxtun*, but could not sail close enough to aid the stricken brig. The next day—17 August

—Carpender floated a dinghy through the surf with a few supplies for Hunter and his men and a message relaying Carpender's decision to surrender, but setting Hunter free to attempt to reach Antón Lizardo in his prize, if he wished. Carpender then hoisted a white flag on the brig, acceded to General Rosas' earlier demand that he surrender, and led his men safely ashore.

After sending the crew of his prize ashore in the cutter, Hunter did head her for Antón Lizardo. After a long chase on the evening of 18 August, he captured a Mexican schooner, put a prize crew of four aboard her and, with her in company, continued on his way. The following night the two vessels became separated, and Hunter reported on board the *Cumberland* at Antón Lizardo on the 22nd, the day before his prize schooner arrived.

Meanwhile, at five bells of the afternoon watch on 19 August, the lookouts in the *Cumberland* had made out the *St. Mary's* standing in to Antón Lizardo under full sail. When the latter came within full sight of the flagship, she began signaling: "Truxton is ashore at Tuxpan. Wants a steamer." The *Truxtun's* plight was known aboard the *St. Mary's* because she had picked up Lieutenant Berryman's boat earlier in the day. As soon as Conner had received a firsthand report, he ordered the *Princeton* and the *Falmouth* to Tuxpan. The *Princeton* put to sea almost immediately, but bad weather prevented the *Falmouth* from leaving port for four days.

In the early afternoon of the 20th, the *Princeton* sighted the stricken brig on Tuxpan Reef and anchored a mile and a quarter from her. Commander Engle, captain of the *Princeton*, sent Lieutenant Charles S. Boggs ashore under a flag of truce. Although he was told that Carpender had surrendered three days previously, Boggs informed the Mexicans that they would not be allowed to board the *Truxtun* until after the Americans had visited her.

The next day, Engle sent two boats to the *Truxtun*, but high seas made it impossible to board her. When Boggs managed to board her on 22 August, he found that she was bilged and that, with the exception of some spars and the anchor chain, everything of consequence had been removed by the Mexicans. He salvaged some of the spars, then set fire to the brig, and she burned down to the water's edge. The *Princeton* arrived back at Antón Lizardo on 23 August.

In the first week of September Conner reported that he had received a Mexican offer to exchange Commander Carpender and the crew of the *Truxtun* for General Rafael de la Vega and his officers, who had been captured at the Battle of Resaca de la Palma on 9 May, the day after the action at Palo Alto. While waiting for Washington formally to accept the exchange, Conner arranged for the *Truxtun's* crew to be paroled and, on 22 September, four of the officers and thirty-eight of the men were delivered to him. He sent the revenue cutter *Forward* to Tuxpan to pick up the other three officers and thirteen men. On 7 October, Conner notified the Mexicans that the U.S. government had given its assent to the exchange.

Three days after the *Truxtun* had left on her ill-fated voyage to Tampico, Conner ordered Lieutenant Hunt in the *Porpoise* to Carmen to get wood, water, fresh fruit, and vegetables for the crew of the *Porpoise*, and cattle or sheep for the squadron. He was also to find out whether the port might be a source of vegetables and fruit for the whole squadron, and, en route, to check on Alvarado and Frontera, the latter being the port at the mouth of the Tabasco River.

After eight days of sailing, in the course of which he seized the Mexican schooner *Nonata*, Hunt reached Carmen on 24 August. He consulted the local authorities about their attitude to the war and learned that they intended to remain neutral, then after loading his prize with wood and vegetables he left on 3 September to return to Antón Lizardo, where he reported that Carmen was not a good source of supplies, and that Yucatán would probably remain independent of Mexico. When Conner forwarded Hunt's information to Washington on 12 September, he added that in spite of the likelihood that Yucatán would remain neutral, he would frequently send vessels to keep a close watch on that rebellious state.

Retaining her Mexican name, the *Nonata* was taken into the U.S. service and placed under the command of Lieutenant Samuel F. Hazard. Her 122 tons made her larger than the schooners fitted out in the United States and, after she had been given a battery of four 42-pounder carronades, she was also better armed.

It will be remembered that about the middle of May, Conner had received orders to let General Santa Anna pass through the blockade. The Commodore knew enough of the General's movements to expect him to arrive aboard the British mail packet the *Arab*, due at Veracruz on 14 August. However, when the *Arab* identified herself to the *St. Mary's* off Veracruz and proceeded into the port, she was two days behind schedule. Her clearance had already been secured by Captain George R. Lambert, the Senior British Naval Officer in the area, who pledged that she would neither land nor take on cargo. It was a Sunday afternoon when the greatest of Mexico's generals returned to his native land with the blessing of a U.S. government, whose confidence that, once he returned to power in Mexico, he would make peace, was soon to be shattered. A month after his arrival, on 14 September, Santa Anna became Commander-in-Chief of the Mexican Army, and on 6 December he was elected President of Mexico.

Conner's squadron spent most of the summer doing little besides keeping up the blockade, as it waited impatiently for the promised small steamers to arrive from the United States. However, two letters that Secretary of the Navy Bancroft wrote to him on 29 August must have given the Commodore reason to hope that his squadron would soon be taking a more active part in the war.

The first letter relayed rumors that there were Mexican privateers off Key West, and ordered Conner to keep a watch for them. The second requested information which the government needed to implement its decision to seize both Tampico and Veracruz as soon as the yellow-fever season was over. The information sought concerned the condition of the road from Tampico to San Luis Potosí; how much assistance would be needed from the Army, in order to take and hold Tampico; the best time of year to disembark troops at Tampico; the best landing place near Veracruz; the state of the road from Veracruz to Mexico City; the general topography of Veracruz; the number of troops that would be required to take and hold Veracruz; the possibility of cutting off supplies bound for Veracruz; and the possibility of an expeditionary force being provisioned from the country.

Before Conner could supply the requested information, which he did not do until 7 October, Bancroft had been replaced as Secretary of the Navy. He had made himself unpopular by attempting to eradicate the many abuses that had crept into the service during the thirty years of peace. He had neither the commanding presence nor the force of character necessary to fight successfully the well-entrenched interests in the Navy Department, nor did he have administrative ability. His outstanding contribution to the Navy was the establishment of the Naval Academy at Annapolis. On 9 September 1846, he was succeeded by Attorney General John Y. Mason, who had previously served a short term as Secretary of the Navy under President John Tyler and, consequently, was familiar with the operations of the Navy Department. Though Mason was a far better administrator than Bancroft, he had neither the intellectual brilliance nor the political standing of his predecessor, who was appointed U.S. minister to England.

When the *Truxtun* failed in her mission to relieve the *John Adams* on the blockade off Tampico, Conner had sent the *Falmouth* in her place. But the *Falmouth* needed to go to Boston for urgent repairs, so on 12 September Conner ordered the *Porpoise* to replace her at Tampico. He was now so short of vessels that he wrote the Secretary of the Navy to say that he was going to delay the dispatch of the vessel earlier ordered to Brazil until he heard from the Department again, and on 15 September he was forced to borrow the *Forward* again from Captain Webster's revenue cutter squadron. These measures were expedients, at best. Conner had to have more vessels if he was to undertake any extensive operations. Nevertheless, he added

JOHN Y. MASON

Tabasco to the ports under blockade, and on 30 September extended the blockade southeast to the Rio San Pedro y San Pablo, halfway between the Tabasco River and Laguna del Carmen.

A very somber event occurred aboard the *St. Mary's* on the morning of 17 September. On order from the flagship, the *St. Mary's* hoisted a yellow flag at her fore royal yard, and assembled her officers and crew. Commander Saunders then read the warrant for the hanging of Seaman Samuel Jackson, who had been convicted of striking Lieutenant William R. Taylor, threatening his superior, and using mutinous and seditious language. Jackson's sentence was too severe for his offense but, since the *St. Mary's* was a disaffected ship, Conner considered it important to make an example of the sailor, and the hanging took place immediately after the reading of the warrant. It is perhaps remarkable that no other such incidents took place, because this one was a direct result of the tedium of blockade duty and the uninterrupted confinement aboard ship to which the men of the squadron were subjected. Fortunately, that tedium was to be broken in the course of the next few months.

Although the decision to seize Tampico had been made in Washington on 29 August, the Cabinet did not agree to order Conner to do so until 20 September. Two days later, General Taylor was ordered to send a column of troops under Major General Robert Patterson to occupy the state of Tamaulipas and its capital, Tampico. He was given the options of sending the column by land or by sea, since "the probability is that the place Tampico will be captured in advance of General Patterson's movement" by Conner. On 27 September, the new Secretary of the Navy, John Y. Mason, informed Conner that another sloop would replace the *Falmouth*, then alerted him to the movement of Patterson's column, and counseled "the capture of Tampico by the Naval Forces, will be of the utmost importance to its success."

On 7 October, Conner replied to Secretary Bancroft's letter seeking information concerning the areas where action was about to take place: there was no road from Tampico to San Luis Potosí; Tampico could be captured by a naval force alone; the winter months were the best for coastal campaigning; there were two good landing places near Veracruz, one at Antón Lizardo and the other west of the Island of Sacrificios; Veracruz could be cut off from its water supply; with the possible exception of beef, there were no supplies to be had in the vicinity. He declined to estimate the number of troops that would be needed to take Veracruz.

The day after dispatching that information, Conner advised Washington that when all the promised small steamers and gunboats had arrived he would have enough light vessels to resume operations against Mexican ports. He noted, however, that it was risky to expose small vessels to the northers, and that the replacements for the *Falmouth*, the *Truxtun*, and the *Flirt*— the last-named was scheduled to leave the squadron—should be vessels capable of holding their stations during the stormy season. Throughout the war, the squadron was hampered by the lack of appropriate vessels and at this time, October 1846, Conner had a weak force with which to blockade and attack the Mexican ports: pending replacements for the *Falmouth*, the *Truxtun*, and the *Flirt*, he had three frigates; two sloops of war; three brigs; one small steamer; five schooner-gunboats; and two very efficient large steamers. The small steamer and the gunboats were too small for blockade duty, the frigates were too large and unhandy to be useful, and the large steamers were too valuable to be squandered on the blockade anywhere but at Veracruz where they could be relieved quickly if they were needed for special missions. Thus, in effect, to blockade the Mexican coast all the way from the Rio Grande to Yucatán, Conner had two sloops and three brigs, and one of the latter, the *Perry*, had been blown ashore on Bahia Honda Key, Florida, by a hurricane.

When Commodore Conner's normal term as commander of the Home Squadron was drawing to a close in the fall of 1845, Secretary Bancroft selected Commodore Matthew C. Perry as his successor, but events were

The Steamer *Mississippi*

moving so fast that it was deemed wise to delay making the change. Then, on 12 August 1846, for reasons that are not clear, the Secretary offered Perry command of the *Mississippi* while he was waiting to succeed Conner. Perry had the reputation of being a schemer and might have been expected to do something to hasten his own assumption of command of the squadron but, according to Commodore Charles Morris, who was usually well informed, he did not. Although the appointment of Perry was undoubtedly prompted in part by concern that Conner's delicate health might fail, it has the earmarks of a conspiratorial move by Secretary Bancroft, who scarcely concealed his animus towards the commander of the Home Squadron.

Perry accepted command of the *Mississippi* and on 20 August was ordered to take charge of the outfitting of the *Vixen* and the *Spitfire*, lead them from New York to Veracruz, report to Conner as relief for Captain Fitzhugh of the *Mississippi*, and break the red pennant of a junior commodore.

Perry arrived at Veracruz in the *Vixen* on 23 September, but did not take command of the *Mississippi* until 6 October. The *Spitfire*, carrying dispatches for Chagres, was ordered to deliver them before joining the squadron, and came in about six weeks after the *Vixen*. Perry's arrival created a problem not often encountered in the American Navy of the period—two flag officers serving in the same squadron—and it led to considerable confusion about the roles of the two commodores. Some historians, then and now, have suggested that the command of the squadron was split: that Conner commanded the sailing vessels, and Perry the steamers. Even a hasty study of the orders issued and the operations conducted by the two men disproves that contention. The only times Perry issued orders in his own name to the commander of any vessel, sail or steam, were when Conner sent him on independent missions: and there were times when Conner, in person, commanded operations that involved steamers. What did happen was that when the ailing Conner did not wish to lead an operation, he sent his second-in-command and heir apparent—Perry.

With the arrival of the *McLane* early in October, there were two shallow-draft steamers in the squadron, so Conner decided to attack Alvarado again. No doubt Commodore Morris' warning of the previous month that "The administration are very anxious, the Navy should do something which will answer to make newspaper noise . . ." had something to do with his decision, but quite apart from that, Conner was well aware of what a successful attack would do for the morale of his men.

As indicated earlier, Conner's first assault on Alvarado, in early August, awakened the Mexicans and in the interim they strengthened their defenses there. Santa Teresa, the main fort overlooking the bar, had been enlarged and mounted sixteen guns, while one pivoting 30-pounder was emplaced on a hill behind it. These guns, taken from the Mexican squadron in the Alvarado River, were in poor condition and badly mounted. The fort was manned by thirty sailors and nine soldiers under Captain Pedro A. Diaz of the Mexican Navy. Between the fort and the town of Alvarado lay the Mexican squadron, composed of the brigs *Veracruzano Libre* and *Zempoalteca*, the schooner *Aguila*, and two gunboats. These vessels and three small inner forts commanded the approaches to the town. In over-all command was Commodore Tomás Marín.

Marín's plan of defense was excellent. It called for allowing the small craft of the American flotilla to enter the river and sail downstream into a cul-de-sac formed by the Mexican squadron and the three inner forts. The combined fire of the Mexican batteries, he believed, would quickly eliminate the attackers. He was probably right.

Conner intended that his expedition would sail early on the morning of 14 October, but a storm came up and delayed its departure. Shortly before midnight that same day, the *Cumberland* showed a blue light as a signal for the *Mississippi* to light her fires, and as a warning to the other ships that they were to leave before daybreak. Twenty-four hours later than originally intended, the vessels weighed anchor and got under way for Alvarado. The steamer *Vixen*, flying the Commodore's pennant and towing the gunboats

Reefer and *Bonita*, led the way. On her starboard bow steamed the *Mississippi*, and astern of her steamed the *McLane* towing the gunboats *Petrel*, *Forward*, and *Nonata*. Soon after sunrise, they arrived off the mouth of the Alvarado River.

Almost immediately, the plan of attack, which called for the *Mississippi* to shell the outer fort while the steamers towed the gunboats across the bar, ran into trouble. The *Mississippi* could not get close enough to the fort for her fire to damage it; the surf was so heavy that the pilots refused to take the vessels across the bar; and the wind, which the low-powered steamers needed to help them tow the gunboats through the fast-flowing water, died. Conner postponed the assault until after noon, when a sea breeze usually came up. In the meantime, the *Vixen* led the small vessels in a column inshore past the fort, each vessel firing a broadside as her guns came to bear. The bombardment accomplished little, although the *Forward* put two shots into the fort, and the *Mississippi*, firing at long range, knocked a gun from its carriage. Handicapped by their inadequate guns, the Mexicans erratically returned the fire without scoring a hit. When the small vessels ceased firing, they drew out of range, but the *Mississippi* kept up a desultory exchange of fire with the fort for the rest of the morning.

At noon Conner called his commanders to a conference aboard the *Vixen*, at which time it was decided that, since the swell had lessened, the bar should be crossed even if the afternoon breeze did not appear. Earlier, while the fort was being bombarded, Passed Midshipman Henry Rodgers had taken two of the *Mississippi*'s boats and sounded the bar.

For the crossing, Conner ordered the ships to form two columns: the first, consisting of the *Vixen* towing the *Reefer* and the *Bonita*, was to be under his personal command; the second, consisting of the *McLane* towing the *Nonata*, the *Petrel*, and the *Forward*, was to be under the command of Captain French Forrest of the *Cumberland* and was to take its place half a cable length—or some 360 feet—to port of the first. In each column there were six ships' boats carrying men to board the Mexican warships.

As the ships, with the *Vixen* in the lead, approached the bar, the current strengthened "causing the steamers to steer badly, and lessening their progress to not more than a mile or a mile and a half the hour." Nevertheless, the force made steady progress. The *Vixen*'s column arrived at the bar first, crossed it at about 1:45, and opened fire on the forts. The second column was half an hour behind, and as the *McLane* attempted to cross the bar, she grounded and her tows became fouled with one another. This setback completely upset Conner's plan. He turned to the captain of the *Vixen*, Commander Sands, and asked, "Well, Sands, what is to be done now?" Sands, ever impetuous, replied, "Go ahead and fight like hell." The soundness of Sands's advice was questionable and it was not taken by Conner. It seemed

46

evident that it would be a long time before the second division could get across the bar, if indeed it ever could, and Conner did not think that the little division that had crossed could possibly continue the attack alone and capture the Mexican vessels. Consequently, he ordered the *Vixen* to put about and, with her column, recross the bar. After executing its turn, the first division again came within range of the fort, and at 2:30 the *Vixen* opened fire. The *Bonita* and the *Reefer* soon joined in, but Mexican fire was concentrated on the *Vixen* and she took two hits. One hit carried away part of her hammock rail and two buckets, while the second entered her hull and wounded one man. The *Reefer* took a shell near her rudder head, but neither vessel was damaged seriously.

By the time the *Vixen's* column had recrossed the bar, the *McLane* had been refloated. She was not damaged by her grounding, but it was too late to continue the attack that day. Conner concluded that since the *McLane* had neither the power to breast the current nor shallow enough draft to cross the bar, she was useless and, without her, he did not have the necessary strength to carry out the attack. Therefore, much to the anger and disgust of the officers and crews of the vessels, he ordered the expedition back to Antón Lizardo.

Many of the Commodore's contemporaries took him to task for not pressing his attack after the *McLane's* grounding. Midshipman Parker later suggested that Conner probably could have pushed through to the Mexican vessels, and maybe he could, but it is doubtful that, with only three vessels, he could have seized them all. He was conscious of the likelihood that some of the Mexicans would escape up the river, in which case he would have to repeat the operation. His difficulty in getting light-draft vessels had made him fearful of losing any that he did have, and he was justifiably reluctant to expose them needlessly by going ahead with the attack when he did not have preponderant strength. It cannot be denied that he overestimated the opposition he was likely to encounter, but that is hindsight and does not alter the fact that his decision to break off the engagement was correct, particularly in view of Marín's well-planned defensive strategy.

V

TABASCO AND TAMPICO

Anxious to offset the squadron's lack of success at Alvarado by immediately conducting another operation, Commodore Perry suggested the seizure of Tabasco. Conner accepted the idea and ordered him to reconnoiter the coast from the Coatzacoalcos River to Carmen and, should conditions and circumstances permit, to seize Tabasco and any other river towns he could, to destroy cannon, munitions, other public stores, and any Mexican vessels that were not worth sending to Antón Lizardo.

In order to carry out his mission, Perry was given command of the *Mississippi*, the *Vixen*, the *McLane*, the *Reefer*, the *Bonita*, the *Nonata*, the *Forward*, and a 253-man landing force under Captain Forrest. Late in the evening of 16 October the vessels began leaving their anchorages. The next morning, when they were off the bar of Alvarado, they caught the American bark *Coosa* communicating with the shore, seized her, and sent her to Antón Lizardo as a prize. That same day, they ran into a heavy storm which they had to battle until they reached the Rio San Pedro y San Pablo five days later and turned north to the Tabasco River. The storm separated the *Reefer* from the other vessels and she missed the attack on Tabasco.

Seventy-two miles up the Tabasco River lies the town of the same name, and at its mouth is the port of Frontera. The Mexicans expected that the very shallow water on the bar lying across the approach to Frontera would be better defense than any fortifications they might build. The town of Tabasco was weakly defended: its garrison, commanded by the provincial governor Lieutenant Colonel Juan Bautista Traconis, consisted of only one company each of regular infantry and cavalry, twenty-three artillerymen, and a militia battalion, for a total of less than three hundred men; its only fortification was Fort Acachapan, a breastwork with four 24-pounders, about two miles downstream, near a sharp turn in the river known as Devil's Bend.

Perry's force spent 22 October preparing to cross the Tabasco bar, and the following day at about noon he shifted his flag from the *Mississippi* to the shallower-draft *Vixen*. Shortly thereafter, the *Vixen* towing the *Forward* and the *Bonita*, crossed into the river. The *McLane*, with the *Nonata* and the boats carrying Forrest's landing party in tow, followed her onto the bar but, as had become her custom, she grounded. She cast off the *Nonata*, and the latter, along with the boats, got across the bar and made her way upriver under sail.

At about three o'clock, the *Vixen*, making steady but slow progress against a four-knot current, sighted at the Frontera wharf two Mexican steamers preparing to flee. Casting off her tows, the American steamer churned ahead, and by the end of the afternoon watch was anchored off Frontera with her guns commanding the town and its shipping. The only vessel to get away was the schooner *Amado*, which fled upriver. Another schooner, the *Laura Virginia*, and two steamers, the *Petrita* and the *Tabasqueña*, were captured.

Perry detailed Lieutenant Joseph C. Walsh and a few men to hold Frontera with the distant support of the *Mississippi* and the *McLane*, still lying outside the bar, while the rest of the force went on to Tabasco. "Desirous of reaching Tabasco before they would have time for increasing their defenses," he embarked Forrest's men in the prize steamer *Petrita*, which headed upstream the next morning followed by the *Vixen* towing the *Forward* and the *Nonata*. After steaming for two hours, they sighted ahead of them the *Bonita*, which had pursued and captured the escaped schooner *Amado*. That afternoon and the following night were uneventful, but progress was slowed by lack of familiarity with the river and by a strong current.

At 8:45 on the morning of 25 October, the *Vixen* went to general quarters, and a few minutes later, Fort Acachapan came into view. Admirably located to command the most treacherous bend in the river, the fort would have been troublesome, had not its garrison fled on seeing the American vessels. A landing party went ashore about a mile below the fort, probably near Seven Palms where Perry landed in June 1847, and before noon the guns of the fort had been spiked.

By 1:00 p.m. the squadron was anchored off Tabasco, a sleepy little town of broad streets and one-story brick houses. An hour later, Perry sent Captain Forrest ashore with a peremptory demand for the town's unconditional surrender and a supporting letter from Juan D. Talagar, a Mexican he had brought from Frontera. Traconis refused to surrender and invited the squadron to fire whenever it pleased. Suspecting that the answer was bravado and not wanting to destroy the town, Perry thought that a few shots fired over it would induce surrender. Accordingly, he directed the *Vixen* to shoot at the flagstaff over the barracks. She did so at 3:05 and, on the third round, the flag disappeared from the flagpole—but only because its halyards had been cut.

When Perry found that the Mexican defenders had retired a short distance from the town, he sent Forrest ashore again at about five o'clock, this time with the landing party. The flotilla countered the scattered musket fire that greeted the men ashore as they moved into and occupied the parts of the town within range of the squadron's guns. Meanwhile, the Americans seized the brigs *Yunaute* and *Rentville*, the schooners *Tobasco* and *Alvarado*, and the sloop *Desada*, which were lying in the river. Another sloop, the *Campeche*, and a tow boat were also captured during this expedition, but details concerning when and how have not been recorded. As night approached, Perry ordered the landing party to re-embark because he was afraid that "from the proverbial heedlessness of sailors . . . should they and the marines be attacked in the narrow streets after dark, they would be cut off by sharp shooters from the houses."

In expectation of an attack, Perry kept the squadron at battle stations throughout the night, but no attack came. Moreover, he learned that Traconis not only refused to give in to the inhabitants' desire to surrender, but he prevented noncombatants from leaving the town, and when the landing party had been withdrawn the previous evening, he had posted his troops in buildings from which they could be dislodged only by artillery. Thus, Perry had the choice of abandoning his assault on the town or of continuing it at the risk of injuring noncombatants. Since he did not have enough men to hold the town even if he chose the second course and managed to occupy it, he "determined, from motives of humanity, not to fire again but to pass down to Frontera with my prizes."

However, Traconis forced the Commodore to alter his decision. At daylight on 26 October the Mexicans began shooting at the American vessels in the river and were answered with shrapnel. At seven o'clock, a white flag appeared ashore, and the squadron ceased firing while Forrest went to investigate. He returned with a request from the foreign merchants that the cannonade cease because it endangered their properties. Perry agreed not to fire unless he was fired on and, as an indication of his sincerity, hoisted a white flag on the *Vixen*. He then ordered the prizes to drop down the river and when one of them, the *Desada*, with Lieutenant William A. Parker and a prize crew aboard, grounded in front of the town at ten o'clock, the Mexicans opened fire on her and on the ships of the squadron. Realizing that the *Desada* was in trouble, Perry dispatched Lieutenant Charles W. Morris in one of the *Vixen*'s boats to her assistance. Morris' boat had to run a gauntlet of musketry to reach the stranded sloop and as it did so, he was mortally wounded. However, with support from the *Forward*, the crew aboard the *Desada* defended itself gallantly and managed to free the craft.

In retribution for what he considered the treachery of the Mexicans, Perry ordered his fleet to bombard Tabasco, but told his gunners to avoid hitting the houses of foreigners and other noncombatants. The fire from the shore continued for about thirty more minutes and when that stopped, Perry, having made his point, was ready to resume his plan to return to Frontera. In the skirmish, one American officer—Lieutenant Morris—and one seaman had been killed, two men had been wounded and two drowned. Five Mexican soldiers and four civilians had been killed.

An hour before midday, the *Vixen* hove up anchor and started steaming down the river, firing at the town as she passed it. That afternoon, as the squadron rounded Devil's Bend, the *Alvarado* ran aground, and since she was "a small schooner of little value," her captain, Passed Midshipman John E. Hart, set fire to her, then boarded the *Vixen*. Shortly before one o'clock the next morning the squadron anchored off Frontera.

While at Frontera, Perry sorted out his prizes: he burned the brig *Rentville*, the sloop *Campeche*, and one tow boat; he released the sloop *Desada* because her captain had rendered service to the expedition; he sent on to Antón Lizardo the steamer *Tabasqueña*, the brig *Yunaute*, and the schooners *Telegraph*, *Laura Virginia*, *Tobasco*, and *Amado*; the steamer *Petrita* sailed to Antón Lizardo in company with the *Mississippi*. Then, leaving the *McLane* and the *Forward* to blockade the port and to protect the neutral merchants from Mexican reprisals, he broke his pennant in the *Mississippi* and sailed for Antón Lizardo on the last day of the month. In the course of the one day's sailing, the *Mississippi* and the *Petrita* caught the American brig *Plymouth* landing cargo, and seized her.

The prizes brought back from Tabasco were of considerable value, and two of them were taken into American service: the *Petrita*, built in New York in 1843 to ply between Richmond and Norfolk and originally named the *Champion*, was assigned to Lieutenant Samuel Lockwood, and she made a very useful addition to the squadron; the *Laura Virginia* was renamed *Morris* in honor of Lieutenant Charles W. Morris and assigned to Lieutenant William T. Smith. Several of the others would undoubtedly have been useful, had they not been lost in a gale on 24 November.

Coming as it did after many failures, the successful action at Tabasco infused new spirit into the men of the squadron, and for those who participated, it broke the monotony of blockade duty and made life more bearable.

As noted several times previously, the American war plan called for the seizure of the weakly defended port of Tampico, the principal town of the state of Tamaulipas. The government in Washington was anxious that it be

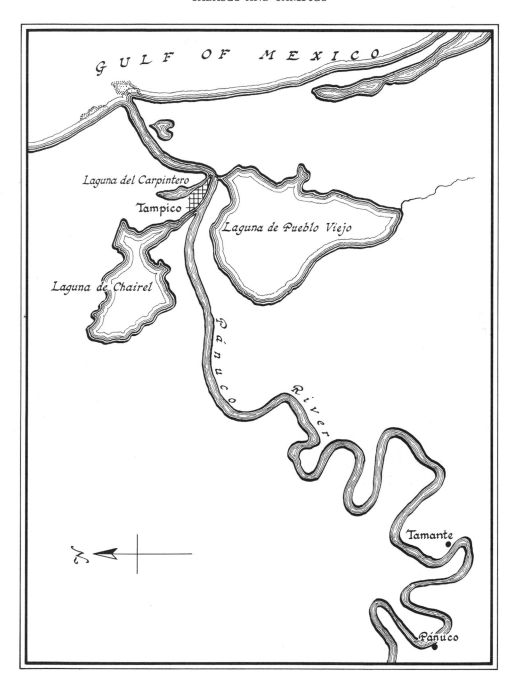

TAMPICO AND THE PÁNUCO RIVER

53

in American hands for three reasons: first, there was still the erroneous impression that there was a carriage road from there to San Luis Potosí; second, Tampico appeared to be a better base for future operations than the Rio Grande; and third, the seizure of Tampico would be a major step towards the conquest of the state of Tamaulipas.

Lying 210 miles north of Veracruz and five miles up the Pánuco River, Tampico is situated on a low ridge with the river in front of it and the lagoon of Carpintero in its rear. In this era, it ranked second only to Veracruz as a port on the Gulf Coast of Mexico but, unprotected as it was, it was considered the most dangerous one. There were normally less than eight feet of water over the bar at the mouth of the Pánuco, and most vessels had to anchor in the completely unprotected waters outside.

On 26 October Secretary Mason sent Conner copies of General Taylor's orders, stressed how greatly a naval attack on Tampico would help the Army, and directed that, if possible, one should be made.

When, through captured dispatches, news of the impending attack fell into the hands of Santa Anna, he ordered that Tampico be abandoned. Almost immediately, Anna Chase, the English wife of the former American consul at Tampico, wrote to Conner to tell him that the garrison had been ordered to evacuate the town and to join Santa Anna at San Luis Potosí. The evacuation, she reported, was set for 21 October and the artillery had already been loaded on the gunboats. On 24 October, four days after Mrs. Chase wrote, Lieutenant Hunt, who was on blockade duty at Tampico in the *Porpoise*, reported to Conner that the defenses of the town had been reduced to 150–200 men and the guns of a small fort. His information about the other guns was the same as Mrs. Chase's—they had been shipped on board the gunboats. In fact, having demolished the defenses and shipped the guns upriver to Pánuco, the garrison of Tampico completed its evacuation on 28 October.

Conner reported to Secretary Mason on 5 November that he could not undertake an expedition against Tampico until the depth of water over the bar increased. Within twenty-four hours, however, apparently because the reports from Hunt and Mrs. Chase had just reached him, he had changed his mind and was issuing orders for such an expedition. He sent the *St. Mary's* to relieve the *Porpoise* at Tampico so that the latter could lay out moorings at Lobos, a small coral island some twelve miles off the mainland and sixty-five miles southeast of Tampico, which he intended to use as a rendezvous.

Fortuitously, on 10 November, while Conner was still preparing for the expedition, the second of the steamers purchased from Brown and Bell, the *Spitfire*, reached Veracruz and, being not only a new vessel but a most efficient and useful one, her arrival immeasurably strengthened the squadron.

The day after she came in, Conner directed Captain Forrest to stay at Antón Lizardo as the Senior Officer Present, designated Lobos as the place where any vessels that got separated from the expedition should rendezvous, and sent the *Potomac* and the *Raritan* out a day ahead of the rest of the squadron with orders to cruise between Lobos and the mainland until further notice. Then, on the morning of 12 November, the *Princeton*, which wore the blue pennant of the Commodore, the *Mississippi*, the *Spitfire*, the *Vixen*, the *Reefer*, the *Bonita*, the *Petrel*, and the *Nonata* stood out from their anchorages. The *Cumberland* remained at Antón Lizardo, but some of her boats and one hundred of her men were embarked in the *Mississippi*.

It took the *St. Mary's* longer than expected to get to Tampico and relieve the *Porpoise*, with the result that when Conner arrived off Lobos the moorings had not been laid. Furthermore, neither the *Raritan* nor the *Potomac* had arrived. But, because the weather had been good for two days and might be expected soon to turn bad, and because he knew that the Mexicans could not offer resistance, he decided to head directly for Tampico without stopping at Lobos or waiting for his missing vessels. He left orders for the latter to join the main body of ships off Tampico.

Early on the morning of 14 November, the *Mississippi* sighted the *St. Mary's* off Tampico bar, and before long the *Porpoise* made out the *Princeton* and the *Mississippi* standing in with the *Spitfire*, the *Vixen*, the *Bonita* the *Petrel*, the *Reefer*, and the *Nonata* in tow. The Commodore had timed his arrival off the bar for daylight and, early in the forenoon watch, the squadron anchored near the *Porpoise*, the *St. Mary's*, and one of the ubiquitous British blockade inspectors, HMS *Daring*.

Conner's original plan was to divide his force into three divisions and to put Commodore Perry, Captain Gregory, and Captain Aulick in command of one each, but because of the absence of the *Potomac* and the *Raritan*, he could form only two divisions. The first division, under his own command, consisted of the *Spitfire*, the *Petrel*, the *Reefer*, and the boats from the *Cumberland*, the *Mississippi*, and the *Princeton*; the second division, under Perry, consisted of the *Vixen*, the *Bonita*, the *Nonata* and the boats of the *St. Mary's* and the *Porpoise*. All the ships' boats, between them, carried about three hundred men.

At 10:45 Conner broke out his pennant in the *Spitfire* and, fifteen minutes later, she signaled the attack by firing a gun. From one of the *Porpoise*'s boats, Lieutenant Hunt directed the Americans across the bar into the muddy Pánuco River. No resistance came from the dismantled fort at the mouth of the river. Pushing upstream between banks lush with tropical vegetation, the vessels passed the old fort below the town and by 12:35 the men could make out the American flag hoisted over the town by the indomitable Mrs. Chase. Fourteen minutes later, a boat flying a white flag put out from Tampico. The *Spitfire* replied with a similar banner, and was soon boarded by a delegation representing the *ayuntamiento*, or city council, sent to arrange for the defenseless town's capitulation.

When, under the interested gaze of hundreds of the townsfolk, the American vessels had anchored, the negotiators—Commanders Josiah Tattnall and Duncan N. Ingraham for the Americans, and Juan José de Sayor, Apolinar Marqués, and Francisco Cervantes for the Mexicans—transferred their deliberations ashore. After the talks had gone on for some time and no agreement had been reached, the Americans broke off the negotiations and informed the Mexicans that, since the landing party had occupied the town, Conner considered a capitulation unnecessary. They promised that, unless they were attacked, they would not interfere with the daily lives of the town's inhabitants. The Mexicans had no choice but to accept those terms. That afternoon, Conner sent Commodore Perry in the *Mississippi* to Brazos Santiago to notify the Army that Tampico had been captured and to ask that men to garrison it be sent as soon as possible.

While the negotiations were going on, the squadron had been busy consolidating its position by seizing three Mexican schooners, the *Union*, the *Pueblano*, and the *Isabel*, former gunboats that had been sold to a local merchant when the town was evacuated. These schooners were taken into the U.S. Navy, the *Pueblano* becoming the *Tampico*, and the *Isabel* becoming the *Falcon*. The merchant schooners *Mahonese* and *Ormigo* were also seized, the former entering the U.S. Navy.

Two days after the capture of Tampico, Commander Tattnall went up the Pánuco River with the *Spitfire*'s and the *Vixen*'s boats. He returned the same day, bringing with him several small prizes. From other sources Conner learned that the guns removed from the Tampico defenses were stored at Pánuco. Accordingly, at daylight on the 18th, he sent Tattnall to Pánuco to seize any usable cannon there, especially those that belonged to the captured gunboats, and destroy the rest. Tattnall sailed in the *Spitfire* and took with him the *Petrel* and a landing party of twenty Marines and twelve sailors.

The town of Pánuco is some twenty-five miles upstream and, after the first day's sailing, the expedition spent the night about six miles below it. Early the next morning, 19 November, the vessels completed their journey. In the course of the next several days, Tattnall and his men received the surrender of the town, dug up and destroyed nine 18-pounders, dumped a large amount of 18-pound shot into the river, and burned some camp equipment. When they left Pánuco on the morning of 21 November, they carried with them one 24-pounder from a gunboat, some copper, brass, and forty large bales of "excellent imported tent pins."

Perry arrived off Brazos Santiago on 16 November and, pausing only long enough to land an officer to notify the commander at Matamoros of the fall of Tampico and to explain the need for a garrison, he hastened to New Orleans. There, he conferred with Brigadier General George M. Brooke and Governor Isaac Johnson, who agreed to provide him with an engineer officer and fifty men, some supplies, and the State of Louisiana's field train of six 6-pounders and two howitzers. With these reinforcements embarked aboard the *Mississippi*, he set sail, and was back at Tampico two weeks after he had left.

At Matamoros the news of the fall of Tampico created a stir. Five days after its receipt, Lieutenant Colonel Francis S. Belton with seven companies—450 men—of the Second Artillery embarked in the steamer *Neptune* and sailed for Tampico. It took the steamer one day to reach her destination, and the following day another steamer, the *Sea*, came in from Matamoros carrying 200 more men and the guns of the men in the *Neptune*. A norther was blowing when the troops landed and on 25 November it sank the *Neptune*, but her crew was rescued by the *Spitfire* and there was no loss of life.

Commodore Conner, busy attending to many details, including the organization of the military government of Tampico, did not leave there until 13 December. However, with the town safely in American hands, he began dispersing the squadron two weeks earlier. The *Mississippi* towed the *Vixen*, the *Bonita*, and the *Petrel* back to Antón Lizardo, and the *Potomac*, having joined the squadron off Tampico on 22 November, a few days later than the *Raritan*, followed. The revenue cutter *Forward*, which had also joined the squadron at Tampico, was sent to New Orleans with dispatches, and the prize schooners, *Union*, *Pueblano*, and *Isabel*, were detached to the squadron's main base, but only two of them arrived: the *Union*, under Lieutenant John A. Winslow, ran on a reef on 16 December and was a total loss, but her crew was saved.

When Conner left Tampico on board the *Princeton*, he directed Commander Tattnall to stay there with the *Spitfire*, the *Reefer*, and the *Nonata*, until 2,000 or 3,000 more troops arrived, and then to return to Antón Lizardo, which he did on 3 January 1847.

The expedition to Tampico had been conceived as a measure to help the Army, which was expected to use the port as a base for an advance inland. In that respect, it was a failure, for the Mexicans realized, as Washington did not, that Tampico was not suitable for such a purpose and, consequently, they did not transfer any troops to defend it. Nevertheless, it was in American hands and a few months later it did play an important part in General Winfield Scott's operation against Veracruz, but only in the role of a staging point. Furthermore, the occupation of Tampico gave Conner's victory-starved squadron another taste of success, and it yielded as many gunboats as Conner had been able to wheedle from Washington in six months.

The Brig *Somers*

While Commodore Conner was at Tampico, the sloop of war *Boston* (Commander George F. Pearson), on her way to join his squadron, was running through North East Providence Channel in the Bahamas, in the early hours of 15 November, when she was caught in a squall and swept onto Eleuthera Island, a total wreck. Her loss hit the squadron hard. Conner had only the frigates *Cumberland*, *Potomac*, and *Raritan*, the sloops *John Adams* and *St. Mary's*, the brigs *Somers* and *Porpoise*, and the large steamers *Princeton* and *Mississippi* that could stay at sea to enforce the blockade during the stormy season. And of these nine seagoing vessels, only the two sloops and the two brigs made satisfactory blockaders: the frigates were too large and the steamers too valuable for blockade duty.

Nine days after the loss of the *Boston*, another misfortune befell the squadron when three of the prizes Perry had taken at Tabasco, the steamer *Tabasqueña*, the brig *Yunaute*, and the schooner *Tobasco*, foundered dur-

RAPHAEL SEMMES

ing a gale. Although none of them as yet had been converted to naval vessels, some would undoubtedly have proven useful to the squadron.

In the same month, Conner had to part with one of his frigates, and he did so in the most economical way possible. As a result of her grounding on Chopas Reef in July, the *Cumberland* needed dry-docking, and because the *Raritan* had served a cruise in the Brazil Squadron before joining Conner, her crew was nearing the end of its time of enlistment. So Conner ordered Captains Forrest and Gregory to switch ships and crews, and when the *Cumberland* sailed for Norfolk, she was manned by the crew and commanded by the captain of the *Raritan*.

While the *Somers*, now under the command of Lieutenant Raphael Semmes, was maintaining the blockade of Veracruz, in the absence of most of the squadron at Tampico, the Mexican schooner *Criolla* evaded her, ran into Veracruz, and moored against San Juan de Ulloa. Some of the *Somers'* officers, notably Passed Midshipman John R. Hynson, wanted to cut out the blockade-runner, and Semmes, chagrined at her escape, apparently agreed. Consequently, on the evening of 26 November, Semmes brought the *Somers* close inshore and put a boat over the side. Into her climbed Lieutenant James L. Parker, Passed Midshipmen Hynson and R. Clay Rogers, and five men.

With muffled oars, they pulled for the Mexican vessel and boarded her shortly before midnight. They had no trouble overcoming and securing her crew, but they did not do it without creating noise, and a sentinel on San Juan de Ulloa hailed to ask what was going on. In excellent Spanish, Parker replied that his men were drunk and he was putting them in irons. When they were ready to take their prize back to the *Somers*, the Americans found that there was not enough wind to sail her, so they set fire to her and taking with them seven prisoners, rowed back in their own boat amid a hail of shot and shell from the castle. This venture did not have too happy an ending, for it turned out that the *Criolla* was a spy ship, and that she had passed the blockade with Conner's blessing.

Not many days later, the *Somers* and Midshipman Rogers figured in another escapade near Veracruz. Rogers and Surgeon John N. Wright, having learned from British officers that a certain building near the beach was a Mexican powder magazine, volunteered to search out a path through the chaparral in which it stood, so that a landing party would be able to reach it. Their offer was accepted, and they spent the nights of 3–4 and 4–5 December in fruitless search. The next night, they went back to try again, and were seized by a Mexican patrol. Wright managed to escape, but Rogers did not, and concern for his safety mounted when the squadron heard that the Mexicans were threatening to try him as a spy, even though he was in full uniform when captured. They did not do so, but refused to parole him. Four months later, when General Scott went to Mexico City, Lieutenant Semmes went with him for the express purpose of securing Rogers' release. However, before Semmes had a chance to negotiate, Rogers escaped.

It was apparently that episode, which led to the capture of one of his officers, that moved Conner to forbid the squadron to make any more landings or even to approach close to the shore.

Almost immediately after the ill-fated landing by Wright and Rogers, the *Somers* furnished the squadron with more excitement: while chasing a blockade-runner on 8 December, she was caught by a sudden squall and thrown on her beam ends. Her captain and crew were unable to right her, and she quickly filled and sank. Thirty-two of her crew of seventy-six drowned, seven were captured by the Mexicans, and the rest were picked up by boats from British, French, and Spanish men-of-war stationed at Sacrificios.

Conner hoped to raise the sunken brig but there was not time to do so. Scott's projected landing at Veracruz was imminent and was making increasing demands on the shorthanded squadron, and a pro-Mexican revolution in Yucatán made it necessary to extend the blockade to that coast.

Nearly all the clandestine contraband trade between Yucatán and the rest of Mexico moved in small coasting vessels through the Laguna de Terminos and, therefore, had to pass the town of Carmen. Conner planned to cut that trade by placing a few small vessels at Carmen and on 16 December he ordered Commodore Perry to go there in the *Mississippi* and to take with him the *Vixen*, the *Bonita*, and the *Petrel*. Perry's orders were to destroy or bring off all cannon and public stores at Carmen, and to leave the *Vixen* and the *Petrel* there, then to go on to the Tabasco River and drop off the *Bonita*, which would replace the *Forward* and assist the *McLane*.

Perry sailed on 17 December and three days later his ships anchored off Carmen bar. The *Mississippi* drew too much water to cross the bar, so Perry transferred his pennant to the *Vixen* and, in company with the *Bonita* and the *Petrel*, sailed the five miles to the town of Carmen. The next morning, he demanded and received the town's unconditional surrender. Then, after having the powder found ashore loaded aboard the *Mississippi* and other munitions destroyed, he named Commander Sands military governor of Carmen. Sands was instructed to consider Carmen a captured town, to keep its inhabitants under surveillance, and respect lives, private property, and religion; but he was to stop trade with other places, to prevent any vessel from leaving port without a pass, to stop the taxing of commerce by the local authorities, and to consider the Yucatán coast to be under blockade. Further, Perry warned him to be on guard against surprise attack, to keep the *Vixen* coaled, and to see that both she and the *Petrel* always had full water tanks: he was told to be watchful, but to cultivate the friendship of the natives.

Perry recrossed the Carmen bar in the *Bonita* on 22 December and broke his pennant in the *Mississippi* again, then with the *Bonita* in tow, the flagship steamed for the Tabasco River. After having her water supply replenished, the *Mississippi* left the Tabasco on Christmas Day and cruised along the coast in search of Mexican shipping. After two days' cruising, she was off Alvarado, where she took two prizes, the Spanish schooner *Isabel*, which was later released, and the Mexican schooner *Amelia*, both outbound for Havana. That same day, having completed her ten-day mission, the *Mississippi* anchored once again at Antón Lizardo.

Two days before Perry left Carmen, Conner had addressed a message to Sands advising him of reports that the pro-American party had returned to power in Yucatán, and directing him to lift the blockade but to continue the occupation. Thus, fortunately for the squadron's resources, the need to blockade the coast of Yucatán was of short duration.

Nevertheless, a shortage of vessels and logistic problems still plagued Conner. On 17 December he reported to the Navy Department that the *Mississippi* was in urgent need of repairs to her boilers and would have to go to Norfolk, and four days later he once again reminded the Secretary of his need for more supply vessels. In late December the supply situation at Antón

Lizardo became so critical that the *Potomac* and the storeship *Relief* (Lieutenant Oscar Bullus) had to be sent to Pensacola for provisions and water. The water shortage was somewhat alleviated when the Commodore contracted with Nathaniel Hoyt of Galveston for 50,000 gallons of it to be delivered at Antón Lizardo by mid-February.

Although the forthcoming attack on Veracruz introduced a host of problems for the squadron in the Gulf of Mexico, the difficulties of supply began to ease after the turn of the year. The first of the replacement warships, the beautiful, clipper-lined sloop of war *Albany* (Captain Samuel L. Breese), reached Antón Lizardo on 8 January 1847, and in February a number of storeships came in with an array of stores and munitions and with water. The supply bureaus had finally begun to function effectively.

Before censuring the bureaus too severely for their slow response to the needs of a distant war, it should be remembered that their organization and their operating procedures did not lend themselves to hasty conversion to wartime conditions, and that the Mexican War presented logistic problems without precedent in American naval experience. Nor did the fleet commanders show great awareness of the need for them to estimate in advance what their requirements would be.

To put the American performance in perspective and judge the validity of complaints made by the Gulf Squadron, and by the Pacific Squadron also, about the deficiencies in their logistic support, one need only look at the fiasco in British logistics during the Crimean War some eight years later.

VI

FROM WASHINGTON TO LOBOS

After President Polk learned on 19 September 1846 that Santa Anna had no intention of concluding a peace treaty, he and his Cabinet, while leaving the door open for negotiations, began to lay plans for new campaigns, the first of which had resulted in the capture of Tampico.

The Cabinet met on 10 October to consider the "manner of prosecuting the Mexican war." Most of the discussion concerned a revived suggestion for an expedition against Veracruz, because the President had "recently received" information that a landing could be made near the island of Sacrificios, and that Veracruz could be invested from the rear. That information put a new light on the operation, and the President called Francis M. Dimond, the former American consul at Veracruz, to Washington for consultation. Dimond met with Polk a week after the Cabinet meeting and confirmed that what the President had been told was correct. That evening, 17 October, the President, Secretary of State Buchanan, Secretary of War Marcy, Secretary of the Navy Mason, Paymaster General Brigadier General Nathan Towson, and Chief of Ordnance and Hydrography Commodore Lewis Warrington met with Dimond at the White House and spent about two hours discussing an operation against Veracruz.

Ten days later, the Commanding General, U.S. Army, Major General Winfield Scott, wrote a paper entitled "Vera Cruz and Its Castle," in which he pointed out that to capture Veracruz and not advance inland would be meaningless and not worth the cost, and he assessed methods of capturing it:

> To take the castle of San Juan d'Ulloa would, no doubt, be a virtual and prompt capture of the city lying under its guns. The reverse . . . would probably, not be equally certain. . . . The castle, after the loss of the city, might still hold out for many weeks, perhaps months, until compelled to surrender from the want of subsistence and water, unless earlier reduced by land and water batteries, escalade, &c.

It is believed that the castle, with a competent garrison, cannot be taken by water batteries alone; or by the latter and an escalade, without a very heavy and disproportionate loss of life. . . .

For these reasons, it seems decidedly preferable to capture the city first and by its means . . . to attack the castle by land and water, including joint escalades —unless it should be found probably that the want of food and drinking water would lead to an early surrender.

Scott estimated that the plan to take the city first would require an army of 10,000 men, including 2,000 cavalrymen and 600 artillerymen, enough special landing craft to put ashore 2,500 men and two light batteries at the beginning of the operation, and the addition of bomb brigs to the squadron in the Gulf of Mexico. In his opinion, such a force could be put afloat off Veracruz by 1 January 1847. Elaborating on his earlier proposals, Scott estimated on 12 November that the 10,000-man army might be made up of 1,200 men drawn from the blockading squadron, and the remaining 4,000 regulars and 5,000 volunteers from Major General Zachary Taylor. Again concluding that "the expedition of 10,000 men may be put afloat, at the latest by the first of January," he commented that, since the yellow-fever season did not begin in the coastal region until May, that would be early enough for even a protracted siege to begin.

Scott was still working out his plan and estimates when the War Department received a letter from General Taylor, dated 15 October, suggesting a defensive stand in the north and a landing near Veracruz or Alvarado for a march to the Mexican capital. He was of the opinion that at least 25,000 men, including 10,000 regulars, would be needed for the landing and march to Mexico City. Four days after the receipt of Taylor's letter, on 16 November, Scott raised his estimate of the forces needed for an expedition to Veracruz to: 4,000 regulars, 10,000 volunteers, 1,000 Marines and sailors from the fleet; 50 transports of from 500 to 750 tons; a pontoon train; and 140 flat boats, sufficient to put ashore simultaneously 5,000 men and 8 guns.

After considering Scott's memoranda and the supporting views of Senator Thomas Hart Benton of Missouri, with whom the President had discussed the operation earlier in the month, the Cabinet agreed that an attack should be made on Veracruz and, on 19 November, President Polk, with the concurrence of Secretaries Marcy and Mason, appointed General Scott to command the expedition. Scott was, without doubt, the ablest general then in the U.S. Army, and one of the ablest in the history of the United States. Yet, Polk had grave misgivings about appointing him, for not only was the new commander a professional military man, but he was an active Whig, and it has never been determined which Polk distrusted more. Scott was given the command because no other general of sufficient rank was acceptable to the

WINFIELD SCOTT

administration, and because the proposal to make Senator Benton a lieutenant general and place him in command failed in the Senate.

Early on the day of his appointment, General Scott called on the President at the White House, and the two men discussed the forthcoming operation and the need for confidence between the government and the commander in the field. They parted cordially and with expressions of a mutual confidence which was to evaporate even before the Commanding General left the country.

For the next four days Scott was in a whirlwind of activity as he prepared for his departure for the south, and later lamented that he had been allowed only four days "when twenty might have been most advantageously spent in the great bureaux" of the War Department. Nevertheless, he did manage to draw up and submit to the Secretary of War a memorandum detailing his requirements in men and supplies.

Of particular importance and interest among the items Scott requested are the flatboats, or surfboats, for carrying his assault troops. Designated by a naval officer, Lieutenant George M. Totten, and built in the vicinity of Philadelphia for the Quartermaster Department of the Army, they were the first specially built American amphibious craft and were admirably suited to their purpose, their only weakness being their rather light planking. They were double-ended, broad-beamed, and flat-bottomed, with frames built of well-seasoned white oak and thwarts of pine. They were built in three sizes, so that they could be stacked for transport: the largest was 40 feet long and could carry 45 or more men; the medium size was 37 feet 9 inches long and could carry 40 or more men; while the smallest was 35 feet 9 inches long and could not carry as many as 40 men. Each one carried a crew of six oarsmen, one coxswain, and a skipper.

Richard F. Loper, the Army agent who negotiated the contracts for the purchase of the surfboats, stipulated a price of $795 per piece and completion within one month. Forty-seven sets, or 141 boats, were ordered and were to be shipped to the Gulf in vessels with oversize hatches which allowed them to be stowed in the hold.

To reinforce the Home Squadron for the forthcoming operation at Veracruz, the Navy Department ordered the crack ship-of-the-line *Ohio* (Captain Silas H. Stringham), destined for the Pacific, to temporary duty in the Gulf, while the sloops *Germantown* (Commander Franklin Buchanan), *Saratoga* (Commander David G. Farragut), and *Decatur* (Commander Richard S. Pinckney) were made ready to serve a cruise in Conner's squadron. Also, four brigs or schooners and one bark, the *Electra* (ex-*Rolla*), were purchased. The *Electra* was to serve as a supply vessel, and the brigs, the *Etna* (ex-*Walcott*), the *Stromboli* (ex-*Howard*), the *Hecla* (ex-*I. L. Richardson*), and the *Vesuvius* (ex-*St. Marys*), all coastal freighters of about

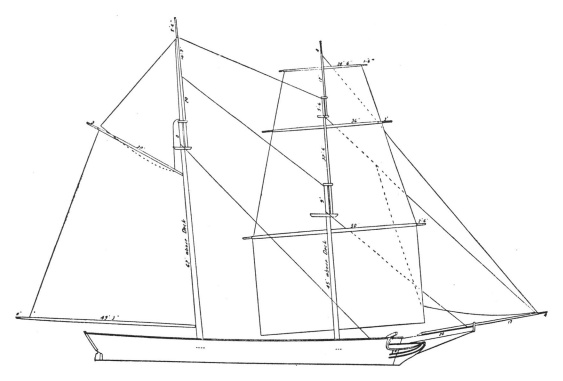

The Bomb Brig *Etna*
Howard I. Chapelle

180 tons, were outfitted as bomb brigs. The first two underwent conversion at Boston, and the last two at New York. Each vessel was armed with one 10-inch columbiad on a pivot mounting amidships.

However, in spite of these efforts, none of the naval reinforcements reached Veracruz in time to participate in the landing there because, as Commodore Morris explained to Conner on 4 March 1847, "The inclemency of the weather and other causes . . . delayed them much longer than anticipated." President Polk later charged that there had been a lack of coordination between the services, a charge amply supported by the record.

In the winter of 1846–47 the fortifications at Veracruz were in poor condition. Strategic points in the city walls were in need of repair, many of the guns were unserviceable, and powder and provisions were very scarce. The official return of ordnance supplies dated 10 November 1846 showed only 65 *quintales** and 80 pounds of powder in Veracruz and 349 *quintales* and 82 pounds in the Castle of San Juan de Ulloa. The same report showed that 54 guns in the city and 12 in the castle were unmounted. The powder short-

* A *quintale* was approximately 100 pounds.

age was alleviated somewhat when the French blockade-running bark *Anax* arrived on 5 January 1847 and unloaded 1,000 *quintales* of it.

General Scott left Washington on 23 November 1846 and headed for the scene of action in Mexico. He traveled via New York and New Orleans and carried with him Secretary Marcy's orders of 23 November:

> The President several days since communicated in person to you his orders to repair to Mexico, to take command of the forces there assembled, and particularly to organize and set on foot an expedition to operate on the Gulf coast, if on arriving at the theater of action you shall deem it to be practicable. It is not proposed to control your operations by definite and positive instructions, but you are left to prosecute them as your judgement, under a full view of all the circumstances, shall dictate. The work is before you and the means provided, or to be provided, for accomplishing it, are committed to you, in the full confidence that you will use them to the best advantage.

Six days after he left Washington, Scott wrote from New York to advise General Taylor that he would soon be joining him on the Rio Grande and to break the news that the forthcoming expedition would probably take most of Taylor's seasoned troops. The letter was couched in terms intended to acquaint Taylor with unwelcome facts without unnecessarily hurting his paper-thin vanity. When he arrived in New Orleans, Scott wrote again to Taylor on 20 December and gave him more detail about the impending operation:

> . . . . Your advice is invited and will be highly acceptable. Perhaps you may be able to meet me on the Rio Grande, say at Camargo, or lower down the river; and I shall send an officer to you, at an early day, who will be able to communicate my views to you in greater detail.
> To make up the force for the new expedition, I foresee that I shall, as I intimated in my letter . . . be obliged to reduce you to the defensive. . . .
> Including the regulars and volunteers at Tampico, or on their way thither, I may now say that I shall want from you, say [Brigadier General William J.] Worth's division of regulars, made up to 4,000 men; two field batteries . . . and 500 regular cavalry; besides 500 volunteer cavalry and as many volunteer foot as you can possibly spare—leaving you a sufficient force to defend Monterey and maintain your communications with Camargo, the mouth of the Rio Grande and Point Isabel. The whole of this force will be needed at the latter points by the middle of January.

In New Orleans, Scott learned that the Island of Lobos would make a good rendezvous for his transports. Accordingly, on 23 December he began making arrangements to collect them there, and notified Conner that:

> Every effort will be made to get afloat off the Brazos San Iago, and off Tampico, in time, the necessary number of troops. I have estimated twelve or fifteen thousand, besides the numbers you may be able to supply from the blockading squadron, to be highly desirable; but you may expect me, if I can get

afloat, in time to meet you early in February, ten, eight, or even five thousand men. . . . I have appointed the 15th of the next month for the assemblage . . . off the two points mentioned above; but do not hope that more than three regiments of the new volunteers will be up so early. I shall, therefore, have to draw more largely upon the forces already on and beyond the Rio Grande.

He went on to ask Conner about the strength of any Mexican field army he would be likely to face after the landing, and requested that any reports from his—Scott's—spies in Mexico be forwarded to him. It is interesting to note that Scott's letter did not mention the point of descent—Veracruz.

After writing these letters, Scott boarded the Army steamer *Alabama* and sailed for Brazos Santiago. The day after Christmas, while still at sea, he wrote Conner again and disclosed his plans in greater detail than he had done in the earlier letter:

> The point of descent will not be determined until I shall have looked at the coast, and had the benefit of a full conference with you; but I now suppose that the nearer to the city [Veracruz] we land will be the better. Your knowledge of the beach (its shoals and surf) is, probably, already sufficiently minute. I, however, throw out the suggestion that you may, if necessary, make a particular study of the subject before my arrival. Every transport will bring open boats sufficient to land her troops, and there will be others for the field guns needed at the first moment.
>
> . . . I have done all in my power to favor the speculation that my purpose is to attack San Luis de Potose, from Tampico, after forming a junction with Major General Taylor, and it is important that this belief should prevail up to my arrival off Vera Cruz.
>
> I wish I could name a day, certain, for our meeting. The 1st of February may be about the time; but, I fear, a little too early. I shall certainly be infinitely chagrined if I am not in a condition to attempt the descent, with your cooperation, before the 15th of that month.

Like most of Commodore Conner's letters, the one in which he responded to General Scott, dated 18 January 1847, was overoptimistic, but the facts it contained were reasonably accurate:

> The present would be the most favorable time for the contemplated attack upon Vera Cruz. . . . Provisions for the garrison are obtained with the greatest difficulty, and in quantities sufficient only to last from day to day . . . I am of the opinion, that if four or five thousand troops could be landed in the neighborhood of Vera Cruz by the end of this month or the beginning of the next, so as completely to invest the place, and cut off all communication with the country, its surrender, in less than ten days, with that of the castle, would be certain, and probably without the necessity of firing a gun. . . . In my opinion there are but two points at all eligible for this purpose [the landing]—one on the beach, due west from Sacrificios; the other on the shores of this anchorage [Antón Lizardo]. . . .

Although the landings at Veracruz were imminent, Conner could no longer delay sending his best vessel, the big steam frigate *Mississippi*, to

Norfolk for the repairs which he had termed urgent in December. She reached Norfolk on 13 January, and when a board of survey reported that it would take six weeks to make the repairs, Perry, impatient to be back in the Gulf in time for the Veracruz operation, hurried to Washington and talked Engineer-in-Chief Charles H. Haswell into making a personal survey of the situation. Haswell's conclusion was that the work could be completed in two weeks if it was done on a round-the-clock basis. He was wrong, it still took six weeks.

After arranging for his ship to be repaired as Haswell suggested and under his supervision, Perry hastened back to Washington to report to Secretary of the Navy Mason. Just what he told Mason is uncertain, but many of his contemporaries believed that he presented Conner in an unfavorable light and pushed his own claims for command of the squadron. Such intrigue would have been in keeping with his character. In any event, when he left Washington he was carrying orders for him to succeed Conner.

While Perry was waiting for his ship to be repaired, Secretary Mason used his services in a capacity for which he was well fitted—to supervise the outfitting of the small vessels intended for the Home Squadron—and gave him authority to "communicate to the heads of the Bureaux to hasten them and give their commanders any necessary orders."

General Scott reached Brazos Santiago on 27 December and a week later, on 3 January 1847, called for the detachment of most of General Taylor's troops—1,000 cavalry, 4,000 regular and 4,000 volunteer infantry, less those already at Tampico and some other detachments. They were to move to the mouth of the Rio Grande without waiting for further orders from Taylor.

Meanwhile, the troops and supplies that Scott had requested before he left Washington were being prepared. According to a summary made on 15 December 1846 by the Secretary of War, Scott's requirements called for, among other things, the chartering of 41 transports: 12 to carry the volunteers, ordnance, and supplies scheduled to sail from ports on the Atlantic; 5 to carry surfboats; 10 to go out in ballast from ports on the Atlantic and pick up troops scheduled to sail from ports on the Gulf; and 14 to be supplied by the Quartermaster at New Orleans.

Following General Scott's instructions of 3 January 1847, Major General William O. Butler issued orders on the 8th for the various detachments to move towards their respective ports of embarkation, and on 12 January Scott reported to Secretary Marcy:

In a week I shall begin to expect the arrival, off this place, of ships with troops and supplies, destined for the expedition against Vera Cruz. After replenishing their water tanks, if necessary, from the Rio Grande, they will be ordered to rendezvous behind the Island of Lobos. . . . I do not at present doubt my arrival off Vera Cruz, with a respectable force, by the 15th, I hope, the 10th of next month. The delay will be in getting down, and embarking in this vicinity, the troops called for from Saltillo, and Monterey, and perhaps in the march from Victoria upon Tampico. . . . I shall attempt the descent, &c., with even half the numbers I should wish to give to any one of my juniors for the same service. . . . A mail from New Orleans is expected on the abatement of this raging norther— by her I hope to hear that the volunteers, boats for debarkation, &c., &c., are in a state of forwardness. . . .

Scott soon learned that his expectations far outdistanced reality. A series of unforeseen developments upset completely the plans for providing the transports. Bad weather delayed the sailing of most of the vessels by 25 to 30 days, and a misunderstanding resulted in the chartering of the ten vessels that were to go out in ballast being countermanded. He did not have enough troops, supplies, and surfboats to allow him to think of making the descent until a month after he made his report to Marcy.

Finally, 53 vessels were furnished from Atlantic ports and 163 from Gulf ports, but it is surprising, and a tribute to one of America's greatest soldiers, that, with his logistic support totally disorganized at the very start, the expedition to Veracruz ever got under way. Nevertheless, on 15 January, he directed the transports carrying troops directly from the United States to rendezvous at Lobos.

On 23 January General Worth reached Brazos Santiago, followed in a few days by his division. Two days later, the division under Major General Robert Patterson completed its move from Victoria to Tampico, and on 28 January part of the South Carolina Regiment left Mobile aboard the *Ellerslie* bound for Lobos.

When he wrote to Marcy again, on 26 January, Scott was still optimistic about his chances of getting the expedition afloat by the middle of February: "The embarkation of Brevet Brigadier General Worth's division I hope to commence at the mouth of the Rio Grande and at this place [Brazos Santiago] within three or four days." He added that Colonel Joseph G. Totten, who had just arrived from New Orleans, expected that sufficient ordnance, ordnance stores, and surfboats to make the landing would reach Lobos by 10 February, then expressed his own hope that the *Ohio* would arrive at Veracruz in time to assist in the attack.

With the embarkation about to get under way, the lack of transport that was to plague the whole operation began to make itself felt. When Major Abner R. Hetzel, the Chief Quartermaster at Brazos Santiago, reported on 2 February that twelve vessels chartered at New Orleans to pick up troops at the Brazos and transport them to Lobos had not yet appeared, Scott directed him to charter locally enough vessels to get the troops at the Brazos afloat by 10 February and to get those at Tampico afloat within the following five days.

One transport came in to Brazos Santiago on 5 February, embarked some of the men of the 8th Infantry, and left the next day for Lobos. However, there was no sign of any others, and on 9 February Scott lamented to General Patterson:

All the transports for the reception of the 8,000 men, regulars and old volunteers, here and at Tampico, were expected to leave New Orleans the 24th ultimo, and to touch at this place, by the 1st instant. But one has yet arrived! . . . . As transports may arrive at Tampico, I wish you to embark the troops under your command as follows: 1. [Brigadier General David E.] Twiggs brigade. 2. [Brigadier General Gideon J.] Pillow's brigade, and 3. [Brigadier General John A.] Quitman's . . . I cannot leave this place for Tampico, &c., until some of the cruel uncertainties, in respect to the approach of transport, ordnance and ordnance supplies, shall be removed. Sixty odd surfboats, out of one hundred and forty, are already up. I will make the descent near Vera Cruz if not another should arrive.

Six days after writing the above, when Scott broke out his red and blue pennant in the Army steamer *Massachusetts* and sailed for Tampico, the transports were still missing. Worth waited at Brazos Santiago so that he could complete the embarkation of his division as transports arrived, but even when he sailed on 25 February he had to leave behind six companies of dragoons.

Meanwhile, the regiments of new volunteers were assembling at Lobos. On 3 February, when the elements of the South Carolina Regiment that had left Mobile on 28 January arrived, they found the Louisiana and First Pennsylvania regiments already there. Scott's original intention was to take only four of the new regiments—the First and Second Pennsylvania, the Louisiana, and the New York—to Veracruz, but since a mistake had been made and the South Carolinians had gone directly to Lobos, he included them in the expedition. Then, when Scott found that another mistake had been made and, instead of going to Brazos Santiago, the Second Mississippi Regiment had gone to Tampico and from there to Lobos, he sent it back north to the Brazos so that, when the regiment was disembarked, its transports could be used to help bring up Worth's veteran troops.

Scott reached Tampico on 18 February and the following day he wrote to tell Conner that, although he was short of transports, he intended to go on down to Antón Lizardo and hoped to be there by the end of the month. He stayed at Tampico only two days, then went on to Lobos. Patterson's force left for Lobos nine days later, on 29 February.

Upon receipt of Scott's letters of 23 and 26 December, Conner sent Commander Saunders in the *St. Mary's* to Brazos Santiago with instructions to assist Scott and to protect the incoming transports, which would be inviting targets for any privateers that might be operating out of Cuba. When

The *St. Mary's* (right) stands by as
General Scott's transports rendezvous
off the island of Lobos.
Franklin D. Roosevelt Library, Hyde Park, New York

Saunders got there on 14 January, Scott asked him to stay off the Brazos
and to communicate with the transports that touched there. On 1 February
he told Saunders, "I hope to be at Tampico by the 6th instant, at Lobos by
the 10th, and up with Commodore Conner [at Antón Lizardo] by the 15th,"
and he asked Saunders to go to Lobos "to give protection, advice and it
may be assistance, to any of the ships of my expedition ordered to await
further orders at the general rendezvous."

Following the dispatch of the *St. Mary's*, Conner wrote a long letter,
dated 11 January, to Scott informing him that there were 1,800 Mexican
regulars and fewer than 1,000 militiamen in the town of Veracruz and
another 1,000 men in the Castle of San Juan de Ulloa, and that there was no
reason to expect much opposition either during the landings or during the
siege. He offered 600 seamen and Marines from the squadron for the landing force. Three days after writing, he sent the *Porpoise* to Tampico with
dispatches for Scott and later information on the garrison at Veracruz. Still
another message for the General was carried by Captain Breese in the *Albany*
which left for Tampico on 18 January, and Captain Breese was instructed
to lend any assistance he could to the Army. However, both the *Porpoise*
and the *Albany* returned to Antón Lizardo after delivering their messages.

The *St. Mary's* arrived at Lobos on 5 February to assist the transports, as
requested by Scott. Late that night, Captain Russell P. Mace of the Louisiana

Regiment and the master of the transport *Ondiaka*, boarded her to report that his vessel carrying Colonel Lewis G. De Russey, 140 men of the regiment, and 60 tons of powder, had gone aground on the mainland north of Cape Royo. The Colonel and his men had gone ashore and were being besieged by a brother-in-law of Santa Anna, General Martín Perfecto de Cos, an old war-horse who had played an important role in Texas, and a force of 980 men. Because the pilot claimed that the *St. Mary's* was too big a ship for him to take out in the dark, her departure was delayed until daylight. When she reached the wrecked ship at noon, Saunders found that Colonel De Russey and his men, using the classic ruse of lighting their campfires and then marching off into the darkness, had made their escape to Tampico earlier that morning. There was then nothing Saunders could do but order the *Ondiaka* to be burned.

On 5 February Conner relayed to Scott rumors that Santa Anna was going to march to Mexico City, where the Army would declare him dictator. He also reported that 1,000 militiamen had arrived at Veracruz to strengthen its defenses, and suggested that the transports should assemble at Antón Lizardo preparatory to the move to the landing place.

As the time set for the landing approached, Conner began calling in his scattered vessels. On 8 February, he sent Lieutenant Hunt in the *Porpoise* to collect the *Vixen* and the *Petrel* from Carmen and the *Bonita* from Tabasco. Ten days later, the *Albany*, which had been cruising off Punta Delgada, was recalled. By the middle of the month, the squadron was assembled and ready to assist an army which Conner expected to arrive any day.

VII

LANDING AT VERACRUZ

Major General Winfield Scott reached the anchorage off the island of Lobos in the *Massachusetts* on 21 February. The First and Second Pennsylvania, the South Carolina, and parts of the Louisiana, Second Mississippi, and Second New York regiments were already there, but more men were due and most of his train was missing. Nevertheless, the day after his arrival, he informed Conner that he was sending ahead to Antón Lizardo two vessels with ordnance supplies, two with surfboats, and some transports, and requested him to have the troops landed and encamped ashore. When the surfboats got there, they were landed, inspected and readied by naval officers, then arranged in divisions of ten on Salmedina Island.

Although Scott grew more and more impatient for his men and supplies to arrive and became fearful of the approach of the yellow-fever season, he took advantage of the delay to drill his troops—except the men of the smallpox-infected Second Pennsylvania. Also, he advised the Secretary of War that his being held up at Lobos was due to "no want of foresight, arrangement or energy on my part."

On 26 February he wrote to Conner again and told him that as soon as the regulars, one-third of his siege train, and some more surfboats arrived, he would leave for Antón Lizardo and attempt a landing. Two days later, he reported to Secretary Marcy:

I cannot wait more than forty-eight hours for any body, except Brevet Brigadier General Worth, and [Captain James] Duncan's and [Captain Francis] Taylor's horse artillery companies, or for anything behind; and two thirds of the ordnance and ordnance stores, and half the surf boats, are yet unheard of. . . .

When February ran out and Scott had still not arrived at Antón Lizardo, Conner sent Lieutenant Hunt in the *Porpoise* to find out what was keeping

75

him at Lobos and when the Army might be expected to arrive off Veracruz. The brig reached Lobos on 2 March, the day after Patterson's volunteers had come in from Tampico and about the same time as Worth's division of regulars came in from Brazos Santiago, so she was just in time to escort the leading contingent of troops south. After breakfast that same day, the *Massachusetts* signaled each transport to send an officer aboard. There, they received sailing orders for Antón Lizardo.

Flying the General's red and blue pennant at her main truck, the *Massachusetts* got under way during the afternoon and the transports fell in behind her. As the fleet sailed south, the *Massachusetts* moved among the ships and the troops cheered and the sailors sang:

We are bound for the shores of Mexico,
and there, Uncle Sam's soldiers, we will land, ho, ho!

Anticipating the arrival of Scott's force, Conner had ordered Captain Aulick on 27 February to take the *Potomac* up to Isla Verde and direct the incoming transports to the anchorage between Salmedina and Antón Lizardo. Later, he sent the *Albany* and the *John Adams* to assist in that service. Aulick was instructed to put an officer who could act as pilot on board each transport, then, when he ran short of officers competent to do that, to give the masters of the transports the information they needed to pass safely inside Blanquilla Reef to their destination.

For almost two days, the voyage of the *Massachusetts* and her accompanying vessels was uneventful, but on 4 March the transports were tossed about by a moderate norther that sprang up before daylight and speeded them along. The gale was still blowing during the first dog watch when lookouts in the *Potomac* sighted two sails, which they correctly assumed to be the vanguard of Scott's transports. In the course of that night and the following day, some forty transports touched at Isla Verde, took aboard pilots or were given instructions, and stood in for Antón Lizardo. A soldier who had witnessed the scene from the deck of his transport remembered that, "The whole eastern horizon looked like a wall of canvas," and Midshipman Parker later recalled, "The first thing that excited our astonishment was the great amount of sail carried by the transports, and the next the skillful manner in which their captains threaded their way between the reefs!" Be that as it may, the records show that at least one transport ran aground and had to be pulled free by the *Princeton.*

Among the ships that came in to Antón Lizardo on 5 March were the *Massachusetts*, the *Porpoise*, and the *St. Mary's*, but Conner did not find time to write Secretary Mason that Scott had arrived until two days later, at which time he anticipated that the landing would probably take place in two or three days and would "scarcely be opposed. . . ."

Immediately upon arrival, General Scott conferred with Commodore Conner and, as the latter reported to Mason on 10 March, "a speedy disembarkation was resolved upon; it being important that we should effect a landing before a norther should come on, as this would delay us two or three days." The two commanders decided to make a joint reconnaissance of the potential landing places before going ashore. Consequently, at nine o'clock on the morning of 6 March the little steamer *Petrita*, carrying the Commodore, Generals Scott, Worth, Patterson, Twiggs, and Pillow, and Scott's staff, including Captains Robert E. Lee and Joseph E. Johnston, and Lieutenants Pierre G. T. Beauregard and George G. Meade, got under way for Collado Beach, which Conner considered the best place for the landings.

A gently curving strip of sand paralleled by a line of sand hills about 150 yards inland, Collado Beach lies behind Sacrificios Island, two and one-half miles southeast of Veracruz. When the inspection of that beach had been completed, the *Petrita* steamed north along Blanquilla Reef towards Veracruz, a route which the small craft of the squadron had often taken without getting into any trouble. However, on this occasion, when the *Petrita* came within a mile and a half of San Juan de Ulloa, its big guns opened on her. The first shell went over the steamer, the second short of her, and the third burst high over her. Lieutenant Lockwood did not wait for a fourth. He turned his frail vessel, with her valuable cargo, out of range. By the time the Mexicans stopped firing, they had aimed about ten shells at the *Petrita*.

Since the reconnaissance had not revealed any defensive preparations at Collado Beach, Scott concurred in Conner's recommendation that the landings should be made there. Although its anchorage was the most protected and was in other respects the most suitable for the operation, it had one considerable drawback—it was too small safely to hold all the transports. Conner suggested, however, that if the large naval vessels were used to carry assault troops, the only transports needed would be the Army's five steamers. Thus, the number of vessels to be crowded into the anchorage would be reduced. Scott concurred, and the Army transports were placed temporarily under naval control. The plan also called for the transports, once they had debarked their troops, to leave the anchorage and thus make room for the supply vessels.

Scott's correspondence with Conner and his orders, particularly General Order Number 28 of 23 February which contained detailed instructions for the signals to be used during the operations at Veracruz, indicate that he thought of the landings as a venture that would involve the Army alone. Not until reconnaissance of possible landing beaches showed that the troops would have to land from naval vessels, does he seem to have realized that it would have to be a joint operation.

With the site for the landings decided, Conner's next move was to put as much strain as possible on the food supplies of Veracruz by completely shutting the port—not allowing even fishing vessels to leave it. This mission he gave to Commander McCluney in the *John Adams*, on 6 March.

While he was at Lobos, Scott organized his troops into three divisions: one division of regulars under General Worth; volunteers under General Patterson; and a second division of regulars under General Twiggs. He planned to use the first division of regulars as the assault troops, the volunteers as the follow-on wave, and to hold the second division of regulars in reserve. Conner assigned these troops to the ships that were to carry them to the landing beach: Worth's men in the *Raritan*, the *Princeton*, and the Army transport *Edith*; Patterson's men in the *Potomac* and the Army transports *Virginia* and *Alabama*; and the reserves under Twiggs in the *Albany*, the *St. Mary's* the *Porpoise*, the *Petrita*, and the Army transports *Massachusetts* and *Eudora*. The surfboats, each manned by a junior or petty officer and seven seamen, were formed into groups of ten with an officer in charge of each group. Captain Forrest of the *Raritan* was assigned to superintend the transshipment of the troops from the transports in which they had arrived, and was to be assisted by Lieutenant Hunt of the *Porpoise* and as many other lieutenants as he might need.

On the evening of 7 March orders went out to prepare for a landing the next day. No copy of the landing plan settled upon by Conner and Scott has ever been found—it may, indeed, never have been committed to paper—but the plan can be deduced from the written orders that have survived and from what took place. The light-draft gunboats and steamers were to sail towards the beach and form a line as close inshore as possible and, if any Mexican troops appeared, they were to shell them. Although it was recognized that the crowded anchorage would probably limit their effectiveness, the larger warships were to join in any such bombardment. The surfboats were to form a line of departure offshore and, when the naval gunfire had dispersed the enemy or silenced his fire, they were to start landing the first wave of assault troops: on entering the breakers, they were to let go kedge anchors from their sterns, so that they could work off the beach and return to the fleet for more men—a process to be repeated until all the troops had been landed. Once ashore, the men were to seize the beach; regroup, and seize the Mexican positions. Insofar as they were able, the guns of the squadron would support the attack.

At the appointed hour on 8 March, the steamers lit off their boilers, and boats carrying crews for the surfboats were dispatched to Salmedina Island. But, amid the preparations to depart, came signs that a norther was approach-

The U.S. Army leaves the Home Squadron.
The city of Veracruz and the Castle
of San Juan de Ulloa can be seen in
the background.
Franklin D. Roosevelt Library, Hyde Park, New York

ing and, before the morning watch ended, Conner had called off the operation for that day. No storm came, however, and the landings were rescheduled for the following day.

General Scott later remembered that on 9 March "the sun dawned propitiously on the expedition," and Lieutenant Semmes, who was aboard the *Raritan,* had a similar recollection of that morning: "If we had the choice of weather, we could not have selected a more propitious day. The sun shot forth his brilliant rays in a cloudless sky, and a gentle breeze from the south-east, which was favorable, and just sufficient for our purposes, rippled, without roughening the sea." Not only was the day perfect for the landings, but it was the thirty-third anniversary of the Commanding General's promotion to the rank of general.

At daylight, crews were sent back to Salmedina to prepare the surfboats, while, "On board the vessels," wrote J. B. Robertson, a member of the First Tennessee Regiment, "an activity of unmistakable significance prevailed: the salt sea rust was cleared from the arms; rations were issued, canteens filled, ammunition was distributed and the men formed upon the decks with arms at hand." As soon as the surfboats had been made ready, they were used to ferry the troops from their transports to the vessels which were to carry them to Sacrificios. Then, when the ferrying had been completed, the empty surfboats made fast to the steamers for the tow to the landing area: fifteen boats were manned by the *Raritan* and made fast to the *Spitfire;* twenty were manned by the *Potomac* and made fast to the *Vixen;* ten were manned by the *Albany* and ten by the *St. Mary's* and were made fast to the *Eudora* and the *Petrita* respectively; and the *Princeton* manned ten boats and took them in tow herself.

Fifteen minutes after the schooner-gunboats *Reefer, Bonita, Petrel, Tampico* (Lieutenant William P. Griffin), and *Falcon* (Lieutenant John J. Glasson), which were to form the inshore covering force, had hoisted anchor and stood out for the landing area, the flagship *Raritan* at 10:00 signaled the main body of ships to prepare to get under way. About an hour later, she broke the signal to sail and, in a gentle breeze from the southeast, Conner in the *Raritan* and Scott in the *Massachusetts* led the fleet in single file through the narrow exit from the anchorage. As the reefs at Antón Lizardo were cleared and the whole force headed for Sacrificios, the *Princeton* took the *Raritan* in tow and, at about the same time, the big transport steamer *New Orleans*, with part of the Louisiana Regiment embarked, came in and took station in the fleet. With Scott, in dress uniform, clearly distinguishable on the quarterdeck, the *Massachusetts* moved among the ships, and the Commanding General was cheered loudly by both the soldiers and the sailors.

To one eyewitness, the scene was memorable: "The tall ships of war sailing leizurely along under their topsails, their decks thronged in every part with dense masses of troops whose bright muskets and bayonets were flashing in the sunbeams; the jingle of spurs and sabres; the bands of music playing; the hum of the multitude rising up like the murmers of the distant ocean; the small steamers plying about, their decks crowded with anxious spectators; the long line of surfboats towing astern of the ships."

Less than three hours after the *Reefer* and her accompanying schooner-gunboats had arrived off Sacrificios at 12:45 p.m. and found that little surf was running on the landing beach, all the rest of the vessels had come in and taken their assigned places in the crowded anchorage with surprisingly little disorder or confusion. As the steamers anchored, they cast off their surfboats, and the latter pulled for the ships whose troops they were to carry. At 3:30 the *Spitfire,* the *Vixen,* and the five schooner-gunboats closed to within about ninety yards of the shore. At the same time, three flags were hoisted on the main truck of the *Massachusetts*—the signal to prepare for the landing of Worth's division—and soldiers began clambering down into the surfboats.

As each boat filled, she shoved off and lay-to waiting for the others of her group to fill. When each detachment was ready, it was to form in a line

The U.S. Army lands on Collado Beach.
Franklin D. Roosevelt Library, Hyde Park, New York

off the landing area, abreast of the *Princeton*, which was at anchor about 450 yards offshore, but a strong current that was swirling around Sacrificios threw the heavily laden surfboats into confusion. Some order was restored when hawsers were thrown out from the *Princeton* and the boats made fast to them in two long lines on each of her quarters. Nevertheless, the units were mixed up and, rather than try to sort them out boat by boat, General Worth arranged only the boats carrying regimental colors and ordered the others to pull for their appropriate flags when they cast off.

While these preparations were going on, Mexican cavalry could be seen among the dunes behind the beach, and to the anxious Americans it appeared certain that the landing force would have to fight its way ashore against strong opposition. About five o'clock, the *Tampico* fired at what were assumed to be Mexican cavalry behind the sand dunes, but the shot had no visible effect. Thirty minutes later, the *Massachusetts* fired a gun and broke the signal for the surfboats to cast off and head for shore.

A deathlike stillness hung over the scene as the long line of boats swept in closer and closer to the beach—when would it be shattered by the first flash from the Mexicans waiting behind the dunes? Suddenly, a gig sped out from the left side of the mass of boats, raced ahead, and grounded on the beach. A lone figure leapt into water up to his armpits and, with his braid glistening in the setting sun, waded ashore. It was Brevet Brigadier General William Jenkins Worth, commander of the first wave of assault troops.

In a matter of moments, as their surfboats grounded, more and more men, holding their unloaded arms and accoutrements above their heads, were jumping into the water and wading ashore. All 2,595 men landed—still no fire came from behind the ridges—rushed up the first range of sand hills, and planted the American flag. When the sailors in the ships and the men waiting to land saw this, they gave a shout and, to quote an English soldier who was on the expedition, "a dozen bands of music, at the same time, as if actuated by an impulse struck up the Star Spangled Banner." Only ten minutes had passed since the signal for the surfboats to head for shore had been hoisted to the yard.

When the men reached the top of that first range of hills they found out why they had met no Mexican fire. The Mexicans had fled. Why they chose not to defend the beach, thus losing an opportunity to inflict heavy losses on the attacking troops without sustaining comparable losses, has never been satisfactorily explained by Mexican historians. The probable explanation is that General Juan Morales, the commander of Veracruz, was unwilling to risk any of his small force in an open battle fought within range of Conner's naval guns. Very likely, he also overestimated Scott's resources.

After the first assault, the Americans made no attempt to land the troops in a line of battle. Worth's division was followed by that of Patterson, and the division of regulars under Twiggs brought up the rear. By 10:00 p.m. all of them had been landed.

The first phase of Winfield Scott's Mexican campaign was over. In less than five hours, more than 8,600 men had been put ashore without the loss of a single life. Even in the second half of the twentieth century, with all its technical advances in amphibious warfare, that would be a considerable achievement; in 1847, it was a tremendous accomplishment. The two commanders truly deserve that laconic but meaningful accolade, "well done."

To Commodore Conner must go the credit for bringing off an extremely difficult and complicated operation: it was he who selected the landing place and the method of transporting the troops to the debarkation point, and he handled the details of the landing. General Scott, on the other hand, deserves credit for conceiving and planning by far the most difficult operation that American troops had faced up to that time: moreover, he undertook to land on a hostile shore before most of his logistic support had reached him and with fewer than the number of troops he considered minimal.

VIII

VICTORY AT VERACRUZ

Many people considered the fortifications of Veracruz to be among the strongest, if not the strongest, in North America, and few military experts believed that it would be possible to take the Castle of San Juan de Ulloa without a long, hard, and costly struggle.

That massive castle situated on Gallega Reef, one thousand yards offshore, dominates the harbor of Veracruz. It consists mostly of a large quadrangle with a bastion at each corner, the southernmost of which had a tall cavalier, or raised platform that gave the defenders command of the adjacent area of the fort and of the water outside it and allowed them to fire over their own exterior parapets. On its eastern front, the side that runs along the reef, the fortress was defended by a type of detached bastion, known as a demilune, and by redoubts, in front of which a wide water battery extended across almost the whole face of the work. A garrison of 1,030 men manned the fortress and its 135 guns.

A massive granite seawall stretched along the waterfront of the city of Veracruz and was strengthened at its northern end by Fort Concepción, and at its southern end by Fort Santiago. On the land side, the city was defended by nine small but well-built bastions connected to one another by a musket-proof masonry curtain and each mounting from eight to ten guns. However, many parts of the curtain, which was about fifteen feet high, were in disrepair, and many of the guns were mounted on carriages that were too small. The garrison of 3,360 men was none too large to handle the defenses with their 86 guns.

Immediately around Veracruz, a sandy plain, bounded by sand hills, stretches inland for distances varying from about one thousand yards in the southwest to nearly two miles in the north. Some of the sand hills that are far inland rise as high as three hundred feet. Southwest of the city, whose

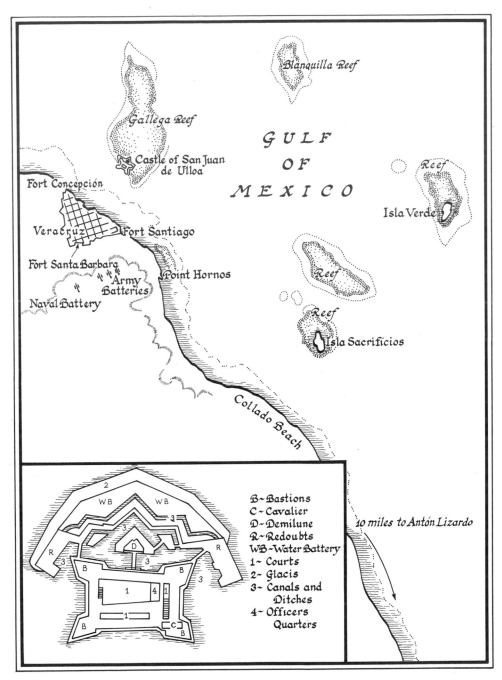

Blanquilla Reef

Gallega Reef

GULF
OF
MEXICO

Castle of San Juan
de Ulloa

Reef

Fort Concepción

Isla Verde

Veracruz — Fort Santiago

Fort Santa Barbara

Point Hornos

Army
Batteries

Naval Battery

Reef

Reef

Isla Sacrificios

Collado Beach

B ~ Bastions
C ~ Cavalier
D ~ Demilune
R ~ Redoubts
WB ~ Water Battery
1 ~ Courts
2 ~ Glacis
3 ~ Canals and
     Ditches
4 ~ Officers
     Quarters

10 miles to Antón Lizardo

VERACRUZ AND ITS ENVIRONS

Inset: PLAN OF THE CASTLE OF SAN JUAN DE ULLOA

walls formed an irregular hexagon, a complex of ponds and marshes then drained into a small stream that passed near its walls. The cisterns that stored water for the city's 15,000 inhabitants were filled from that stream.

Neither San Juan de Ulloa nor the city was amply stocked with powder and provisions.

By the morning of 10 March—the day following the landings—the only troops destined to take part in the siege who had not been landed were the few volunteers and cavalry stranded at Brazos Santiago and Tampico by lack of transports. During that morning, General Scott transferred his headquarters to shore. General Morales expended little effort either in resisting the American advance or in setting up the siege lines, and the first clash ashore, which took place in the early hours of 10 March, was inconclusive and served only to keep the Americans awake.

Soon after daylight, the Army began encircling the city and Commodore Conner sent Commander Tattnall in the *Spitfire* to make a diversionary attack on San Juan de Ulloa. At 5:20, the steamer anchored to the east of the castle and opened a fire, which, ten minutes later, was answered. The steamer did little or no damage to the castle, but she fulfilled her mission of distracting the Mexicans from Scott's actions, and after about half an hour of firing, Conner ordered Tattnall to take his ship out of range.

Captain Forrest, who had been assigned to supervise the embarkation of the troops when they were preparing to leave Antón Lizardo, had been designated officer in charge of landing operations when the expedition reached Collado Beach, but at about the time General Scott moved his headquarters ashore, Forrest was replaced in the latter assignment by Commander Sands. One of the tasks of the officer in charge of landing was to designate which supply ships were to be unloaded. When the weather permitted, stores were landed, mostly by surfboats, from early morning until late in the evening, and as each ship completed discharging her cargo, she left for the United States. While the quantity of material to be handled was small compared with what was needed, it was large in the aggregate. Indeed, one observer recalled seeing supplies piled up along a mile of the beach. At the time Sands took over from Forrest, worsening weather made the task of landing supplies increasingly difficult.

This situation did nothing to ease one of the greatest difficulties facing the Army—a shortage of carts and draft animals. As late as the morning of 12 March, when a strong norther set in and the landing of provisions and stores had to cease, only fifteen carts and one hundred draft horses had been landed. This shortage slowed the advance of the siege line because it meant that nearly everything had to be moved by hand across sand hills covered with stunted, thorny mimosa, prickly pear, and other plants, which formed chaparrals through which it was often necessary to cut a path. Furthermore, the men had either to wade through the pools of water that interspersed the thickets, or to make lengthy detours to bypass them.

In spite of his transportation problems and the bad weather, which hampered the operations ashore almost as much as it did those afloat, Scott pushed on with the investment of Veracruz, and shortly after noon on 13 March the division of regulars under the command of General Twiggs reached the sea northwest of the city, thereby completing its encirclement. During the course of that day, the winds abated long enough to allow four mortars and a small amount of ammunition to be landed, but they returned with even more force.

When the storm finally blew itself out on 17 March, the landing of supplies resumed, and the troops dug trenches around the city. Then, with Twiggs's division entrenched to the north, Patterson's in the center, and Worth's to the southeast, the Army was in position for the siege, but it was still short of supplies, particularly ordnance and transport. The shortages were alleviated but not cured the following day when six mortars, four 24-pounder siege guns, some 8-inch siege howitzers, a large amount of ammunition, some horses, and some quartermaster supplies were landed. In a report written that day to the Secretary of War, General Scott lamented that only one-fifth of the guns he was expecting had arrived: he had enough artillery, he wrote, to take Veracruz, but not enough to take Ulloa.

The siege batteries were planted in front of Worth's lines to the southeast of the city, about half a mile from its walls, and the soldiers went to work to make them ready. The General expected to be able to open fire by noon on 21 March. He arranged with Commodore Conner for a naval bombardment of the seaward defenses to coincide with the opening of the Army's batteries, and when word of this plan reached the men in the fleet, many of them began to devise means of being included in the attacking force. Commander Saunders of the *St. Mary's* went so far as to propose transferring his ship's 8-inch shell guns to surfboats. His idea was romantic but not practical, since the frail surfboats would have been knocked apart by the recoil of the big guns.

Early in the afternoon of 20 March, the *Mississippi*, having completed her repairs at Norfolk, arrived off Sacrificios. She carried Commodore Matthew C. Perry and orders, dated 3 March 1847, from Secretary of the Navy Mason informing Conner that: "The uncertain duration of the war with Mexico has induced the President to direct me no longer to suspend the rule which limits the terms of command in our squadrons in its application to your command of the Home Squadron." Conner was directed to turn his command over to Perry and to proceed to Philadelphia in the *Princeton*.

These orders arrived at a very unfortunate time, for they prevented

Conner from carrying to completion his most successful operation, which was also the most important single operation undertaken by any naval commander during the war. Thus, they deprived him of much of the recognition that he deserves.

His term as commander of the Home Squadron was highly creditable. His handling of the squadron during the period of protracted diplomatic negotiations was above reproach. If his conduct of operations after the outbreak of the war was overly cautious, there were extenuating circumstances. He was in a position faced by many naval commanders before and since: compared with his adversary, he had tremendous superiority in numbers of ships, yet, because his base was far away, because major repairs could not be made locally, and because, when the war started, the Navy did not have the types of ships he needed, most of his operations had to be conducted on a shoestring. Although maintaining an extensive blockade was his main mission, he was so short of vessels that if he lost one, the effectiveness of the blockade would be impaired. When he did attempt offensive operations, as at Alvarado, misfortune dogged him, and he incurred the scorn of his more impetuous subordinates as well as of the press.

Not until the late fall of 1846 did Conner have enough light-draft vessels to undertake an offensive operation with a reasonable margin of superiority. By that time, his activities were circumscribed by orders from Washington for the capture of Tampico and by the preparations for the landings at Veracruz. In neither of those cases did the Mexicans offer resistance, so Conner's victories were bloodless and lacked public appeal. Two months after issuing the orders relieving him of his command, Secretary Mason offered him, as a reward, appointment as Chief of the Bureau of Construction, Equipment, and Repair, but the Commodore refused on the grounds that he was not in good health.

The new commander of the Home Squadron was a man whose career marks, in many ways, a milestone in American naval history. More than any of his contemporaries, Perry bridged the gap between the officers who were trained in the War of 1812 and those who received their training after that war. He was an experienced officer and, in his time, was probably the Navy's greatest authority on steam warships. He was the first commander of the second steamer *Fulton* and was largely responsible for the design of the *Mississippi* and the *Missouri*, the two most efficient steamers of their day. Ambitious and unscrupulous, yet, according to Franklin Buchanan, commander of the sloop *Germantown*, "respected and esteemed," Perry brought to the squadron a spirit of offense that it had lacked under Conner—and much better luck.

As the morning watch ended on 21 March 1847, Commodore Perry relieved Commodore Conner as commander of the Home Squadron. A furious norther was raging and Perry had hardly taken command when he learned that the chartered steamer *Hunter*, her prize, the French bark *Jeune Nelly*, and an American schooner were aground on the northeast point of Isla Verde and their crews and passengers were in danger of being swept away by the seas. The winds were so high and the seas so heavy that neither the squadron's sailing vessels nor the British steamer, HMS *Daring*, which was lying near the wrecks, could risk leaving their moorings to offer assistance. Perry took the powerful *Mississippi* out into the teeth of the storm, drove through to the wrecks, and rescued the survivors. But the storm was costly to the squadron, for it drove thirty of the irreplaceable and still-needed surfboats up on the beach and damaged them.

When Perry returned from his rescue mission, he and Commodore Conner went ashore to visit General Scott, and the three men discussed the part the Navy would play in the siege, particularly a previous offer of Conner's to land some of the Navy's heavy guns. Ever anxious to uphold the prestige of the Army, Scott wanted that part to be as limited as possible. He had told his staff:

> We, of course, gentlemen, must take the city and castle before the return of the vomito. . . . [Storming would cost] some two thousand, perhaps three thousand of our best men . . . [and] although I know our countrymen will hardly acknowledge a victory unaccompanied by a long butcher's bill, I am strongly inclined to forgo their loud applause and aves vehement and take the city with the least possible loss of life. . . .

This placed the General in a dilemma. He had already asked for a naval bombardment; now he had to accept the offer of naval guns, since he did not have any heavy enough to breach the walls of Veracruz. He asked for six guns. Commodore Perry, as anxious to preserve the prestige of the Navy as Scott was to preserve that of the Army, replied, "Certainly, General, but I must fight them." Scott said that he had enough artillerymen, and it would be necessary for the Navy only to land the guns. But Perry was adamant in his stand that wherever the guns went, their officers and crews must go. Scott had no choice but to accept those terms.

When Perry left the conference, he boarded his barge and was rowed among his squadron announcing that guns and their crews were to be landed. The manner in which his announcement was received made an impression on Midshipman John H. Upshur: "I shall never forget the thrill which pervaded the squadron, when . . . [Perry] announced from his barge, as he pulled under the sterns of the vessels of the fleet, in succession, that we were to land guns and crews . . . cheer after cheer went up in evidence of the enthusiasm this promise of a release from a life of inaction we had been leading . . . inspired."

On 22 March, the day after the meeting between the commanders, Scott issued a formal demand that Veracruz surrender within two hours. Simultaneously, Perry disrupted communications between the town and the neutral men-of-war in the harbor by forbidding boats from the latter to ply back and forth with messages. As required by protocol, General Morales refused to surrender.

Scott's demand had been issued in the early afternoon and, when the time limit expired, he ordered the three completed batteries, which all together mounted seven 10-inch mortars, to open fire. They did so with much spirit and effect. An eyewitness described the effect the sound of the guns produced on the men in the ships lying at anchor off Veracruz:

> . . . While the crews of the squadron were all at supper, a sudden and tremendous roar of artillery on shore proclaimed that the battle had begun. The tea things were left 'to take care of themselves' and pell mell tumbled sick and well up the ladder to the open deck. . . . Some two hundred sail of vessels were lying immediately around us, their tops, cross-trees, yards, shrouds—everything where a foothold could be obtained—crowded with human beings.

As soon as Commodore Perry observed that the firing had started, he sent Commander Tattnall in the *Spitfire* with the *Vixen*, the *Bonita*, the *Reefer*, the *Petrel*, the *Falcon*, and the *Tampico* to bombard the city, and they stood out for Point Hornos, about one mile from the walls of the city. En route, the *Petrel* collided with the *Falcon* and ran aground but at 5:45, less than two hours after Scott's batteries had opened fire, the rest of the flotilla dropped anchor in the lee of Point Hornos. The destructive bombardment that the American vessels opened on the city was returned from San Juan de Ulloa. Fire from the guns of the *Spitfire* was particularly accurate: it reached into the heart of the city and scored hits on the plaza and in the neighborhood of the market gate.

When the flotilla had spent most of its ammunition, it ceased firing and hauled out of range. It had been under the fire of Ulloa for eighty minutes; none of its vessels had been damaged; and its fire had brought response from several guns whose existence was not previously known—for which General Worth sent his thanks. When the bombardment was over, the crew of the refloated *Petrel*, at least, celebrated by splicing the main brace.

That night, while the flotilla was replenishing its magazines and making ready to renew the bombardment, there was unusual activity aboard the *Spitfire*. Her executive officer, Lieutenant David D. Porter, who later conducted successful operations on the Mississippi River in the Civil War, had volunteered to find out whether the southern channel into the harbor of Veracruz would be a better place from which to launch the next day's bombardment, by going out in a boat and sounding it. He handled his special and highly dangerous task with skill, and returned with the information that the channel could be used.

An artist's conception of the flotilla under
Commander Tattnall attacking San Juan de Ulloa.
Left to right: the *Falcon*, the *Reefer*, the *Vixen*,
the *Petrel*, the *Bonita*, the *Spitfire*,
and the *Tampico*.
Franklin D. Roosevelt Library, Hyde Park, New York

When morning came, 23 March, and Perry ordered the flotilla in again, Tattnall asked him where he should engage, to which Perry replied, "Where you can do the most execution, sir." Tattnall followed his orders scrupulously. At dawn, the *Spitfire* towing the *Petrel* and the *Tampico*, and the *Vixen* towing the *Bonita* and the *Reefer*, stood out once again for Veracruz in company with the *Falcon*. They dropped the *Falcon* off at Point Hornos, where she was to serve as a decoy, then stood out from the land as though they were returning to Sacrificios. But, once they were clear of the shoals off Point Hornos, Tattnall ordered them to steer directly toward Ulloa until they were about 600 yards from it and within grapeshot range of Fort Santiago. They reached that position and anchored without drawing the fire of a single gun ashore, but at 5:20 when they opened fire on the town and on Ulloa, the Mexicans immediately replied with every gun that would bear. Shot and shell thrashed to foam the water around the frail vessels of the American flotilla.

Tattnall's rashness was too much for Perry who watched the action for

JOSIAH TATTNALL
U. S. Naval Academy Museum

more than an hour, then signaled his commander to withdraw. Tattnall either did not see the signal, or did see it and refused to recognize it. Half an hour later, at 7:00, Perry sent his message again and sent Captain Isaac Mayo in a boat to ensure that it was obeyed. At last, the flotilla withdrew, amid cheers from the troops ashore and from the sailors in the neutral warships. The only damage sustained by Tattnall's little vessels was a stove-in gig in the *Spitfire* and several pieces of shell imbedded in the *Petrel's* starboard quarter. Undoubtedly, the reason so little damage was done was that the vessels were so close to the Mexican batteries that it was impossible for the latter to bear properly.

Ashore, more American batteries had been completed and, by noon on 23 March, three more mortars had been emplaced and had begun firing on the city. However, during the afternoon, the high seas of a norther interfered with the landing of ammunition and, in order to preserve their dwindling supply of shells, the gunners slackened their fire. In spite of high winds that filled the trenches and mortar batteries with sand almost as fast as they could be cleared, one more battery, mounting three 24-pounders, was completed during the night. However, the norther was still blowing the next day and fire again had to be restricted: one shell was fired every five minutes.

In the evening the seas calmed sufficiently to allow the landing of ammunition to be resumed, and to permit the ship-of-the-line *Ohio*, which had been waiting for two days for the weather to moderate, to reach her anchorage. Her eight 8-inch shell guns, forty-four 32-pounders, and twenty-eight 42-pounder cannonades made her an important addition to the squadron as it fought to subdue the Castle of San Juan de Ulloa.

To make good Conner's offer of guns to General Scott, Perry chose two 32-pounders from the *Potomac* and one from the *Raritan*, and one 8-inch shell gun each from the *Mississippi*, the *Albany*, and the *St. Mary's*, and had them ferried ashore in ships' launches on 22 March, the day after the meeting between the three commanders. For the overland trip to the battery, the guns were slung under the axles of two-wheel trucks. Getting them to their destination was a lengthy operation not only because there were only two two-wheel trucks available, but also because, by main force, 200 men had to tug, pull, haul, and shove the trucks across three miles of loose, deep sand, and through a lagoon two feet deep. Furthermore, the movement had to be made at night, in order to conceal it from the Mexicans.

Meanwhile, Captain Robert E. Lee, an engineer on Scott's staff, supervised the construction of the battery to house the naval guns. The work—designated Battery Number Five by the Army, but known to the Navy as simply the Naval Battery—stood on a sand ridge about seven hundred yards from Fort Santa Barbara, at about the middle of the American line. It was built of sandbags, and the guns, mounted on ships' carriages on platforms, were run out with side tackle and handspikes. There was a sandbag traverse, six or more feet thick, between each pair of guns, and sandbags were used to check recoil.

In order to raise morale, depressed by long inactivity, Commodore Perry wanted as many men as possible to serve the battery, so he assigned two crews to each gun and rotated them every twenty-four hours. There was, he said, "a great though generous strife" for places on the gun crews. The battery was completed and the guns emplaced during the night of 23–24 March and, at ten o'clock the next morning, Captain Lee transferred it to its first naval commander, Captain John H. Aulick of the *Potomac*.

While it was being built, the battery had been well screened from the

Mexicans, but soon after it was completed it was discovered and fired upon by the defenders of Fort Santa Barbara. Aulick ordered his gunners to return fire, and Midshipman Allen McLane and two volunteers went out in plain view of the Mexicans and cleared away the masking brush in front of the battery. The range to various targets had been determined by triangulation and, consequently, fire from the battery was very effective. The 32-pound shot, fired at the brittle coral walls of the city at the short range of seven hundred yards, broke them down, while the shell guns focused on the casements and barracks. Mexican fire, too, found its mark but since five batteries concentrated their fire on the Naval Battery without inflicting serious damage, it could not have been as effective as claimed by an eyewitness who reported that every shot either hit the battery or passed through its embrasures. Nevertheless, on the first day of action, four Americans were killed and six wounded.

Fort Santa Barbara, the nearest, strongest, and best-served of the Mexican batteries, was manned by Mexican Marines and seamen under the command of an able German Lieutenant of Marines, Sebastian Holzinger. When a lucky shot fired from one of the *Potomac*'s 32-pounders severed the fort's flagstaff, Holzinger and one of his men leaped onto the exposed wall, rescued the flag, and nailed it to the stump of the flagstaff. Before the two men could take cover, a second shot struck the wall and nearly buried them in an avalanche of rubble, but they escaped unharmed amid the applause of the Americans. It is a rare act of courage that wins mention in the enemy's dispatches, but Aulick was so impressed by Holzinger's bravery that he recounted the incident in his report of that day's action.

Only fifty rounds of ammunition for each gun in the battery had been landed and at 2:30 in the afternoon, when it had all been expended, the gun crews closed the gun embrasures with sandbags and waited to be relieved by Captain Mayo's detachment, which would bring up fresh supplies of ammunition.

During the night of 24 March, Army engineers repaired the Naval Battery, and shortly before sunrise next morning, the Mexican batteries again opened up on it. In the course of the day, their fire became so accurate that one 13-inch mortar shell fired from San Juan de Ulloa landed about five paces to the rear of the Naval Battery and exploded a copper tank containing five rounds of powder but, amazingly, neither damaged the battery nor injured any of the men. Many shells narrowly missed the walls, and Midshipman Thomas B. Shubrick was killed as he sighted a gun. The naval guns responded so steadily that, at one time, firing had to cease for an hour to allow them to cool. However, when they did so, the newest Army battery, Number Four, filled the gap by opening up with its 24-pounders and an 8-inch howitzer.

The Naval Battery bombards Veracruz.
Library of Congress

By 2:30 p.m., the Mexican guns had fallen silent and the Naval Battery again ceased firing. Captain Mayo, having seen the Mexicans evacuate Fort Santiago, told his men, "If the enemy intends to fire another shot, our cheers will draw it," and ordered them to climb the sandbag walls of the battery and give three cheers. When no answering shot came, he turned command of the battery over to Lieutenant Simon B. Bissell, mounted a horse he had somehow acquired, and rode off to report to Commodore Perry. As he rode past Scott's headquarters, he saw the General, reined up in front of him, and said, "General, they are done, they will never fire another shot." Naturally concerned, the General asked, "Who? Your battery, the Naval Battery?" "No, General," answered Mayo, "the enemy is silenced. They will not fire another shot." In his joy, Scott nearly pulled Mayo off his horse. "Commodore," he said, "I thank you and our brothers of the navy in the name of the army for this day's work." The Captain finally disentangled himself from Scott's clutches and continued on his way.

Mayo's announcement that the Mexicans would not fire another shot turned out to be slightly premature. Less than an hour after his men had stood on the parapet and cheered, there was another exchange of fire, but it did not last long because the Naval Battery ran out of ammunition, and

94

A norther batters the squadron on the
night of 25–26 March.

the Mexicans shifted their fire to more immediately threatening targets. In spite of the heavy fire that was exchanged on that second day of action, 25 March, only two of the men in the Naval Battery, including Midshipman Shubrick, were killed and three wounded.

Successful as the bombardment was, Scott decided that if no surrender proposal came from the Mexicans the following day, 26 March, he would send three columns of men to storm the city. He and Perry agreed that one of the columns, whose mission would be to assault the wall protecting the sea side of the city, would be composed of seamen and Marines. Perry had apparently made a plan of his own before he conferred with the General, for he mentions in his later correspondence that he had been waiting only for a dark night to lead a boat expedition to spike the guns of the water battery at Ulloa, and he had ordered the construction of the scaling ladders he would need for that purpose.

Much damage had been done in Veracruz, and the carnage had been great. As 25 March wore on, it became evident that the city would soon have to surrender for the sake of its noncombatants. Then, about five o'clock, all firing ceased so that a truce proposal drawn up by the foreign consuls stationed in the city could be delivered to General Scott. However, since the proposal had not originated with the Mexican authorities, Scott refused it and shortly before midnight, the truce-bearers having returned to the city, firing resumed.

That night a council of war called by General Morales advised surrender, a course which he obstinately opposed. Consequently, he resigned. General José Juan Landero became the commander of Veracruz and immediately made overtures to General Scott.

Afloat as well as ashore the night was filled with activity. A norther that Perry, who was accustomed to vicious storms, considered one of the worst he had ever experienced, was battering his fleet. Both the *Raritan* and the *Potomac* had vessels across their hawses, and the *Raritan* lost her foresail and spritsail yards. The *Mississippi* parted one of her chains, many vessels had boats blown from their decks, and before the storm dissipated twenty-three vessels had gone aground. Even the Naval Battery was affected: the storm whipped up and blew about so much sand that its guns could not be sighted and Captain Breese of the *Albany*, whose detachment was then serving the battery, ordered them masked.

Another result of the norther's fury was that Scott was prevented from consulting Perry as to who should be appointed to negotiate with the Mexicans and what instructions the negotiators should be given. Consequently, the instructions that were given reflected only the Army's desires and did not include the Navy's wish for the terms of surrender to include a special provision insuring the release of Midshipman Rogers, who had been captured by the Mexicans early in the previous December.

On 26 March before the Naval Battery could resume fire and participate in the bombardment that had begun in the pre-dawn hours, General Scott ordered all firing to cease. During its two days of operation, the Naval Battery had made serious inroads on the squadron's supply of ammunition. It had fired 1,000 shells and 800 round shot—or about 45 per cent of the number and one-third of the total weight of shot and shell fired by the American batteries.

Captain Aulick was to have represented Commodore Perry at the surrender negotiations, but he was delayed by the storm and arrived in time to take part only in the signing of the Articles of Capitulation for Veracruz, which took place at Point Hornos on 27 March 1847. Commander Mackenzie who, it will be remembered, had been sent to Havana the previous June to interview Santa Anna, and who was a brother-in-law of Perry, acted as interpreter for the American negotiators. The formal ceremony of surrender was set to take place two days after the signing of the Articles. Full honors were to be accorded the surrendering garrison, which would march out of the city and be put on parole; the Mexican flag would be saluted as it was lowered; and Mexican officers would be allowed to keep their arms and personal effects, including horses and trappings.

On the morning of the appointed day, 29 March, the sun rose in a cloudless sky and a gentle breeze blew in from the southeast. The ceremonies began early in the morning when a salute of twenty-one guns was fired from the Castle of San Juan de Ulloa and the Mexican flag flying over it was hauled down. The flotilla and the boats of the Home Squadron carrying the American Marines then entered the harbor and, when they had anchored inside Point Hornos, a salute of twenty-one guns was fired from the city and the Mexican flag flying over it was hauled down. When the American flag went up over the fortifications of the city at 11:10, it was given a twenty-nine-gun salute by both the Army and the Navy. This was followed by another twenty-nine-gun salute from the assembled warships when the American flag was hoisted on the flagpole of the castle at noon. The surrender of Veracruz was complete.

It came as a pleasant surprise to the Americans that Ulloa was included in the surrender, for they had anticipated that, even after the capture of the city, they would face a long and bloody struggle to reduce the castle.

In the afternoon, the *Princeton* carrying Commodore Conner and Colonel Totten, a courier for General Scott, stood out for Pensacola. She arrived there on 3 April and, a week later, the news of the fall of Veracruz reached Washington in the form of a telegraphic dispatch from Baltimore.

Thus fell what was considered to be one of the strongest fortifications in North America, and the cost to its besiegers was only fourteen killed and fifty-nine wounded.

In his General Order Number 80, dated 30 March, General Scott said: "Thanks higher than those of the general-in-chief have also been earned by the entire Home Squadron, under the successive orders of Commodores Conner and Perry, for prompt, cheerful, and able assistance from the arrival of this army off this coast."

IX

ALVARADO AND TUXPAN

Before he left Washington to take command of the Home Squadron, Perry had submitted to Secretary of the Navy John Y. Mason a plan for the prosecution of the war: the occupation, colonization, then annexation of California; the withdrawal of all troops from the interior of Mexico and the establishment of a military cordon along her northern frontier; and the occupation of her principal Atlantic and Pacific ports, which would be declared open to all friendly shipping for trade in noncontraband goods. He suggested that his plan for victory through economic strangulation would be "more congenial to the institutions and professions of the American people" and would reduce the cost of the war by three-quarters.

Perry's plan received scant consideration. On 17 March 1847, while he was on his way to join the squadron, Secretary Mason issued orders concerning the operations the squadron was to undertake after the seizure of Veracruz: maintain the blockade and seize any Mexican ports that might be beneficial to the United States.

"The naval forces under your command," Mason noted, "form the largest squadron, it is believed, which has ever been assembled under the American flag." The Secretary was undoubtedly correct for, including the vessels en route to the Gulf, Perry had under his command: one ship-of-the-line, the *Ohio*; one steam frigate, the *Mississippi*; two sailing frigates, the *Potomac* and the *Raritan*; six sloops of war, the *St. Mary's*, the *John Adams*, the *Albany*, the *Germantown*, the *Decatur*, and the *Saratoga*; two brigs, the *Porpoise* and the *Washington*; six small steamers, the *Vixen*, the *Spitfire*, the *Petrita*, the *Scourge*, the *Scorpion*, and the *McLane*; seven schooner-gunboats, the *Reefer*, the *Bonita*, the *Petrel*, the *Tampico*, the *Falcon*, the *Morris*, and the *Mahonese*; four bomb brigs, the *Etna*, the *Stromboli*, the *Hecla*, and the *Vesuvius*; and a number of store and supply vessels.

CHARLES G. HUNTER
U. S. Naval Academy Museum

Immediately after the surrender of Veracruz, General Winfield Scott ordered Brigadier General John A. Quitman to march his brigade to Alvarado and seize it, an operation in which the Navy would participate. Scott wanted to neutralize the area by assuring the inhabitants safety of person and property and, more importantly, to secure a source for the horses, mules, and beef cattle, that the Army would need for transportation and food on its forthcoming march to Mexico City. He did not expect Alvarado to be defended, but the force he sent was large enough to overcome any resistance that might be offered.

Since Commodore Conner's attack on the town the previous October, its seaward defenses had been greatly strengthened by the addition of six forts along the banks of the river, making a total of eight. Between them, the forts contained forty-nine guns, most of which had been taken from the Mexican squadron bottled up in the river. But the rear, or land side, of Alvarado was vulnerable to assault, and the fall of Veracruz had increased that vulnerability to the point where the town was untenable.

Quitman and his column left Veracruz in the afternoon of 30 March and spent that night encamped at the mouth of the Madelin River. The crossing of the river was made the next morning in boats from the squadron.

While the soldiers were marching to the Madelin, the steamer *Scourge*

(Lieutenant Charles G. Hunter) sailed for the Alvarado River to await their arrival. She reached there shortly before dusk on 30 March, and as soon as she had taken station off the bar, she fired her 32-pounder at Fort La Vigia, which guarded the mouth of the river. However, after she had fired a few rounds, threatening weather forced her to withdraw, and she spent the night steaming to and fro off the river mouth. At nine o'clock the next morning, she came in again towards the bar and fired another shot at Fort La Vigia. Immediately, a white flag was run up in the fort, and before long the captain of the port put out in his boat to inform Hunter that the garrison of the town had been evacuated during the night, that all naval vessels had been burned, and that the Americans were at liberty to enter.

Hunter lost no time in taking the *Scourge* across the bar and upstream. Before noon, she dropped anchor off the town, and Lieutenant Matthias C. Marin went ashore to secure its surrender. The *Scourge* then hoisted an American flag, fired a twenty-one-gun salute, and landed Passed Midshipman William G. Temple and five men to hold the town.

Upon learning that several vessels loaded with munitions had retreated up the river, Hunter got his ship under way and went in pursuit. He soon sighted a Mexican schooner aground. The *Scourge* closed in to seize her, but when it proved too difficult to refloat her, she was burned. However, as the American vessel churned her way on up the river, she captured three other vessels. Before dawn on 1 April, she arrived off the sleeping village of Tlacotalpán and Lieutenant Marin landed to take its surrender.

On the same morning Commodore Perry's force stood out from Antón Lizardo to support General Quitman's capture of Alvarado. By noon the *Mississippi*, the *Porpoise*, the *St. Mary's*, the *Albany*, the *Spitfire*, the *Vixen*, the *Reefer*, the *Falcon*, the *Tampico*, the *Bonita*, the *Petrel*, the *Vesuvius* (Commander George H. Magruder), and the *Hecla* (Lieutenant Archibald B. Fairfax) swung at anchor off the Alvarado bar. Not knowing that the town had already fallen, Perry sent a messenger in a boat to demand its surrender. While waiting for the answer, he made ready to ascend the river by transferring his pennant from the *Mississippi* to the *Spitfire*. The latter then cast off from the *Mississippi* and, with the *Bonita* and the *Petrel* in tow, headed for the bar. The *Vixen*, towing the *Reefer*, the *Tampico*, and the *Falcon*, followed. When the first of the vessels anchored off Alvarado in the middle of the afternoon and it became known that the town had already been taken, the gunboats immediately landed a force of Marines to relieve Temple's tiny garrison and to safeguard the town pending the arrival of the Army. Quitman arrived shortly after the Marines had been landed and, before long, the *Scourge* also came in with one of her prizes.

The following morning, Perry in the *Spitfire*, accompanied by the *Scourge*, the *Bonita*, the *Petrel*, the *Reefer*, the *Tampico*, and the *Falcon*, headed upriver for Tlacotalpán, apparently in search of the Mexican garrison that had withdrawn from Alvarado. He got there in the early afternoon and left a few hours later, having found no garrison, but having received the unconditional surrender of the village and neighboring countryside, and a promise of at least 500 horses at low prices. Except for the *Reefer*, which had parted tow, the squadron was back at Alvarado before midnight.

General Quitman and his men stayed at Alvarado only a couple of days and were back at Veracruz by 6 April. So it fell to the Navy to garrison the town, and Perry designated a small force under the command of Captain Isaac Mayo to hold both Alvarado and Tlacotalpán.

Lieutenant Hunter's premature seizure of Alvarado upset completely the plans of his superiors for, although the Mexicans had left the area in a hurry when Hunter arrived, they had not only burned their naval vessels but had driven off the horses that the expedition had been designed to secure. On 8 April a 300-man expedition set out by water from Veracruz in search of horses in the area of Alvarado and Tlacotalpán and returned partially successful a week later. A court-martial ordered by Perry sentenced Hunter to be reprimanded and dismissed from the squadron—a sentence that many men in the squadron considered unduly harsh. The press at home made a hero of "Alvarado" Hunter.

With forthcoming campaigns in mind, Commodore Perry took stock of his needs and, on 5 April, reported to the Navy Department that he had no further use for the *Ohio*, which had been sent out specially for the operation against Veracruz. The *Raritan*, he reported, should be replaced, preferably by a frigate that had flag quarters, and the rest of the squadron was needed in the Gulf.

On 15 April, five days after ordering the *Ohio*, the *Raritan*, and the *St. Mary's* to be returned to Norfolk, Secretary Mason advised Perry that Nicholas P. Trist, Chief Clerk of the State Department, who had that day been appointed commissioner to negotiate peace, was being sent to Mexico, and that if and when he, Perry, learned that Trist had succeeded in concluding an armistice, he was to "suspend actual hostilities until further orders from the Department."

After the fall of Alvarado, the only ports on the Gulf that were still in Mexican hands were Tuxpan, Tabasco, Coatzacoalcos, and a few insignificant ones between Alvarado and Tabasco. Tuxpan was the most important of these, and it was well fortified and well garrisoned.

The town of Tuxpan lies on the left bank of the Tuxpan River, about six miles from its mouth. The river, which empties into the Gulf some 180 miles north of Veracruz, averages no more than two hundred to three hundred yards in width, and for the first four miles between its mouth and the town, is bordered by extensive marshes. Farther upstream, its banks are firm and thickly covered with trees and chaparral.

Midway between the town and the river mouth, a hill, sixty feet high, juts out from the right bank into the stream. Atop that hill stood La Peña, a battery mounting one 9-pounder and two of the *Truxtun*'s 32-pounder carronades, that commanded the course of the river for two miles or so. Approximately equidistant from the town and from La Peña, stood La Palmasola, a water battery containing two 18-pounders. Near the base of a steep knoll that rises on the lower edge of the town and was known to the Americans as Hospital Hill, a single 9-pounder had been emplaced and, at its summit, a pivoting 32-pounder. These defenses were manned by from three hundred to four hundred men under the command of General Martín Perfecto de Cos.

Besides the obvious reasons for reducing the last Mexican stronghold on the coast, Perry considered it a point of honor to reclaim the guns which the Mexicans had salvaged the previous August from the wreck of the *Truxtun*, and soon after his return from Alvarado, he began coaling his steamers for an expedition to Tuxpan. He decided that it would be extremely hazardous to steam all the way to the town without taking any action from the land against the formidable defenses along the river. Consequently, 1,519 officers and men were drawn from the crews of the squadron's vessels and formed into a force for action ashore, under the command of Captain Breese of the *Albany*. Two guns from the *Mississippi* and one each from the *Vesuvius* and the *Hecla* were assigned for support of the landing force, and the steamers *Spitfire*, *Vixen*, and *Scourge*, and the schooner-gunboats *Bonita*, *Petrel*, and *Reefer*, were to provide its naval support.

Designating Lobos Island as the rendezvous, Perry sent ahead the sailing vessels *Raritan*, *Albany*, *John Adams*, *Germantown*, *Decatur*, *Vesuvius*, *Hecla*, and *Etna* (Commander Gershom J. Van Brunt). On the morning of 12 April he left the anchorage at Sacrificios aboard the *Mississippi* and in company with the small steamers and gunboats. The steamers arrived in the protected waters off Lobos on the evening of 13 April and while they were awaiting the slower sailing vessels, the landing party spent the time training. Some twenty-four hours later, the whole squadron was under way for the port of Tuxpan.

Although the vessels were scattered by a norther that came up during the second night at sea, one by one they all arrived off the bar at the mouth of the Tuxpan River during the morning of 17 April. The eight feet of water that flowed over the bar were scarcely enough even for the shallow-draft steamers and gunboats, and the small craft spent the afternoon and a good

Commodore Perry's flotilla ascends the Tuxpan River.
U. S. Naval Academy Museum

part of the night lightening ship. While boat parties sounded and carefully buoyed the channel, the *Raritan* hoisted out the masts of the two deepest-draft vessels scheduled to take part in the action, the *Spitfire* and the *Vixen*.

Early the next morning, the landing party boarded the craft that comprised the attack force—the *Spitfire*, the *Vixen*, the *Scourge*, the *Bonita*, the *Petrel*, the *Reefer*, and thirty barges—and, under cover of the *Mississippi*, which was anchored in five fathoms of water about a mile from the bar, the loaded vessels stood in. By noon, the flotilla had crossed the bar. A small party was landed at the mouth of the river, then the vessels dropped anchor and waited while the *Vixen* went back to the *Mississippi* to take aboard the latter's field piece.

That afternoon at about 1:40, the *Spitfire*, in which Perry wore his pennant, the *Vixen*, and the *Scourge*, each towing one of the gunboats and ten barges, began steaming upriver. They had been under way for about fifty minutes when they came under fire from La Peña. Since a sea breeze had just sprung up and the sailing vessels and barges would be able to proceed under their own power, Perry halted the column long enough to allow the steamers to disencumber themselves of their tows. Then, before returning the fire from La Peña, the flotilla moved on up the winding river to get within closer range and to have a clearer view of their target. Soon after the American vessels did fire on the fort, the detachment under Commander Buchanan of the *Germantown* landed and captured it without difficulty. As the American flag was run up over La Peña, three cheers rang out from the men of the flotilla.

The *Spitfire* had not gone far beyond La Peña when she was hit by a volley of musketry that came from the chaparral along the bank, and Commander Tattnall and three of his officers were wounded. At about 2:45, the guns of La Palmasola began firing at the Americans and the *Vixen* took a shot in her bow. The flotilla again returned the fire, then landed a party to seize that fort.

When the American vessels came within range of Hospital Hill, Perry sent still another detachment of men ashore and it took them only until 3:10 to secure the position. Some twenty minutes after that, the flotilla was off Tuxpan, and although a landing party quickly secured the town, in the chaparral beyond, there was a running fight, in which two Americans were killed and nine wounded.

Except that the sailors went on a spree with General Cos's champagne, the night passed quietly, and the next day, 19 April, Captain Forrest led an expedition upstream in search of Mexican vessels. They were away only one day and they brought back a few small prize ships, and accounts of the rich and wild country through which they had passed.

The Commodore did not intend to occupy Tuxpan permanently, he wanted only to make it useless to the Mexicans, so he set his men to work destroying its fortifications and any military equipment that could not serve his force, and taking off guns and anything else that was usable. He assigned a battalion of sailors and two guns to garrison the town, then evacuated it on 22 April. As the flotilla headed back to Antón Lizardo, the *Albany* and the *Reefer* were left to cover the mouth of the Tuxpan River.

Back at his base, Perry began to prepare for the operation he intended to launch against Coatzacoalcos, including the organization of a landing force of 2,500 men and ten guns, and attended to the administrative details that had accumulated during his absence. On 1 May he advised Secretary Mason that the order of 10 April to send the *Ohio*, the *Raritan*, and the *St. Mary's* to Norfolk was about to be complied with, and that the *Porpoise* would follow as soon as she could be spared. When the *St. Mary's* left, she carried trophies in the form of guns captured at Veracruz, Alvarado, and Tuxpan.

Writing from on board the *Mississippi* on 10 May, Perry told the Navy Department that he needed engineers and medical officers, and he wrote again the next day to say that his steamers were in poor condition: the *Vixen* and the *Spitfire* were fast breaking down and would soon require thorough overhauling; the *Scourge* was useless because she had broken her propeller shaft; and the engines of the *Scorpion* (Commander Abraham Bigelow) could not be depended upon. He asked that the *Fulton* and the *Water Witch* be sent to reinforce his squadron.

A rumor that, following his defeat by General Scott at Cerro Gordo on 18 April, Santa Anna was fleeing to Coatzacoalcos to board a Mexican vessel and sail to Cuba, led Perry to disperse his force along the coast on blockade and holding stations. He sent the *Hecla* to blockade Soto la Marina; the *Etna* to close the Tabasco River; the *Porpoise* and the *Vesuvius* to watch Carmen; and the *Germantown* to watch the coast north of Lobos. The *Albany* and the *Reefer* were already on station at the mouth of the Tuxpan River. The rumor was proved unfounded on 30 April, when the *Bonita* captured the vessel, the schooner *Yucateca*, that Santa Anna was supposed to have boarded.

The appearance of so many American vessels along the coast spread alarm among the Mexicans. Tabasco being one of the only two ports of any significance still in Mexican hands, the people of that area feared that they were about to be attacked and brought in a concentration of troops to protect them. Since fear that he might attack was keeping a considerable body of troops from reinforcing Santa Anna's army, Perry decided that there was no need, at that time, for him to take action against the port. He was, however, concerned about the trade that had developed between Tabasco and Carmen since the blockade of the latter had been lifted in December. Accordingly, he sailed for Carmen on 10 May in the *Mississippi* accompanied by the *Vixen* and the *Scorpion*.

Two days after leaving Antón Lizardo, the flotilla reached Coatzacoalcos, where it was joined by the *John Adams*, the *Decatur*, and the *Stromboli* (Commander William S. Walker). At the mouth of the Coatzacoalcos River there was a well-constructed fort that had been recently evacuated. The carriages of the twelve guns the fort contained had been burned, and the Americans completed the demolition by destroying the guns and burning the fort. On 13 May an expedition that Perry ordered to survey the river halted on its way long enough to hoist the American flag over the ruins of the fort.

Commander Bigelow of the *Scorpion* led the *Vixen* and several barges upriver. Aboard the vessels were Commanders Henry A. Adams and Alexander Slidell Mackenzie and a group of surveyors. The party went as far as the village of Minatitlán, twenty-four miles inland, then, after filling their water casks, headed back to Coatzacoalcos. The intelligence they brought back would have been valuable, had a plan that Perry later submitted for a joint Army-Navy expedition from the headwaters of the Coatzacoalcos River to the Pacific materialized.

Early on the morning of 14 May, the *Mississippi*, the *Vixen*, the *Scorpion*,

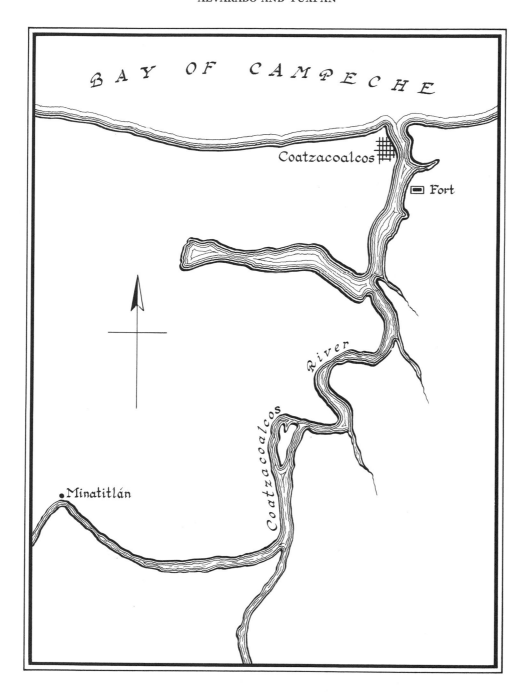

BAY OF CAMPECHE

Coatzacoalcos

Fort

River

Coatzacoalcos

Minatitlán

THE COATZACOALCOS RIVER

the *John Adams*, and the *Decatur* stood out from Coatzacoalcos to continue on their way to Carmen, but Commander Walker in the *Stromboli* was left to guard the port. When the flotilla reached Frontera, the *Vixen* was ordered to take two launches in tow and make a thirty-mile side trip up the Tabasco River to get fresh water for all the vessels. On arrival off Carmen bar on 16 May, Perry found that the brig *Washington* (Lieutenant Samuel P. Lee), having been sent to relieve the *Porpoise*, had already joined that brig and the *Vesuvius* there. A party of sailors and Marines landed, and Perry took formal possession of the town and island of Carmen the day after his arrival. He named Commander Magruder of the *Vesuvius* as naval commander and military governor of Carmen and its dependencies, and instructed him to permit American and neutral vessels not carrying contraband to enter the port on payment of duty to the United States. Later, these regulations were amended to allow logwood and other products to be exported on payment of an *ad valorem* war tax of ten per cent.

Perry stayed at Carmen only two days, then sailed for Frontera in the *Mississippi* and arrived there on the evening of 18 May. He found the *John Adams* and the *Decatur*, which had left Carmen ahead of him, the *Germantown*, which had come south from Lobos, the *Raritan*, the *Albany*, and the *Bonita*, which he had ordered to come south from Antón Lizardo, all riding at anchor outside the bar. Inside, were the two blockaders stationed there, the *Etna* and the *McLane*, along with the *Vixen*, which had completed her water-fetching mission. In the morning, the Commodore landed and paraded the Marines of his flotilla, opened the port to trade, and designated Commander Van Brunt of the *Etna* civil and military governor of the area. Besides the *Etna*, he left the *Bonita* with Van Brunt, and instructed him to keep a careful watch over activity on the streams emptying into the river.

Before Perry left the Tabasco River, he ordered Commander Mackenzie to accompany Captain Breese, who was going to Campeche in the *Albany*, to see once again what the situation was in Yucatán. When they got there, they were assured by the local authorities that Yucatán was independent and neutral, and, indeed, Yucatán so remained until the end of the war.

The *Raritan*, the *John Adams*, the *Decatur*, and the *Germantown* delayed at the Tabasco long enough to replenish their water tanks before returning to Antón Lizardo, but Perry led the few ships still with him back up the coast to Coatzacoalcos on 20 May. The day after he got there, he embarked in the *Scorpion* and steamed upriver to take formal possession of Minatitlán and the villages of Cosaleaque and San Cristóbal de Jhantlan.

Coatzacoalcos was the last stop Perry made on this cruise, as a result of which he reported on 24 May that "there is no particular object to be gained by a second attack on the city of Tabasco, as we have quiet possession of the mouth of the river, which, with the occupation of Laguna, completely shuts the Tabascans from the sea." When he left Coatzacoalcos to return to Antón Lizardo, he assigned an armed barge to remain there with Commander Walker and instructed the Commander to open the port: he also detached the *Scorpion* and ordered Commander Bigelow to search the small inlets along the coast for Mexican ships.

Meanwhile, decisions that would greatly affect the operations of the Home Squadron were being made in Washington. On 13 May, President Polk noted in his diary:

Gen'l Henderson stated that 6 companies of marines could be spared from the navy for land service. I have written an order to the Secretary of the Navy to transfer them to the land forces under the immediate command of Gen'l Scott. I requested Gen'l Henderson to execute the order without delay, as I deemed it important that Gen'l Scott's column should be re-inforced by all our available forces with as little delay as possible.

The Navy could not spare "6 companies of marines" without depleting the Marine detachments aboard the vessels of the Home Squadron. In vain did Perry protest that if he was deprived of his Marines, he would be compelled to withdraw the garrisons he had left in the captured ports. Indeed, on 29 May, at the very time when the Navy Department and the White House were deciding to take away his garrisons, he asked the Secretary of the Navy to send him more Marines to handle the guerrilla warfare that was becoming a source of concern, particularly at Tampico and Alvarado.

Thus, Perry's hold on the Mexican ports along the Gulf coast was threatened from two directions: the impending departure of several of his vessels scheduled to go home for repairs, and actions being taken in Washington.

X

BACK TO TABASCO

Shortly after reporting that there was "no particular object to be gained" by making a second attack on Tabasco because it could be easily neutralized, Commodore Perry changed his mind and decided to make just such an attack. In theory, his first opinion was correct, but in practice it was not, for supplies for Santa Anna's army continued to flow through the town. He was aware that the Tabascaños, moved to haste largely by his concentration of vessels in southern waters in May, had considerably strengthened their defenses since his first attack in October and that, consequently, he would be wise to act before the *Raritan* and the *Albany* left for the United States.

Tabasco's defenses were well planned to withstand assault by a force advancing up the river. At Seven Palms, just above the treacherous Devil's Bend, the newly built La Colmena breastwork stretched seventy-five yards from the river to the chaparral on the left and commanded some obstructive piles that had been driven into the river bottom, four hundred yards downstream. One mile upstream from La Colmena, lay the principal work—Fort Acachapan, where Perry had met opposition during his earlier attack—which extended inland about two miles and mounted only two guns, its original four 24-pounders having been spiked by the Americans during their previous visit. About a mile and a half farther upstream there was a new earthwork, La Independencia, which stretched some seventy-five yards along both the river bank and the road that paralleled it. A quarter of a mile beyond La Independencia, the road was obstructed by an abatis, and a quarter of a mile beyond that, one mile below the town proper and three hundred yards back from the river, stood Fort Itúrbide, a breastwork four and a half feet high. Fort Itúrbide mounted three 28-pounders that commanded the river for a mile and a half downstream, two 6-pounders that swept the road from Acachapan, and a single 18-pounder carronade that stood ready to spray

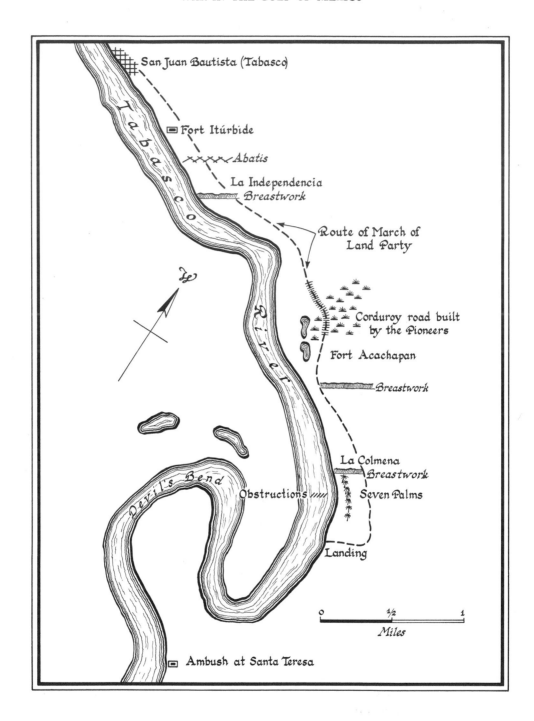

San Juan Bautista (Tabasco)

Fort Itúrbide

××××× *Abatis*

La Independencia
Breastwork

Route of March of
Land Party

Corduroy road built
by the Pioneers

Fort Acachapan

Breastwork

La Colmena
Breastwork

Obstructions

Seven Palms

Landing

Tabasco River

Devil's Bend

0 ½ 1
Miles

Ambush at Santa Teresa

TABASCO AND ITS DEFENSES

grapeshot at vessels passing along the river. The final defense was a small breastwork built on a rise in front of the house of the inept and corrupt commanding general, Domingo Echegaray, who had a force of some 900 soldiers with which to man these extensive fortifications.

Except for Fort Itúrbide and the small breastwork in front of Echegaray's house, all the defenses extended from the river to the almost impenetrable chaparral. All faced downstream only, their rearward—or upriver—sides were unprotected, and Fort Itúrbide alone mounted artillery trained on the river. Although they had been hastily thrown up and their construction was consequently not of the best, and although they were deficient in defensive artillery, they probably could, if resolutely defended, have withstood attack by a very large infantry force, provided that force was not well equipped with artillery. Echegaray's most serious lack was men, but he had made the best possible disposition of the means at hand.

With that appraisal of the defenses in mind, Perry estimated that if a naval force could break through the obstructions in the river below La Colmena, it would be able easily to run past the various works and attack them from their defenseless rear sides: there would be nothing to stop its progress upriver until it came to Fort Itúrbide. Then, if it could get past the guns of that fort, the town would be defenseless.

According to his biographer and ardent admirer, William E. Griffis, Perry "prepared the plan of attack with great care. Every contingency was foreseen and provided against, and the minutest details were subject to his thoughtful elaboration." Whether or not that is an overstatement, Perry certainly did prepare for the expedition with more than his usual thoroughness. His earlier visit to Tabasco had made him aware of many of the problems facing him, and the accuracy of the intelligence with which he was provided can be deduced from the fact that he knew about the obstructions that had been sunk in the river above Devil's Bend. It was that foreknowledge that prompted him to take along on the expedition the merchant schooner *Spitfire* carrying George W. Taylor and his inflatable "patent India-rubber camels," but they were, in fact, never used. Also, because he expected strong opposition from Echegaray's garrison, he took the entire Naval Brigade—the landing force he had organized when he returned from Tuxpan —to handle the fighting ashore.

The *Etna* and the *Bonita* had been at Frontera at the mouth of the Tabasco River, since Perry's visit there in May, and at the beginning of June had been joined by the steamer *Spitfire*. All other vessels of the squadron that could make the voyage to Frontera and could be spared from other duties were called up for the attack on Tabasco. Perry left Antón Lizardo aboard the *Mississippi* on the morning of 9 June and, sailing independently, the *Vixen*, the *Scourge*, the *Raritan*, the *John Adams*, the *Albany*, the

The *Scorpion*, the *Spitfire*, the *Vixen*,
and the *Scourge* cross the bar at the
mouth of the Tabasco River.
The Mariners' Museum, Newport News, Va.

Germantown, the *Decatur*, and the *Washington* followed. In the course of 12 and 13 June all the vessels reached the mouth of the Tabasco River, where they were joined by the *Stromboli* from Coatzacoalcos, and the *Scorpion* and the *Vesuvius* from Laguna del Carmen.

Early on the morning of 14 June, the small steamers *Scourge*, *Scorpion*, *Spitfire*, and *Vixen* towed the *Washington*, the *Stromboli*, the *Vesuvius*, and the schooner *Spitfire*, carrying Taylor's camels, across the bar to join the *Bonita* and the *Etna* at anchor off Frontera. Then, having cast their tows, they returned beyond the bar in order to begin towing in the surfboats and ships' boats. Though the deep-draft vessels—the *Mississippi*, the *Raritan*, the *John Adams*, the *Albany*, the *Germantown*, and the *Decatur*—stayed at anchor outside the bar, as usual, they contributed men to the expedition. Shortly after noon, Perry transferred his pennant to the *Scorpion*.

The steamers spent the afternoon coaling at Frontera and, at 5:25 when that operation had been completed, Perry signaled the force inside the bar to head upriver. The flagship *Scorpion*, towing the *Vesuvius*, the *Washington*, and the boats of the *Mississippi* and of the *John Adams* led the way, and the steamer *Spitfire*, with the *Stromboli*, the *Bonita*, and the boats of the *Albany* in tow, followed in her wake. Then came the *Scourge* towing Taylor's schooner *Spitfire* and, bringing up the rear, were the *Etna* and the *Vixen*, the latter towing the boats of the *Raritan*, the *Germantown*, and the *Decatur*. Between them, the forty ships' boats carried 1,173 men. Also included in the tows were seven surfboats, each holding a field piece.

"The clear sky and bright sunshine," wrote Francis Winslow, a young officer aboard the *Washington*, "the blue water ripping with the sea breeze, the green foliage and graceful palm trees on the banks, the dark steamers and the boats crowded with men and marines (a small field piece in the larger ones) with the white awnings and ensigns streaming gallantly out on the breeze, formed one of those spirit stirring scenes not readily forgotten."

There was a good deal of activity aboard the craft, as gun crews checked their weapons and the Marines and sailors of the landing party rechecked their equipment. In the *Scourge*, Lieutenant Lockwood's crew worked at piling sandbags and bags of coal around the steam drum to protect it from Mexican shot, one of the earliest known attempts to protect the exposed machinery of a steamer.

During the night, as the squadron worked its way cautiously up the river, halting every now and again, probably to sound bars, it had little cause for concern, other than an occasional grounding. But, during the mid watch, when it was about thirty miles below Tabasco, two Indians in a canoe came down upon it and reported that the Mexicans, in the hope of ambushing the expedition, had thrown up breastworks at three points in the thick chaparral that lined the river. When Perry heard this, he ordered a halt and waited for daylight.

After resuming its slow movement up the river, the squadron steamed for seven hours before clearing for action at two o'clock in the afternoon. Some two hours later, the leading vessels came abreast of the first of the ambushes reported by the Indians, Santa Teresa, about twelve miles below Tabasco. There, from the vantage of a high hill, one hundred and fifty men under Colonel Miguel Bruno opened fire, but their bullets passed harmlessly over the vessels. The squadron returned the fire and continued to churn peacefully on its way for two more hours, by which time it was nearing Devil's Bend. As the *Scorpion*, leading the squadron, reached the elbow of the bend, three or four ineffectual shots rang out from the thickly wooded left bank. The fusillade that followed those opening shots riddled awnings and pinged against the flagship's superstructure, but no one was injured, not even the Commodore who was standing in an exposed position under the awnings on the upper waist deck. The *Scorpion*, her tow, the *Washington*, and the boats astern all opened on the Mexicans and their fire was silenced. Not long after that episode, the masthead lookout of the *Stromboli* spotted a body of cavalry behind the chaparral, but it soon dispersed when a 10-inch shell from the *Vesuvius* fell nearby.

In Lieutenant Winslow's opinion, excited Americans were responsible for most of the damage done to the flagship. He commented that had the Marines stationed on the *Scorpion*'s paddle boxes gone to the engaged side of their ship, they would not have had to fire across her deck. As it was, he reported, they "fired away, without going once to the right side of the quarter deck, and shaved one of the Commodore's whiskers and knocked a cigar out of another officer's mouth."

Approaching darkness found the squadron one hundred yards below the obstructions in the river, which Perry knew his ships would not be able to pass at night and, if it proved that they could not pass them at any time and the Naval Brigade had to be landed, that operation also would have to take place in daylight. Consequently, although an incident that occurred at dusk, when a lone Mexican on the river bank shot a man on the forecastle of the *Vesuvius* and escaped unscathed amid a hail of shots, pointed up the danger of spending the night in the narrow Devil's Bend, that is what Perry decided his force would have to do. As the river was no more than eighty yards wide and the channel in which the vessels had to anchor was only ten to twenty yards from the chaparral-covered left bank, the men spent the night on deck behind barricades made of hammocks, and slept with their arms beside them. This arrangement exposed the men to Mexican fire, but even if there had been room for them all to sleep below decks, some of them would have had to go up on deck to reach their battle stations and, as they emerged through the hatches to do so, would have made excellent targets. Further, the hit-and-run tactics of the Mexicans made it imperative for the guns to be ready to fire in the shortest time possible. As it turned out, the precautions were unnecessary, for only once during the night did the vessels fire, and that was when the *Spitfire* and the *Vesuvius* responded to what turned out to be a false alarm.

A fragrant and balmy breeze was scarcely disturbing the surface of the water as dawn broke on 16 June, and Perry sent two experienced survey officers, Lieutenants William May and James Alden, to reconnoiter the obstacles in the river. Meantime, he shifted his vessels into position to cover the landing that would have to be made if May and Alden reported that the river was impassable.

However, at 6:40, before the surveyors had completed their mission, the Mexicans at La Colmena opened fire on them severely wounding Lieutenant May, and they were forced to return to their ships. Convinced by this experience that, at best, it would take some time for his steamers to get beyond the obstacles, Perry immediately prepared to land the Naval Brigade and advance overland. Having instructed Commander Buchanan of the *German-town* to select the landing place, he ordered his force to prepare to land.

The surfboats and ships' boats embarked their passengers and got into formation opposite the foot of a steep bank just below Seven Palms, which Buchanan had chosen as the site, and the *Spitfire*, the *Scourge*, and the *Bonita* swept the area with grape, shells, and musketry. The Commodore boarded his barge and, with his broad pennant flying, moved ahead of the line of boats. He was the first man ashore, and the three cheers from the sailor army that greeted his order to land were repeated when his pennant was unfurled atop the high bank, in sight of the whole expedition. An anonymous naval officer reported that "such spirit, such enthusiasm, I am confident, never were surpassed," and Lieutenant Winslow suggested that the noise was "enough to frighten the Mexicans to death without firing a shot."

By the end of the morning watch, the whole Naval Brigade was ashore. It had taken ten minutes for 1,173 men and seven 6-pounders to land and form—no mean accomplishment when it is considered that the men had to climb a precipitous bank, twenty feet high, and drag their artillery up after them. While boats went back and fetched three more guns, one each from the *Etna*, the *Stromboli*, and the *Vesuvius*, the Pioneers, or engineers, looked for and found the road to Tabasco. Twenty-five minutes after the landings had begun, the whole force was on the march. The Pioneers, commanded by Lieutenant Lafayette Maynard, doubled as scouts and led the way. To them fell the difficult task of making the road passable for the artillery: that meant frequently felling trees to corduroy soft spots in the road, and sometimes having to build bridges. Behind the Pioneers, came the Marines under the command of Captain Alvin Edson, and the Marines were followed by Commodore Perry, his suite, and the detail carrying his pennant. Following Perry, came the artillery commanded by Commander Mackenzie and supported by an infantry detachment under Commander Buchanan. Behind the artillery, was the main body of infantry in two divisions under Captains Breese and Forrest. An ambulance party brought up the rear.

As the column advanced, it moved first through a narrow band of chaparral, then across about a mile of level plain before finding itself in more chaparral. High grass on the plain, the tangled thickets of the chaparral and, as the morning wore on, especially the excessive heat, made progress slow. Since the route being taken led northward, away from the river, before turning westward to parallel the river, it bypassed La Colmena and the first obstacle encountered was Fort Acachapan, the Mexicans' main defensive work, where Echegaray had stationed Colonel Claro Hidalgo with three hundred infantry, three hundred irregular cavalry, and two guns. When the van of the sailor army came within range of the fort, Perry ordered it to halt until the artillery came up. Then, as the guns were moved into their places, he drew up the rest of his force in a long line facing the work and, heedless as usual about his personal safety, took an exposed position in front. A few rounds from the artillery brought no response and Perry, sensing that the defenders were faltering in their resolve to stand and fight, ordered a charge. With great spirit but little organization, the sailors and Marines rushed forward. At the sight of an overwhelming mass of yelling men bearing down upon them, the Mexicans broke and fled.

Meanwhile, under the personal direction of Taylor, the crews of the vessels still lying at anchor below La Colmena were busy opening a passage through the piles in the river. They placed drums of powder around the bases of the piles, ran wires from the powder drums to a galvanic battery, then fired the powder: the resultant explosion loosened the logs. The *Spitfire*, temporarily commanded by Lieutenant David D. Porter, then towed them away. At about the same time as the land party began its march towards Acachapan, the *Scorpion*, the *Spitfire*, the *Scourge*, and the *Vixen* worked their way through the opened passage and headed upstream.

It so happened that, at the breastwork of Acachapan, the road ran for a short distance along the river bank, and many of the hot and thirsty sailors and Marines on land rushed down to the water for a drink. The men on the steamers mistook them for Mexicans and opened fire on them. Fortunately, none of the shots found their mark, and when the men ashore showed an American flag, the firing gave way to cheers.

After re-forming, Perry's little army again took up the march, but the condition of the road and the heat of the day made progress slow. The heat was particularly hard on the artillerymen, who had to pull the guns over the rough road as well as carry all the ammunition on their backs. "Many of the officers," reported Commander Buchanan, "carried canteens with liquor and the moment they saw a poor fellow fall they would give him 'a drop of comfort' which had an astonishing effect on him. . . ."

At 10:32 the steamers, with the *Scorpion* in the lead, rounded Cachas Bend and approached La Independencia. Musket fire from that work was answered by the Americans as they passed on up the river. Five minutes later, the *Scorpion* reached Point Commandra and ran into raking fire from nearby Fort Itúrbide. The fourth shot from the fort carried away some of the flagship's rigging and wounded Passed Midshipman William H. Hudson. Undeterred, the Americans forced their way through the continuing fire. The *Spitfire* was hit in her wheelhouse and in her starboard paddle wheel, and the *Scorpion* also took a hit in her wheelhouse, but none of the damage was serious enough to stop the vessels. In a few minutes, when they had passed Fort Itúrbide, the steamers opened rapid and accurate fire on it from behind. Noticing that the defenders seemed shaken by this attack, Lieutenant Porter led sixty-eight men ashore and drove the garrison from the fort.

Mexicans fire on the squadron as it
works its way up the Tabasco River.

With the last of the river defenses behind them, the vessels steamed on for
the town of Tabasco. There was no Mexican flag to be seen when the
Scorpion dropped anchor there, so Commander Bigelow sent messengers
ashore to fetch the local authorities. They brought back the Prefect of
Tabasco, and he surrendered the town unconditionally. A few minutes after
noon on 16 June, Bigelow went ashore to attend the ceremony of hoisting the
American flag, but had to wait while Passed Midshipman Isaac N. Briceland
provided a place to plant the flagstaff by making a hole in the roof of the
governor's house. While the ceremony was taking place, the *Scorpion* exchanged fire with some Mexicans in the chaparral beyond the upper end of
the town, and a little later the *Scourge* moved upstream to that area in order
to provide more fire power against such guerrilla attacks.

Perry and the land force reached the abatis above La Independencia at
two o'clock and, finding it undefended, proceeded on their way, after halting

The capture of Tabasco
Left to right: the *Bonita*, the *Spitfire*, and the *Scorpion*
Franklin D. Roosevelt Library, Hyde Park, New York

only long enough for stragglers to catch up. Very soon, the American flag flying over Fort Itúrbide came into view. Glad as they were to see it, they were also disappointed at this evidence that they would not be the first to arrive at Tabasco. "Cheers, hearty cheers passed along the line," reported Buchanan, "but the disappointment to all hands you may imagine; the field pieces became a thousand pounds heavier at once."

No sooner had they marched into Tabasco, about an hour later, than it began to rain and, in order to have sheltered quarters, they had to break down the doors to the public buildings because no keys could be found. They parked their artillery under cover of the arcade in the plaza, where it commanded the approaches to the town.

Scarcely more than 1,100 men, poorly trained for campaigning on land, had routed some 900 men from behind strong fortifications. They had inflicted some 30 casualties upon the Mexicans, at a cost of five of their own men wounded. The expedition was conducted in a manner that reflected great credit on Commodore Perry, and every Mexican port of consequence on the Gulf was now in American hands.

Perry stayed at Tabasco until 22 June superintending the destruction of contraband, the transfer of guns from the forts to the flotilla, the blowing up of the magazine, and the demolition of the fortifications. He had to decide whether to hold the town and open a customhouse there, or abandon it and hold Frontera alone. There were sound arguments for both courses. If he held it, the United States would control a rich, populous town situated in a very fertile region, it would have effective control over the states of Oaxaca and Chiapas, and more revenue would flow into American hands: on the other hand, it would need a large garrison to hold it, and the men would be exposed to a vicious climate and to yellow fever. He decided to hold it pending instructions, which he would request from the Navy Department, and garrisoned it with Marines under Lieutenant William B. Slack. In the river, off the town, he stationed the *Spitfire*, the *Scourge*, and the *Etna*, each with a field piece and ammunition aboard. He gave Commander Van Brunt of the *Etna* over-all command and named him governor and collector of the port.

On 24 June a force of Mexicans made a night attack on Tabasco. They were driven off, but the garrison was not strong enough to pursue and disperse them and they hung about the outskirts of the town waiting to harass any Americans who ventured into that area. For instance, the next day, Lieutenant Porter, now in full command of the *Spitfire*, led a party of his men ashore and they were attacked. Two nights after the attack on the town, Commander Bigelow arrived from Frontera in the *Scorpion*. As senior officer, he took command and immediately notified the Commodore that the garrison at Tabasco badly needed reinforcing.

When Perry responded by sending the *Vixen* with forty-four Marines, fifty sailors, and one gun, Bigelow decided to attack the enemy's quarters at Tamulté, about four miles upriver from Tabasco. He formed his expedition into two parts: a land force of some 200 men with two 6-pounders, and two steamers, the *Scourge* and the *Vixen*, on the river. As the land party neared Tamulté on the morning of 30 June, they came up against the Mexicans and a skirmish ensued. After twenty minutes of fighting, the Mexican force was scattered and the Americans marched on into the village. One American had been killed and five wounded. The few arms found in Tamulté were worthless, so Bigelow had them destroyed before leading his men back to Tabasco. When the *Scourge* and the *Vixen*, having been slowed by many groundings in the shallow river, finally reached Tamulté, the land party had already left.

In spite of the successful expedition upriver, the garrison at Tabasco continued to be daily harassed, so on the night of 14 July Bigelow decided to set an ambush for the Mexicans and try to cut them off before they reached the town. However, the effort ended in failure when the two detachments that were landed, one from the *Spitfire* and one from the *Etna*, fired on each other in the darkness. In another attempt to put an end to the attacks on Tabasco, Bigelow sent the *Spitfire* and the *Scorpion* to attack Tamulté again. Lieutenant Porter of the *Spitfire* burned the barracks there, before returning to Tabasco on 19 July, but little else was accomplished. The pressure on Tabasco was not eased.

On the sixteenth, shortly after Porter's expedition left for Tamulté, the Mexicans, probably assuming the strength of the garrison greatly depleted, made an unprecedented daylight attack on Tabasco. They got within musket range of the town's plaza before being driven back.

Meanwhile, on 17 July Perry, who had come down from Veracruz, told Bigelow that he was concerned about the health of the garrison and, although he wanted to hold Tabasco, he did not want to do so at the "expense of many valuable lives." He gave Bigelow permission to evacuate the town if and when the latter felt such a step was necessary. Bigelow replied that he had not been able to stamp out guerrilla raids on the town but, in spite of a very long sick list, he did not consider it necessary to evacuate. Nevertheless, two days later, on the recommendation of his surgeons, Perry ordered Tabasco evacuated, and the sickest of the men and some of the stores were embarked on 21 July. That night the Mexicans again approached the town and one American was killed and three wounded in a skirmish between the garrison and the guerrillas. The next morning, protected by the Marines under Lieutenant William L. Shuttleworth, the main body of men, the rest of the sick, the artillery, and what stores remained were embarked, and the vessels reached Frontera that evening.

In an attempt to soften the loss of Tabasco and make its neutralization more effective, Perry made Commander Van Brunt commanding officer and collector of the port of Frontera, and left him there with the *Scourge*, the *Bonita*, and the *Etna*, and instructed him to cut off all trade with Tabasco.

Thus, Tabasco fell victim to yellow fever, with which one-third of its garrison was afflicted, as well as to the decision to transfer Perry's Marines to General Scott's army, which made it impossible to provide a garrison large enough to eliminate harassment by marauding Mexicans.

XI

YELLOW FEVER AND YUCATÁN

All through the war, the U.S. government was concerned lest the Mexicans license privateers. Most responsible officials realized that the Mexican merchant marine was too small to provide many privateers, but Mexican law allowed the granting of letters of marque and reprisal to foreigners who would swear allegiance to the Republic of Mexico, and provided for the issuing of commissions in foreign ports. The U.S. government refused to recognize such commissions, and a new piracy statute, providing that all foreigners caught using Mexican letters of marque would be treated as pirates, was pushed through the Congress.

A Spanish felucca, *El Unico*, is the only privateer with a Mexican commission known to have seized an American vessel. Early in 1847, she was sailing near Gibraltar when she captured the *Carmelita* and took her to Barcelona. The Spanish government promptly returned the American vessel to her master and arrested the crew of *El Unico* on charges of piracy. It also seized the Spanish steamer *La Resita*, which was being fitted as a privateer at Oran, Algeria. Despite these resolute actions on the part of the Spanish government, the United States sent the sloop of war *Marion* (Commander Lewis E. Simonds) from her station off the coast of Africa to Gibraltar, where she was later joined by the steamer *Princeton* (Commander Frederick Engle) and the revenue cutter *Taney* (Lieutenant Charles G. Hunter).

After the abandonment of Tabasco, Commodore Perry reorganized his squadron and sent home the ships he no longer needed. The frigate *Raritan*, carrying three guns captured at Tabasco, was the first to leave. Perry suggested that two of the trophies be sent to the Naval School at Annapolis in recognition of the part its graduates had played in their capture. The *Poto-*

mac, the *Albany*, the *Washington*, the *Flirt*, and the storeship *Supply* (Lieutenant John De Camp) followed. On 23 July Secretary of the Navy Mason informed Perry that the *Cumberland* would be sent out to replace one of the departing frigates, but that the Department could not send any more small vessels.

The decision reached by the Cabinet in Washington in May—to add every available Marine to General Scott's army—obviously would have far-reaching effects on the operations of the Home Squadron: without any Marines, Perry would not only be prevented from undertaking any more amphibious operations, but he would have to reduce his garrisons to below the danger point, and this at a time when Mexican guerrilla warfare was on the upsurge. On 4 July Perry wrote to Mason reporting on a conversation he had had with Brigadier General Franklin Pierce, to whose command the squadron's Marines were to be attached: Pierce agreed with Perry's contention that the number of men involved was too small to make any difference in his, Pierce's, command, whereas their withdrawal from the squadron would have serious consequences. Perry advised Mason that he would await instructions from the Department before he parted with the Marines on garrison duty in the captured ports, but would send all the others to the Army. On 23 July the orders to transfer the Marines of the Home Squadron to General Scott's command were canceled, and few of the Marines attached to the vessels of the squadron fought under Scott.

During the summer of 1847, Commodore Perry ran into two other problems that sharply curtailed his operations. The first was a shortage of junior officers, particularly midshipmen, and the second was a shortage of steamers. Now that the squadron had fewer steamers, it had more coal at Antón Lizardo than it needed, and supply vessels that were needed to carry other goods to the squadron were needlessly tied up. When the storeship *Supply* left for Pensacola on 9 July, she carried excess coal and Perry ordered her commander to stay there until he heard from the Department whether he was to proceed north or return to Veracruz. Moreover, several of the vessels that arrived in the tropical waters of the Gulf had not had their bottoms coppered, with the result that they quickly attracted the dreaded teredo, or shipworm. In July Perry had to send the storeship *Electra* (Lieutenant Timothy A. Hunt) home to be coppered, as well as the sloop *Albany*, which was due for routine repairs.

The necessity of sending the *Albany* home for routine repairs points up a problem which confronted the Home Squadron throughout the war. The closest Navy yard with a dry dock was at Norfolk. The yard at Pensacola, which should have been the base for the squadron, was not satisfactory even as a supply center, and it would be more accurate to describe it as an advanced supply depot than as a base supply point. As a repair base, it was useless. A naval appropriations act passed on 3 March 1847 provided $250,000 for building a dry dock there, but it was not finished until after the war.

In July there was an outbreak of yellow fever in the squadron and, while it caused few deaths, it incapacitated so many men, including the Commodore, that the activities of the squadron were crippled for the rest of the summer. Worst hit were the crews of the *Mississippi*, the *Decatur*, and the *Saratoga*. Perry wanted to send the *Mississippi* north to a cooler climate, to Norfolk or Boston, for instance, the standard procedure for infected vessels, but could not because so many firemen and coal heavers were sick. By early August, enough men had recovered to allow him to send her to Pensacola to have her hold fumigated and whitewashed—not an ideal solution but, under the circumstances, the most practical. Her departure left Perry without a large steamer and further limited his freedom of action.

The medical staff of the squadron, already inadequate, was particularly hard hit by the fever: at one time there was only one doctor well enough to work and he had to serve seven vessels. The Navy Department was able to do little to relieve the shortage of medical officers, but a hospital was set up on Salmedina Island, off Veracruz, and that eased the situation. The sickness reached its peak in late August and early September. It forced the bomb brig *Stromboli* to leave her blockade station at Coatzacoalcos, and she arrived at Antón Lizardo on 26 August with only six healthy men. Three days after she came in, Perry had to give Commander Pinckney of the *Decatur* permission to take his vessel to Pensacola in an attempt to get rid of the malady. The *Saratoga* relieved the *Decatur* off Tuxpan on 1 September and soon had on board more cases of fever than any other vessel, excepting the *Mississippi*. By the end of the month, however, Perry was able to report that the fever was dying out.

The ingenious surgeon of the *Vixen* decided that the epidemic could be stamped out by sterilization, so he had the hatches and ports of the vessels closed, and all the steam that the boilers could generate released. The treatment ended the epidemic, killed the rats and roaches—and ruined all the woodwork.

Even had yellow fever not appeared, the squadron would have been almost impotent during the summer months of 1847, because the *Raritan*, the *Potomac*, and the *Albany* had not been replaced. At the same time, guerrillas were constantly harassing Alvarado and the suburbs of Veracruz and Tampico, and wreaking vengeance on all who traded with the Americans. At Tampico, despite its army garrison, conditions became so bad that the government's money could not be kept safely in the town and Perry had to send the *Petrel* to serve as a floating vault. There was little he could do to provide protection beyond the range of his guns, since he could not spare men from his shorthanded crews to reinforce his garrisons. However, the guerrillas never became more than a nuisance, because of dissension among their leaders.

News that an attack was about to be made on the flotilla lying off Alvarado reached Perry on 14 August, while the yellow-fever epidemic was raging. He immediately sent the bomb brig *Hecla* to support the threatened flotilla, and the following day ordered the *Scorpion*, the *Vixen*, and the *Spitfire* to steam up the Alvarado River as far as Tlacotalpán and make a demonstration that would intimidate the Mexicans.

After relaying the rumor about an attack on Alvarado and a similar one on Coatzacoalcos, Perry told the Navy Department that he did not have enough ships to hold the ports. His only usable large vessels were the *Saratoga*, the *Germantown*, and the *John Adams*. The *Mississippi* had gone to Pensacola and would not return for some time: when the *Decatur* left for that port, the *Saratoga* would have to take her place off Tuxpan, and he would have to keep the *Germantown* at Antón Lizardo as his flagship. Thus, the only cruising vessel available to him was the *John Adams*. Every one of the small steamers was plagued by some kind of engine trouble, and the schooner-gunboats and bomb brigs were too small to keep the sea during a storm. Veracruz and Tampico, which had Army garrisons, were the only ports that would be able to withstand a determined Mexican attack. Although a previous attempt to recruit men in New Orleans and Mobile had been an abject failure, yellow fever was taking such a toll of Perry's crews that, in desperation, he suggested to the Department that temporary recruiting stations again be opened in those cities.

The closest the Navy came to conducting an active operation in the summer and early autumn of 1847 was in September when Commander Adams was sent in the *John Adams* to inquire into a report that Indian uprisings were going on in Yucatán. Having stopped at Frontera and Carmen to land provisions and medicines, Adams reached Campeche on 7 September and conferred with Consul John F. McGregor, who told him that there had not been any Indian uprisings and that Yucatán would remain neutral. Adams relayed this information to Perry and reported also that the authorities in Yucatán were concerned over the lukewarm support given their regime by the Americans and over the American occupation of Carmen. In answer to the latter complaint, Perry was quick to point to experience, which proved that the abandonment of Carmen would mean the development of a flourishing illicit trade between Yucatán and Mexico.

On 4 August Secretary Mason ordered Perry not to seize any more places, and that, naturally, put an end to offensive operations in the Gulf. Nevertheless, the Home Squadron was not idle for the rest of the war. It still had to maintain the blockade and to hold the ports already in American hands.

DAVID G. FARRAGUT

An incident that caused chagrin to all the Americans involved in it took place in Veracruz Harbor on 14 August, when the British mail steamer *Teviot* arrived on her regularly scheduled run from Havana. One of her passengers, traveling under the name of M. Martinez, turned out to be General Mariano Paredes y Arrillaga, ex-president of Mexico. For some unknown reason, the army officer whose duty it was to check incoming mail steamers, did not check the *Teviot* until after General Paredes had gone ashore and escaped. The *Saratoga* was in port at the time, but Commander Farragut did not board the English steamer because he considered that to do so was the duty of the Army. When Commodore Perry reported the episode to Secretary Mason, he blamed Paredes' escape on Farragut's failure to board the *Teviot*, which, not unnaturally, intensified Farragut's animosity towards the Commodore. As a result of the mix-up, Perry issued instructions that all vessels, except Army steamers and transports, arriving in Mexican ports were to be boarded by naval officers.

On 25 September Perry once again wrote to Secretary Mason about the difficulties he was having with regard to vessels. He said he needed the bomb brigs and, therefore, could not comply with a suggestion Mason had made that they be sent to New Orleans and sold. He said further that the small steamers were not seaworthy enough to be sent to New Orleans for repairs and, anyway, in spite of the poor condition they were in, he needed them in the Gulf.

Soon after he had written that letter, the reinforcements that he had so long awaited began arriving. On 27 September, the *Albany* (Commander John Kelly), her repairs having been completed, was ordered to rejoin the squadron at Veracruz, but her return was offset by the detachment on 1 October of the *Decatur*, which had been at Pensacola since early September. The *Mississippi* left Pensacola on 17 October to return to Veracruz, and the steamers *Water Witch* (Lieutenant George M. Totten), which Perry had asked for early in May, and *Iris* (Commander Henry B. Wilson), which had been recently purchased, and the big frigate *Cumberland* (Captain William Jameson) reported to Perry during the course of late October and November. A chartered storeship, the *Monterey*, came in to Veracruz on 11 October bringing Marines and stores.

Thus, by the end of 1847, the Commodore again commanded a squadron large enough to undertake active operations.

About the middle of October Perry proposed to his superiors a joint Army-Navy expedition from the headwaters of the Coatzacoalcos River across the Isthmus of Tehuantepec to the Pacific. He suggested that if a line of posts were established along that route the states of Tabasco and Chiapas would be cut off from the rest of Mexico, and it would then require no more than 2,000 men to subdue them.

In order for his squadron to participate in such a project, he estimated he would need some small one-gun, 100-ton river schooners with flat bottoms and no more draft than 18 inches, three steamers, some Marines with light field-camp equipment, engineering tools, saddles, bridles, and a few mountain howitzers. His plan also called for Tuxpan and Alvarado to be garrisoned by the Army, and Coatzacoalcos, Frontera, and Carmen to be held by naval vessels alone. If that were done, he said, the men released from garrison duty would be available for the expedition.

The government accepted the proposition and plans for its implementation were drawn up. The Pacific Squadron was ordered to cooperate and more Marines were sent to the Home Squadron. However, the imminence of peace negotiations caused the project to be canceled.

Apparently believing that Santa Anna had violated the agreement he made with Commander Mackenzie in the summer of 1846 and might not be entitled to treatment as a prisoner of war, Perry asked for instructions from Washington about what to do with Santa Anna if he were captured. Mason replied on 16 November that, if captured, the Mexican dictator should be sent to New Orleans as a prisoner of war. Five months later, on 5 April 1848,

Santa Anna embarked in the Spanish brigantine *Pepita* at the bar of the Antigua River, north of Veracruz, and sailed for Havana under a safe-conduct pass issued by General William O. Butler, who had replaced General Scott on 18 February. So, Perry never did get his hands on Santa Anna.

Late in November 1847 the *Mississippi*, with the Commodore embarked, the *Water Witch*, and the *Scorpion* left Antón Lizardo for a cruise to Alvarado, Coatzacoalcos, Tabasco, Carmen, and Campeche. At the first four stops, Perry inspected the garrisons, and at Campeche he checked on the state of affairs in Yucatán. When he arrived back at Veracruz on 12 December, he was under the impression that relations between the United States and Yucatán were not likely to improve.

How best to hold the smaller captured ports was a continually vexing problem. They were not important enough to warrant garrisoning at the expense of other operations, yet they could not be left unguarded. Some ports—Tabasco, for example—could not be held without a garrison, while others—Coatzacoalcos, for example—could be most effectively held by naval vessels. Ships on station in the mouth of the Tabasco River could neutralize that area, and the same method would have been effective at Tuxpan had it not been for the fact that a vessel small enough to cross the bar there was too small to ride out a storm. The above probably explains why, soon after he returned from Yucatán, Perry set out for Tuxpan and landed a garrison there—December being the middle of the stormy season. He went in the *Mississippi*, which was accompanied by the *Iris*, the *Vixen*, the *Tampico*, and the *Mahonese*.

Less than a month later, on 10 January 1848, the Commodore requested that he be relieved of his command. He claimed that he had not fully recovered from the yellow fever, and reminded Secretary Mason that, having served a tour with the Africa Squadron before going to the Gulf, he had been away from his family for five years. However, the view of the Navy Department was that, since Perry had not served his full term as squadron commander, a change of command would be undesirable and on 24 February Mason turned down his request. This action may also have been inspired by a feeling that Perry had asked for relief because the war had moved into a passive phase and the chance for him to distinguish himself had passed.

In January 1848, three of the large vessels in the Gulf were withdrawn: first, Secretary Mason ordered the *Mississippi* to Boston for repairs; then, on 15 January, the sloop *Germantown* sailed for Norfolk, her tour of duty in the Gulf having been completed; and five days after that, the *Saratoga*, then at Pensacola, was ordered to return to New York. Early in February Mason authorized the *John Adams* to return to the United States and, about a month later, ordered Perry to send a vessel to Venezuela. Perry complied by sending the *Albany*, and thus the squadron would soon be denuded of most of its large vessels. On top of these incapacitating losses, the steamer *Petrita*, which Perry had captured during his first attack on Tabasco, sprang a leak and sank in the Alvarado River on 14 March. Mason realized that peace would probably be made before any more large-scale operations were needed, and that is most likely the reason why the vessels withdrawn from the Gulf were not replaced.

Before the *Mississippi* left for home, Perry made two more cruises in her. In February he visited Alvarado, Tlacotalpán, and Coatzacoalcos, and on 1 March he sailed for Carmen and Campeche, picking up en route the *Scorpion*, the *Iris*, the *Water Witch*, and the *Vesuvius* from their blockading stations. The purpose of his trip to Yucatán was to investigate an Indian uprising there and to find out whether he could help to suppress it. He arrived off Campeche on 13 March and met with Governor Santiago Mendez, who told him that help was needed to quell the uprising. Except for the coastal settlements, the Indians succeeded in occupying most of the state before they were driven back and defeated late in the year. When Perry got back to Veracruz in late March, he found a message advising him that on 7 March the Cabinet in Washington had authorized him to provide the authorities in Yucatán with powder and muskets for use against the Indians, if he was satisfied that these materials would not find their way into Mexico. These he sent. As a further concession to hard-pressed Yucatán, Mason ordered that all Yucatán vessels should be exempted from paying duty at Carmen. There was little else that the United States could do to help.

Another message from Washington that Perry found at Veracruz when he returned from Yucatán was dated 11 March and in it Mason advised him that on 10 March the Senate had ratified an amended Treaty of Guadalupe Hidalgo. The Secretary went on to point out that, since there was no way of knowing whether the Mexicans would accept the amendments, the detachment of 11 Marine officers and 364 men under the command of Major John Harris, which had been intended for Perry's planned expedition across Tehuantepec, could be distributed according to the Commodore's judgment. At this same time, the two detachments of Marines that had been serving with General Scott returned to the control of the Navy and were stationed at Alvarado and Carmen, where they remained until after the war.

Some two months later, Mason sent Perry instructions concerning the evacuation of Mexico and gave him authority to use his own discretion about both the time of departure and the destination of the squadron's small vessels. On 28 May Perry heard through the British Consul at Veracruz that three days previously the Mexican Congress had ratified the peace treaty as amended, but the next day he advised Mason that he would not begin to evacuate the country until he had been officially notified of the ratification. Nevertheless, on 30 May he issued instructions to his subordinates at Frontera de la Tabasco and Carmen to turn the customhouses back to the Mexicans and to be ready to leave their stations when he gave the order. Between 7 and 9 June, he issued similar orders to his officers at Tuxpan, Alvarado, and Tlacotalpán. The city, fortress, and customhouse of Veracruz reverted to Mexican control on 11 June. Troops embarking for home assembled at Veracruz, and between 30 May and 2 July 1848 the Army, which had sole responsibility for their embarkation and transportation, handled 18,331 men. The last American left Veracruz on 31 July.

Apart from the continuance of the blockade, there had been little action during the final year of the naval war in the Gulf of Mexico. The yellow-fever epidemic in the summer of 1847 had brought operations to a virtual standstill. Then, when the squadron had recovered from that, there was a natural reluctance to undertake any major operations because it seemed that peace would be made.

Perry sailed for New York aboard his flagship *Cumberland* on 15 June, stopping en route at Pensacola. From there, he issued orders for all the vessels of the squadron that did not have orders to go farther north to rendezvous at Pensacola. On 7 July he reported that he had ordered the *Hecla*, the *Vesuvius*, the *Stromboli*, and the *Etna* to Norfolk. Meanwhile, the *Relief* had already left Pensacola for New York, the storeship *Fredonia* (Lieutenant Frederick A. Neville) had been ordered from Veracruz to Norfolk, and the *Electra* to Carmen. The nature of the *Electra*'s mission to Carmen is not specified in the records of the squadron, but she could have been sent to pick up supplies left by the vessels that had been on station there.

No more orders were issued to the Home Squadron in the Gulf of Mexico.

WAR IN THE PACIFIC

XII

FALSE START IN CALIFORNIA

There is a striking similarity between the situation of California and that of Texas immediately prior to the outbreak of the war with Mexico in 1846. California had been a part of the Spanish empire in the Americas, as had Texas. It was one of the last areas to be settled from Spanish Mexico, as was Texas, and both were settled in order to form buffers against foreign threats. Whereas in the case of Texas, the threat came from France, in California, it came from Russia and Britain. Just as Texas did, California became part of Mexico when that country achieved its independence from Spain.

California—then called Alta California to distinguish it from Baja California—had been a fringe area of Spanish Mexico, as it was of independent Mexico during most of the time it belonged to that state. It was too far from the Mexican capital and too difficult to reach for the succession of relatively weak Mexican governments to control it effectively and, in practice, it remained connected to Mexico only by ties of race, religion, and culture. But, being proud, independent frontiersmen, the Californians did not take kindly to being even nominally controlled by centralized governments which offered little in return for the revenue of the Californian customhouses.

To many foreigners—Americans, Britons, Frenchmen—the riches of Mexican California cried out to be exploited. To the American exponents of Manifest Destiny, it was the natural western limit of the United States, and its great potential could be realized only under the enlightenment and divine inspiration of the United States. These men, of whom Senator Thomas Hart Benton of Missouri was probably the leading spokesman, argued that if British designs succeeded, California would belong to a foreign power, when logic showed that it should and must belong to the United States. Moreover, British acquisition of California would mean isolation for the American settlements in Oregon.

It was during the negotiations over the boundary between the United States and Mexico that the former first showed an official interest in California: on 6 August 1835 Anthony Butler, American Minister to Mexico, was instructed by the administration of President Andrew Jackson to try to acquire the area of San Francisco and all of California north of the thirty-seventh parallel. Although nothing came of Butler's effort and it was ten years before an American government made another attempt to acquire it, interest in the territory did not die. In those intervening years, steadily increasing numbers of American merchants settled in California and became landholders. American vessels worked in the hide trade along its coast, which was also a favorite stopping place for whalers operating in the North Pacific. By 1839 the interests of American citizens in California were so substantial that the Pacific Squadron, which spent most of its time off the west coast of South America, was ordered to send a vessel to the waters off California and, two years later, Secretary of the Navy Abel P. Upshur instructed the squadron commander, Commodore Thomas ap Catesby Jones, to station a warship there.

Early in September 1842, as his flagship *United States* (Captain James Armstrong) lay at Callao, Peru, Commodore Jones received what appeared to be reliable information to the effect that war had broken out between the United States and Mexico. Aware of his government's interest in California, particularly its desire to head off British or French occupation of the region, Jones hastened north in the *United States* to seize the port of Monterey. No sooner had he arrived there on 19 October and occupied it, than he discovered that he had acted on false information: there was no war. Consequently, with full apologies and ceremonies, he returned the town to its Mexican authorities two days after he had taken it. Not unnaturally, his premature action cost Jones his command, but it indicated that it would be easy to capture the Californian ports. One cannot help but agree with what Josiah Royce says in his book *California*: "The hasty seizure of Monterey in 1842, although wholly disavowed by our government, was a betrayal of our national feeling, to say the least, if not our national plans . . ."

At Callao on 24 March 1845, Commodore John D. Sloat hoisted his pennant as commander of the Pacific Squadron in the frigate *Savannah*, whose captain was the same James Armstrong who had commanded the flagship *United States*. There were similarities between Sloat and Commodore Conner in that both suffered from ill health and both had the caution born of the thirty years of peace that followed the War of 1812, but with all his caution, the Commander in the Gulf of Mexico was a decisive and effective leader, whereas Sloat tended to vacillate and temporize when faced with making important decisions.

JOHN D. SLOAT

For most of the four years following the abortive seizure of Monterey, the Pacific Squadron's activities in the waters off California were routine. Ashore, however, important events were taking place. Towards the end of 1842, the central government of Mexico sent General Manuel Micheltorena with a motley army of ex-convicts and other disreputable characters to reassert its supremacy over the province of California by serving as its governor. Micheltorena's administration so exasperated the Californians that in February 1845 they drove him out and set up their own state government. The Mexican government made no effort to overthrow the insurrectionary regime, and finally signaled its effective abandonment of California by recognizing that regime as legal.

The local administration was, at best, chaotic and by the end of 1845 California was ripe to be taken over by any movement that could assure it tranquillity and stable government. While many Californians seem to have looked towards the protection of one of the great powers or of the United States, they would not have accepted forcible annexation. The policy of President James K. Polk's administration was to acquire California by infiltration and subversion—in reality, the process that had ultimately brought Texas into the American union. On 3 February 1844, Polk made a move in

THOMAS O. LARKIN
Bancroft Library, University of California

this program of peaceful expansion by appointing Thomas Oliver Larkin, a hardworking Massachusetts businessman with large business interests in Monterey, as U.S. Consul at Monterey. Larkin was on excellent terms with most of the Californian leaders, and was probably the only American in California who had the patience, skill, and local acceptance to carry out a program of conquest by subversion.

Secretary of the Navy George Bancroft sent Commodore Sloat a letter dated 21 March 1845, warning him that war was imminent and directing him to concentrate the Pacific Squadron in Mexican waters. In another letter written on 5 May, Bancroft repeated the warning, but neither message reached Sloat until 29 July.

On 24 June Bancroft, who was in closer touch with events in Mexico than Sloat was, issued instructions to control the operations of the Pacific Squadron in the event of war with Mexico:

"It is the earnest desire of the President to pursue the policy of peace; and he is anxious that you, and every part of your squadron, should be assiduously careful to avoid any act which could be construed as an act of aggression.

". . . should you ascertain beyond a doubt that the Mexican government has declared war against us, you will at once . . . possess yourself of the port of San Francisco, and blockade or occupy such other ports as your force may permit.

Yet, even if you should find yourself called upon . . . to occupy San Francisco and other Mexican ports, you will be careful to preserve, if possible, the most friendly relations with the inhabitants; and, where you can do so, you will encourage them to adopt a course of neutrality. . . .

The great distance of your squadron, and the difficulty of communicating with you, are the causes for issuing this order. The President hopes most earnestly that the peace of the two countries may not be disturbed.

These orders were explicit as to operations in case war broke out, but left the handling of unforeseen developments to the Commodore's discretion. The warning to avoid disturbing relations with Mexico, however, combined with the memory of the Jones affair, made the cautious Sloat fearful to act even after he knew that Mexico had committed an overt act.

After taking command of the squadron, Sloat remained at Callao until July, when he sailed in the *Savannah* bound for Mazatlán, Mexico. He went by way of Hawaii, where he stayed for some six weeks, and where the orders quoted above reached him on 2 October. He did not reach his destination until 18 November. Most of the squadron, which, besides the flagship, consisted of the sloops of war *Portsmouth* (Commander John B. Montgomery), *Levant* (Commander Hugh N. Page), and *Warren* (Commander Joseph B. Hull), the schooner *Shark* (Lieutenant Neil M. Howison), and the storeship *Erie* (Lieutenant James M. Watson), followed to Mazatlán. In the second half of 1845 two vessels sailed from the United States to join the Pacific Squadron: the sloop of war *Cyane* (Captain William Mervine) left Norfolk on 10 August, and the crack *Congress* (Commander Samuel F. Du Pont), the largest frigate in the U.S. Navy, sailed from Hampton Roads on 30 October with Commodore Robert F. Stockton on board. Commodore Stockton was to be second-in-command of the squadron, and he brought with him instructions on what was to be done if the difficulties with Mexico were settled amicably, and permission for Sloat, in case his health should require it, to turn command of the squadron over to Stockton.

Another communication carried by Stockton was a copy of a letter appointing Consul Larkin American confidential agent in California and instructing him to oppose any attempt by a foreign power to take over that territory and to assist the Californians if they tried to establish a government independent of Mexico. Further, the letter informed Larkin that Lieutenant Archibald H. Gillespie, U.S. Marine Corps, was about to leave for California to serve as his assistant.

President Polk's diary reveals that at 4 o'clock on the afternoon of 30 October, the day the *Congress* sailed, he "held a confidential conversation with Lieutenant Gillespie of the Marine Corps . . . on the subject of a secret mission on which he was about to go to California. His secret instructions & the letter to Mr. Larkin . . . will explain the object of his mission." The written instructions to Larkin and Gillespie directed them to assist the Californians in throwing off Mexican rule, and to endeavor to keep them from accepting the protection of any foreign power, other than the United States. The fact that Gillespie's actions far exceeded those instructions has given rise to speculation that the President gave him oral instructions as well as the written ones, but the entry in Polk's diary, quoted above, makes it very unlikely that such was the case. When he left Washington on 3 November 1845, Gillespie carried a copy of the instructions to Larkin, a letter of introduction from Secretary of State James Buchanan to Larkin and one to Brevet Captain John Charles Frémont of the U.S. Topographical Engineers, as well as a packet of private letters to Frémont from the latter's wife and from her father, Senator Benton.

A week after Sloat arrived at Mazatlán, he reported to the Navy Department that he was there with the frigate *Savannah*, and the sloops of war *Portsmouth*, *Warren*, and *Levant*. He informed the Department also that the frigate *Constitution* (Captain John Percival), which was on her way home from a special mission to the Orient and was not a part of Sloat's squadron, was in port. Mazatlán was the principal port on the west coast of Mexico and, as such, was the natural point of concentration for the squadron. Furthermore, it had the fastest and most reliable communications with Mexico City, where an American consul was still at his post, and, thus, would make it possible for Sloat to receive information concerning the actions and decisions of the Mexican government that might influence the operations of the squadron. Less than a month after the squadron had gathered at Mazatlán, Sloat learned that John Slidell had been sent to Mexico to try to reopen diplomatic negotiations, and that Commodore Conner had withdrawn his squadron from Veracruz. Consequently, he ordered the Pacific Squadron to deploy along the west coast of Mexico.

While Commodore Sloat was at Mazatlán awaiting the outcome of the diplomatic maneuverings, events that were to have profound effects on his future operations were taking place in California. The impetuous Captain Frémont, whose mission in the West was to find the shortest route for a railroad to the Pacific, having set out from Walker Lake and crossed the Sierra Nevada Mountains, arrived on 9 December at Sutter's Fort, at the junction of the Sacramento and American rivers (now the city of Sacramento), with some of his men in search of supplies for his expedition.

Towards the end of January 1846, when he realized that he could not get the needed supplies at Sutter's Fort, Frémont went to Monterey to request permission of the Mexican authorities to bring his whole expedition into California to refit. It is certain that some form of agreement was reached, but there is no way of knowing whether it allowed him to survey in California or required that he depart as soon as his men were ready. Participants in the discussions have left such divergent accounts of what happened that it is almost impossible to reconstruct the agreement. It does seem, however, that whatever it allowed Frémont to do, the Mexicans later reneged on it.

After refitting his expedition, Frémont moved south, crossed the Santa Cruz Mountains, and on 5 March, when he was within twenty-five miles of Monterey, he received a peremptory order to leave California. He haughtily refused to comply and he and his men entrenched themselves on Gavilan (modern Frémont) Peak, northeast of what is today the city of Salinas and about thirty miles from Monterey. There, they were besieged by General José María Castro and a force that outnumbered them six to one. After four days of bombastic talk on both sides, and desperate maneuvers by Larkin to prevent bloodshed, Frémont withdrew towards Oregon on 9 March. His high-handed dealing with the Mexican authorities in California did nothing to dispel their suspicions that he was there to aid in the conquest of the country for the United States. There is, however, no solid evidence to support the belief that, at that time, Frémont had any such motive.

Larkin saw Frémont's actions as a grave threat to his own plans for a peaceful conquest of California, and was so disturbed at the strong possibility that they would provoke bloodshed and reprisals, that on 9 March he wrote to ask Sloat to send a warship to Monterey to protect Americans and their property. His plea reached Mazatlán on the first day of April, and Sloat immediately ordered the *Portsmouth* to Monterey.

At the turn of the year, 1845–46, the two vessels that Sloat had left in South American waters when he moved up to Mazatlán, the schooner *Shark* and the storeship *Erie*, rejoined him, and on 21 January the sloop *Cyane*, which had sailed from the United States five months earlier, came in. Also at Mazatlán or nearby were the British razee *America* and three sloops of the British Pacific Squadron.

The Americans realized that their country might, at any moment, be plunged into war with Britain over Oregon, and they suspected that Britain had designs on California. Consequently, a tense situation was created aboard the American vessels by the presence of the British squadron, whose every move was carefully noted. At about this time, Commodore Sloat received a number of communications stressing the seriousness of the crisis over Oregon, and indicating that the administration expected its difficulties with Mexico to be resolved. These messages made such an impact on the Commodore that even after war with Mexico broke out, his actions were motivated more by a fear of what Britain might do than by the necessity of waging war against Mexico.

Such was the situation at Mazatlán on 9 February 1846, when a man, claiming to be a British subject and an agent of MacDougal Distilleries, Ltd.,

JOHN B. MONTGOMERY

of Edinburgh, Scotland, rode into town. He was, in fact, Lieutenant Archibald H. Gillespie, U.S. Marine Corps. He had taken ship to Veracruz and, while at sea, had become so worried about the safety of the official correspondence he was carrying that he committed its contents to memory, then burned it. After landing at Veracruz, he had crossed Mexico in the guise of a British merchant. When he reached Mazatlán he reported to Sloat on board the *Savannah*, but told the Commodore little, other than that he must be sent to California as swiftly as possible. Sloat ordered the *Cyane* to take him there but, in order not to reveal her destination, to sail via Honolulu. However, because some of her officers were sitting on a court-martial, the *Cyane* could not get away until 22 February. Less than a month after Gillespie left, Sloat wrote to the Navy Department on 17 March, asking to be relieved of command of the Pacific Squadron.

Lieutenant Gillespie disembarked from the *Cyane* at Monterey on 17 April after an extremely disagreeable and stormy voyage. Situated at the southern end of a large, protected harbor, Monterey was then a small but thriving town of one-story adobe buildings and, across a carpet of green grass dotted with herds of horses and cattle, was a beautiful view of mountains. But Gillespie had little time to enjoy the scenery. Immediately upon arrival, he conferred with Consul Larkin and conveyed to him the official instructions from Washington that any foreign attempts to occupy California were to be countered and any native independence movements were to be supported. Then, Larkin sent him north to deliver the packet of letters he was carrying to Frémont, who was believed to be near Sutter's Fort. By the time Gillespie got there, however, Frémont and his exploring party had moved on. Gillespie went in pursuit and caught up with them on the shores of Klamath Lake, just north of the Oregon border, on 9 May, the day after General Zachary Taylor had fought the opening battle of the war and defeated a Mexican army at Palo Alto on the Rio Grande. Beyond the fact that Gillespie delivered the letters, very little is known of what transpired when the two men met.

Six days after Gillespie arrived at Monterey, the *Portsmouth* came in from Mazatlán and her captain, John B. Montgomery, told Larkin that the Mexican authorities at Mazatlán were daily expecting war with the United States. Gillespie had already left in search of Frémont, so Larkin relayed that information to him by letter, and added: "I have (as my opinion) said . . . that our flag may fly here in thirty days." This letter reached Gillespie at Yerba Buena*, where he had stopped on his way north. Therefore, although Frémont later put much stress on countering supposed British designs on California, he was aware of the probability that, at the time he met Gillespie, war had broken out between Mexico and the United States.

After his meeting with Gillespie, Frémont started back to California. Whether he was about to do so, anyway, because late snow clogging the passes made it impossible to journey farther into Oregon, or whether he did so as a result of the meeting with Gillespie, is not known.

Although the trouble between Captain Frémont and General Castro had quieted down and there was no need for the presence of a man-of-war at Monterey, Commander Montgomery kept the *Portsmouth* there to await the arrival of Commodore Stockton in the *Congress*.

Meanwhile, on 22 April the *Constitution* left Mazatlán to continue her journey home and, with the *Portsmouth* and the *Cyane* detached to California, and the *Shark* on a cruise to Oregon, Commodore Sloat was left at Mazatlán with only his flagship *Savannah* and two sloops, the *Warren* and the *Levant*, and the storeship *Erie*. The British squadron there, on the other hand, had been enlarged by the arrival of Rear Admiral Sir George F. Seymour in his flagship, the eighty-gun ship-of-the-line *Collingwood*. In order to be in a position to get early news of developments, Sloat had to stay at Mazatlán, where he could make no move without the British having full knowledge of it.

---

* Yerba Buena and San Francisco were villages within what are now the limits of San Francisco. Although Yerba Buena was the more important, the two villages were combined and officially given the name San Francisco on 30 January 1847. In the interests of clarity, that name will hereinafter be used.

The two squadrons at Mazatlán were still watching one another when on 1 May the *Warren*, carrying the squadron surgeon, Dr. William Maxwell Wood, and the U.S. Consul, John Parrott, both on their way home, sailed for San Blas, in the Mexican state of Nayarit. There, the two passengers disembarked and proceeded to cross Mexico by road. When they got to Guadalajara on 10 May and heard that fighting had broken out on the Rio Grande, they sent a courier to carry the news to Sloat. The rider made the trip in five days—half the usual time—and reached Mazatlán on 17 May. The next day, the Commodore wrote to Larkin:

> . . . it appears certain that hostilities have commenced on the North bank of the Rio Grande. . . . It is my intention to visit your place immediately. . . . I am led to hope that you will . . . consult and advise me on the course of operations I may be disposed to make on the coast of California. . . .

Cautioning him not to let the news of war leak out, Sloat chose Captain Mervine in the *Cyane*, now back from carrying Gillespie to Monterey, to take the letter to Larkin. He also told Mervine that if he met a fast-sailing Mexican vessel that could be converted into a cruiser, he should capture her. The *Cyane* departed on 19 May, and on the 20th the *Levant* and the storeship *Erie* sailed for Hawaii, apparently to get provisions.

Although the Commodore had told Larkin on 18 May that it was his intention to visit Monterey "immediately," he was still at Mazatlán a week later, when the *Collingwood* left port. The Americans did not know where she was going, but surmised that her destination was California. On the last day of the month, Sloat received news of the battles fought by General Zachary Taylor at Palo Alto and Resaca de la Palma, and promptly sent a coded message to Secretary Bancroft:

> I have just received such intelligence as I think will justify my acting upon your order of the twenty-fourth of June and shall sail immediately to see what can be done.

"Upon more mature reflection," however, Sloat changed his mind and decided that he could not take possession of California or undertake any hostile action against Mexico until he knew definitely that war had been declared or that the Home Squadron in the Gulf of Mexico had taken offensive action. He advised Bancroft of his decision on 6 June. In taking this stand, he was adhering to the letter of his instructions of 24 June 1845. Those orders had told him not to take action until "you ascertain beyond a doubt that the Mexican government has declared war against us," and had cautioned him to "be assiduously careful to avoid any act which could be construed as an act of aggression." Most military commanders would probably have considered that those conditions had been fulfilled and that they could take action, but Sloat was old and sick. Furthermore, he was, undoubtedly, haunted not only by the experience of his predecessor, Commodore Thomas ap Catesby Jones, but by the treatment accorded to Commodore David Porter following the Fajardo incident, during which Sloat had commanded the *Grampus,* one of the vessels involved. The latter incident occurred in 1824, when Porter, then commander of the West India Squadron, took action against the Spanish authorities in Puerto Rico in retaliation for the seizure and imprisonment of one of his subordinates, was court-martialed, and sentenced to a six-month suspension from duty. In Sloat's defense, however, it must be said that, at the time in question, he had little more to go on than Jones had had—unconfirmed rumors.

The day after notifying Bancroft of his decision not to act in the absence of more official information, Sloat received a letter from Surgeon Wood, who was then in Mexico City, confirming what Wood and Parrott had told him earlier. Coming, as it did, from the Mexican capital, Sloat considered that this information was authentic: "These hostilities [at Palo Alto and Resaca de la Palma]," he later noted, "I considered would justify my commencing offensive operations on the west coast," although "upon my own responsibility," i.e., before he received official notification that hostilities had begun. Leaving the *Warren* to wait for the official announcement that the United States was at war with Mexico, Commodore Sloat sailed for Monterey in the *Savannah* on 8 June, twenty-two days after he had first heard that fighting had started.

When the war did break out, Secretary of the Navy Bancroft wrote new orders for the Pacific Squadron. On 13 May, the same day that President Polk signed the declaration of war, he sent Sloat the long-awaited official notification that war had been declared, and ordered him to carry out the instructions of 24 June 1845. He also directed the naval commander in the Pacific to allow neutral merchant ships twenty days to leave blockaded ports, but to make the blockade absolute, except against neutral armed vessels. Other orders issued that day were to Commodore James Biddle, who was in Chinese waters in the ship-of-the-line *Columbus* (Captain Thomas W. Wyman), to proceed with all possible dispatch to California or to the Mexican state of Sonora to strengthen the forces there and to take temporary command of the Pacific Squadron; and to the sloop of war *Saratoga* (Commander Irvine Shubrick), which had been sent to the Brazil Squadron in December 1845, to join the Pacific Squadron. After rounding Cape Horn on her way to join Sloat, the *Saratoga* was badly damaged in a storm and forced to return to the United States. After being repaired, she was ordered to the Home Squadron in preparation for the attack on Veracruz, and never did serve with Sloat.

Further instructions from Bancroft, dated 15 May, pointed out to Sloat that San Francisco must be seized, and continued: "You will take possession of Mazatlán and of Monterey, one or both, as your force will permit." The Secretary also suggested the seizure of Guaymas, north of Mazatlán, on the Gulf of California, but left the final decision on that and on the seizure of other ports to the discretion of Sloat. "When you cannot take and hold possession of a town," Bancroft added, "you may establish a blockade, if you have the means to do it effectually, and the public interest shall require it." But, he cautioned, a blockade must be widely publicized and strictly enforced. Bancroft concluded by advising Sloat that reinforcements would be sent "as the exigencies of the service may require." These orders which, with only slight modification, controlled the operations of the Pacific Squadron throughout the war, were entrusted to Passed Midshipman Archibald McRae, who went by steamer to Panama, rode across the isthmus, then took a sailing vessel to California.

Frémont reached the Marysville Buttes on the Sacramento River, near Sutter's Fort, on 30 May and sent Gillespie to San Francisco in search of supplies. Luckily for the erstwhile explorer, at this same time the *Portsmouth* had shifted her anchorage from Monterey to San Francisco, apparently at the request of Larkin, who did not know what Frémont planned to do. On being assured by Gillespie that Frémont was preparing to return to the United States, Commander Montgomery supplied Gillespie with most of what he needed from the *Portsmouth*'s stores.

Meanwhile, events that were to influence profoundly the course of Californian history were taking place in the American settlements in the Napa and Sacramento valleys. Most of the settlers there were illegal immigrants, that is to say, they had entered the territory without the permission of the Mexican authorities and had not become Mexican citizens. They became increasingly afraid that the local authorities would enforce the immigration laws. They were aware of an order issued by the central government of Mexico on 10 July 1845 directing Pío Pico, the governor of Alta California, to prevent any more illegal immigration, and Pico had warned them that they were subject to expulsion at the convenience of the government. Frémont's return to California acted as a catalyst for the fear and restlessness that rumors of impending eviction had aroused.

Unrest among the American settlers took concrete form on 10 June when Ezekial Merritt and five or six other men seized a herd of horses that was being taken to General José María Castro's camp at Santa Clara. Four days later, Merritt led another party of Americans into the village of Sonoma, the home of General Mariano Guadalupe Vallejo, titular commander of northern California, and seized Vallejo and the few arms they found there.

In spite of Frémont's later claim that Merritt was his "Field-Lieutenant among the settlers," and his boast that, "I sent Merritt into Sonoma," the degree of his involvement in these raids and his exact relationship to the rebels are moot, and not particularly important, points, because as Hubert Howe Bancroft wrote in his *History of California*: "The revolution broke out after Frémont's return from Oregon; and it would not have broken out at all had it not been for the presence and cooperation of that officer and his hardy followers."

The Californian authorities reacted swiftly to the uprising, and within ten days General Castro had raised a force of 160 men. He began moving his army northwards, but no sooner had the leading detachment of his troops crossed San Francisco Bay on its way to retake Sonoma than it was defeated in a skirmish with the settlers on 24 June, and Castro withdrew to Santa Clara. On the first day of July, Frémont and some of his men went south across San Francisco Bay and spiked the ten guns of the unoccupied Battery San Joaquín, overlooking the Golden Gate. Flushed with success at having turned back Castro's advance, the rebels, or Bear Flaggers as they were called because of their flag, acting at the behest of Frémont, declared California independent on 4 July 1846.

The Bear Flaggers were a source of much embarrassment to Consul Larkin at Monterey and to Commander Montgomery at San Francisco. The Californian authorities, naturally, could not believe that the uprising, led as it was by an American army officer, did not have the sanction of the American government. Larkin had been embarrassed by Frémont's actions before, but Montgomery, having been told by Gillespie in June that Frémont was preparing to return to the United States, insisted that Frémont did not have any connection with the revolt. Moreover, although he sympathized with the rebels, Montgomery preserved strict neutrality and tried to exert a moderating influence on them.

While the rebellious settlers, still unaware that war had broken out, were establishing their own republic, and American naval forces in the Pacific were preparing to seize the ports of California, a third force was being organized in Washington for the conquest of California.

On 30 May 1846 the Cabinet agreed to President Polk's proposal to send an overland expedition to California and to name General Stephen Watts Kearny as its commander. Three days after that, it agreed to send cannon, small arms, and munitions for Kearny's use to California by sea. This material, along with a large shipment of naval supplies, was sent in the storeship *Lexington* (Lieutenant Theodore Bailey). Kearny was instructed to occupy and pacify New Mexico, then advance on California and, when he had conquered that territory, to establish a temporary civil government. As will be seen, when the time came to carry out this last provision, Kearny suffered much unhappiness and difficulty.

Towards the end of June, Secretary of War William L. Marcy authorized Jonathan D. Stevenson of New York to raise a regiment of men who wanted to make California their home. These men, who became the First New York Volunteers, were to go by sea around Cape Horn and join Kearny's command in California.

During the late spring and summer of 1846, three vessels sailed for the Pacific to join Commodore Sloat's squadron: the small sloop of war *Dale* (Commander William W. McKean) left New York on 3 June; the razee *Independence* (Captain Elie A. F. La Vallette) left Boston on 22 August; and on 26 September the sloop *Preble* (Commander William F. Shields) sailed as convoy for Stevenson's First New York Volunteers. On board the *Independence* was Commodore W. Branford Shubrick, who carried orders to relieve Sloat as commander of the Pacific Squadron. Although one of the senior commodores in the Navy, Shubrick was junior to Biddle. Thus, when Biddle arrived in California from the Far East, in accordance with Bancroft's order of 13 May, he superseded Shubrick. This situation piqued Shubrick, as well it might have done, and led to his requesting an early relief.

These arrangements completed the plans for the conquest of California. Indeed, though he had no orders to do so, Frémont had already begun the conquest and, if the damage he had wrought to the government's plans for action in California was not obvious at this time, it would soon become so.

XIII

TOWARDS EMPIRE

During the afternoon of 19 June 1846, while General José María Castro was gathering his forces to move against the settlers in northern California and try to retake Sonoma, Captain Mervine in the *Cyane* arrived at Monterey with Commodore Sloat's letter telling Consul Larkin that fighting had broken out on the Rio Grande. On the strength of Sloat's statement that he intended to visit Monterey immediately, and aware that San Francisco would be one of the prime objectives of the American squadron, Larkin promptly sent word to Commander Montgomery to remain at San Francisco with the *Portsmouth.*

Day by day after the receipt of his letter, Sloat was expected to arrive at Monterey, but eleven days passed and there was no sign of him. Then, in the late evening of 30 June, as she lay off Monterey, the *Cyane* sighted the light of a vessel standing in to the north of Point Pinos, at the entrance of Monterey Bay. About an hour and a half later, the stranger dropped anchor near the *Cyane*, and daylight revealed her to be the *Levant.* But, having left Mazatlán only one day behind the *Cyane*, she brought no news of the missing Commodore.

Two days later, the *Cyane* made out another vessel standing in and soon identified her as the *Savannah.* The long-awaited Commodore had arrived. He immediately went about the business of conferring with Larkin and making the usual courtesy calls on the local authorities. Now, so it was thought, there would be action. But, the next morning, Sloat granted shore leave to some of the *Savannah*'s crew, then went off riding with Larkin. He did nothing to secure the port. Why he delayed the seizure of Monterey is something of a mystery. Apparently, still without official notice of the outbreak of war, he did not yet feel too sure of himself, and Larkin, probably

149

because he was a pacifist and hoped for a peaceful conquest, did nothing to overcome the naval commander's hesitation.

A launch that came in to Monterey on the afternoon of 5 July brought a letter that changed Sloat's thinking. The launch came from the *Portsmouth* at San Francisco, and the letter was from Commander Montgomery to Captain Mervine and reported Frémont's open support of the rebels. Here, reasoned Sloat, was an army officer recently in receipt of news, if not of orders, from Washington, conducting active operations against the Mexicans. Certainly, Frémont must know something the Commodore did not. War must have begun. And, if Frémont was acting prematurely, well, then he, Sloat, would be able to throw a large part of the responsibility for his actions on Frémont. Furthermore, Sloat had seen Admiral Sir George Seymour's flagship *Collingwood* sail out of Mazatlán towards the end of May, and there must have persisted the gnawing fear that the British Pacific Squadron might appear at any moment and raise the British flag in California.

Reassured by that line of thought, Sloat wrote Montgomery on 6 July that he had decided to act, as "I would prefer being sacrificed for doing too much than too little." It would probably have been nearer the truth if he had said he believed that the certainty of war was so great that he could no longer procrastinate. He advised Montgomery that Monterey was to be seized the next day, ordered him to take possession of San Francisco and the area around that Bay, and added: "'I am very anxious to know if Captain Frémont will cooperate with us." That afternoon, the *Portsmouth*'s launch left to return to San Francisco with Sloat's letter to Montgomery, and the next day the instructions contained in the letter were confirmed in a coded dispatch, which was carried overland to San Francisco by messenger.

Sloat had finally committed himself to a course of action and, after the departure of the *Portsmouth*'s launch, the crews of the vessels at Monterey began to exercise their boats and check their arms in preparation for the landing the next day.

At 7:30 on the morning of 7 July, Captain Mervine of the *Cyane* and a small party of men left the *Savannah* and went ashore with a demand for the surrender of Monterey. While they were gone, Sloat had the crews of the vessels mustered and a general order was read to them:

"We are about to land on the Territory of Mexico, with whom the United States are at war. To strike her Flag, and to hoist our own in the place of it, is our duty.

"It is not only our duty to take California but to preserve it afterwards as a part of the United States, at all hazards; to accomplish this, it is of the first importance to cultivate the good opinion of the inhabitants, whom we must reconcile.

I scarcely consider it necessary for me to caution American Seamen and Marines against the detestable crime of plundering and maltreating unoffending inhabitants.

That no one may misunderstand his duty the following regulations must be strictly adhered to, as no violation can hope to escape the severest punishment.

1st. On landing, no man is to leave the shore until the Commanding Officer gives the order to march.

2d. No gun is to be fired or other act of hostility committed without express orders from the Officer Commanding the party.

3rd. The officers and boat keepers will keep their respective boats as close to the shore as they will safely float taking care they do not lay aground, and *remain* in them, prepared to defend themselves against attack and attentively watch for signals from the ships as well as from the party on shore.

4th. No man is to quit the ranks or to enter any house for any pretext whatever without express orders from an officer. Let every man avoid insult or offense to any unoffending inhabitant, and especially avoid that eternal disgrace which would be attached to our names and our country's name by indignity offered to a single female even let her standing be however low it may.

5th. Plunder of every kind is strictly forbidden. Not only does the plundering of the smallest article from a prize forfeit all claim to prize money, but the offender must expect to be severely punished.

6th. Finally let me entreat you one and all, not to tarnish our hope of bright success by any act that we shall be ashamed to acknowledge before God and our Country.

Two hours after they had left, Mervine and his party returned to the *Savannah* with the reply to their demand. It was signed by Captain Mariano Silva, the town's military commandant, and read: "The undersigned . . . is not authorized to surrender the place, having no orders to that effect; the matter may be arranged by the Señor commodore with the commandant general . . . the undersigned withdrawing and leaving the town peaceful and without a soldier . . . according to information from the treasurer, there are no public properties or munitions." Indeed, it turned out later that Silva did not have even a Mexican flag to surrender.

Less than half an hour after Silva's reply was received, the order to land was given from the flagship. Two boats were lowered from the *Levant*, and a launch and the gig from the *Cyane*, and, as soon as they were loaded, they pulled quickly for the *Savannah*, three of whose boats were loaded and waiting. Captain Mervine was in command of the landing party of 85 Marines and more than 140 sailors. The six boats formed in two lines behind the *Cyane*'s gig and, covered by the broadside of the squadron, pulled for the customhouse wharf. As the column neared the wharf, the boats that carried guns peeled off, one to the right and one to the left, to give close cover, while the others ran in and landed their passengers on the wharf.

The landing was unopposed and, at 10:20, when the whole party had formed in front of the customhouse, Purser Rodman M. Price of the *Cyane* read a proclamation from Sloat. The proclamation was straightforward and calm: it promised nothing that could not be delivered:

> . . . although I come in arms with a powerful force, I do come as [the Californians'] best friend, as henceforward California will be a portion of the United States, and its peaceful inhabitants will enjoy the privilege of choosing their own magistrates and other officers, for the administration of justice among themselves, and the same protection will be extended to them as to any other State in the Union.

After extolling the advantages that would come to the Californians under the Stars and Stripes, it went on to guarantee to those who wished to return to Mexico the freedom to do so: it guaranteed Mexican real-estate titles and church lands, and promised fair payment for goods furnished to the occupying forces. Sloat did not have the authority to annex California, but both he and Larkin, who was co-author of the message, knew that the American government desired ultimately to annex the territory.

When Price had finished reading the proclamation, Midshipmen William P. Toler and Edward Higgins ran the Stars and Stripes up the flagpole of the customhouse to the accompaniment of three cheers and a salute from the squadron. Four years previously, Midshipman Toler had performed the same ceremony at the same place for Commodore Jones.

Purser Daingerfield Fauntleroy of the *Savannah* was ordered to organize a company of thirty-five horsemen to patrol the outskirts and hinterland of the town and the road to San Francisco. Then, so as to provide for functioning civil government ashore, Sloat appointed Purser Price and Surgeon Edward Gilchrist justices of the peace, in the place of the *alcaldes* who refused to serve. He made Captain Mervine commander of the garrison and instructed him to repair and occupy the earthworks forming the Presidio. Quarters were set up in the customhouse for the Marines who were to perform garrison duty. To prevent trouble between the sailors and the townspeople, Mervine ordered all stores and shops to close for two days, and strictly forbade the sale of liquor, a move that sent the price of bootleg *aguardiente* soaring skyward.

As soon as Monterey had been occupied, Sloat sent a message to General Castro at San Juan Bautista, northeast of Salinas, demanding his surrender and inviting him to come to Monterey to discuss the terms of capitulation. Another messenger left for Sonoma that day, 7 July, carrying a dispatch from Larkin advising William B. Ide, leader of the Bear Flag "republic," of what had taken place at Monterey and suggesting that no more offensive operations be undertaken. The same dispatch relayed to Frémont Sloat's hope that the explorer would cooperate with the Navy.

Copy

<u>General Order</u>

Flag Ship Savannah
7th July 1846

We are about to land on the territory of Mexico with whome the United States are at war. To strike her Flag and to hoist our own in the place of it is our duty.

It is not only our duty to take California but to preserve it afterwards as a part of the United States, at all hazards: to accomplish this it is of the first importance to cultivate the good opinion of the inhabitants, whome we must reconcile

I scarcely consider it necessary for me to caution American Seamen & Marines against the detestable crime of plundering and maltreating unoffending inhabitants.

That no one may misunderstand his duty the following regulations must be strictly adhered to, as no violation can hope to escape the severest punishment.

1st   On landing no man is to leave the shore until the Commanding Officer gives the order to march.

2   No gun is to be fired or other act of hostility committed without express orders from the Officer Commanding the party.

3   The Officers and boat keepers will keep their respective boats as close to the shore as they will safely float taking care they do not lay aground, and remain in them prepared to defend themselves against attack and attentively watch for signals from the Ships as well as from the party on Shore

4th   No man is to quit the ranks or to enter any house for any pretext whatever without express orders
from

from an officer. Let every man avoid insult or offence to any unoffending inhabitant, and especially avoid that eternal disgrace which would be attached to our names and our Country's name by indignity offered to a single female even let her standing be however low it may.

5th Plunder of every kind is strictly forbidden. Not only does the plundering of the smallest article from a prize forfeit all claim to prize money, but the offender must expect to be severely punished.

6nd Finally let me entreat you one and all, not to tarnish our hope of bright success by any act that we shall be ashamed to acknowledge before God and our Country.

(signed) John D. Sloat
Commander-in-chief of the
U. States Naval Forces in the
Pacific Ocean

Order issued by Commodore Sloat prior to the landing at Monterey
National Archives

The Commodore celebrated the taking of Monterey by parading the Marine garrison, led by a brass band, through the streets of the town.

On 9 July, Castro replied to Sloat's message with a refusal to surrender or even to come and talk.

Henry Pitts, the messenger who carried Sloat's coded message of 7 July to Commander Montgomery, reached San Francisco on the evening of 8 July. Immediately upon receipt of the message, Montgomery prepared to carry out its instructions to seize San Francisco. He notified the U.S. Consul, William A. Leidesdorff, that the landing would be made the next morning and asked

The Stars and Stripes being raised over the
customhouse at Monterey. At middle left, a
Mexican redoubt can be seen, and, at right, the
Cyane, the *Savannah*, and the *Levant*. This
sketch, done by W. A. Coulter, is believed to be
the first ever made of this historic event.

him to translate into Spanish a proclamation from Commodore Sloat. At
dawn the next morning, a courier, Lieutenant Joseph W. Revere, left the
Portsmouth for Sonoma carrying some American flags for that town and for
Sutter's Fort, and a letter announcing the seizure of Monterey.

When Revere left, Montgomery set about trying to find some responsible
official of San Francisco who could surrender the town. As the morning
watch drew to a close and none had been found, he and seventy of his men
went ashore at Clark's Point. The sailors in their white frocks and pants,
black hats and shoes, and the Marines in their dress uniforms, led by one
fifer and one drummer, marched to the customhouse in what is now Portsmouth Square, San Francisco.

There, Montgomery read an address to some thirty or forty interested
inhabitants of the little town. He told them that the American flag was flying
over Monterey, and expressed the hope that it would "this day be substituted
for the revolutionary flag recently hoisted at Sonoma." He promised the

San Francisco at the time of the Mexican
War, with the sloop *Portsmouth* in the
center foreground.
Society of California Pioneers

people that they need have no fear that their new rulers would be oppressive
or would unnecessarily disrupt the life of the town, and he concluded by
asking all those interested in forming a local militia company to meet at the
house of Consul Leidesdorff. When he had finished his own address, Montgomery had his executive officer, Lieutenant John S. Missroon, read Sloat's
proclamation in both English and Spanish. Then the American flag was run
up the pole of the customhouse, as a twenty-one-gun salute was fired from
the *Portsmouth* and the onlookers cheered. When the ceremonies were over,
a garrison of fourteen Marines was left ashore under Lieutenant Henry B.
Watson, U.S. Marine Corps, and the rest of the landing party returned to the
Portsmouth.

Montgomery sent Missroon, Purser James M. Watmough of the *Portsmouth*, Consul Leidesdorff, and several volunteers to inspect the Presidio and

Battery San Joaquín. They found both works in great need of repair, and their armament too old to be of use. Anyway, Frémont had spiked the Battery's ten guns a week or so previously. Francisco Sanchez, the former military commandant of San Francisco, pointed out several places in the area where other guns had been hidden.

On the afternoon of 9 July Montgomery sent Purser Watmough to see Frémont, notify him of the occupation of San Francisco, and tell him that Sloat was anxious to confer with him at Monterey. Meanwhile, Lieutenant Revere reached Sonoma with the news of the seizure of Monterey. He read Sloat's proclamation to the garrison and townspeople, and sent a copy of it and an American flag to Sutter's Fort. By noon, the American flag had been hoisted at Sonoma, and the short life of the Bear Flag "republic" had ended.

Two days later, the appearance of the British sloop *Juno* (Captain F. J. Blake) in San Francisco Bay threatened to upset the peaceful take-over of San Francisco. Hastening to defend his newly won prize, Montgomery withdrew the garrison of Marines, leaving the militia to defend the town proper. However, the scare soon subsided when it became known that Captain Blake had no intention of interfering with the state of affairs. Admiral Seymour, who had not been instructed to take any action in California, had sent Blake there as an observer. On 17 July, six days after she had come in, the *Juno* sailed away again, bound for Mazatlán.

A shortage of land forces did not prevent the Americans from making the two ports in their hands stronger defensively. At Monterey, Sloat ordered the building of a blockhouse—Fort Mervine—mounting three cannon, and by 12 July three hundred sailors and two 18-pounder carronades mounted as field pieces were ashore. At San Francisco, Montgomery had a battery built on Telegraph Hill, which commanded the anchorage, and mounted in it four guns ferried down from Sonoma. The Presidio and the Battery San Joaquín were too far away to be garrisoned by the small force at hand, so Montgomery made no attempt to rehabilitate them, but he did have three of their guns reconditioned and installed in the battery on Telegraph Hill.

Meanwhile, General Castro and Governor Pico, with about one hundred men each, met at Rancho Santa Margarita, near San Luis Obispo, and agreed that in the face of the foreign invasion, they should reconcile their differences. They decided to withdraw to the area of Los Angeles. At Santa Barbara on 16 July, Governor Pico issued an order calling for the conscription of all men between the ages of fifteen and sixty, but the order was merely a manifestation of the face-saving bravado that characterized so much of Mexican administration, and it produced few men.

By the time a long letter that Secretary of the Navy Bancroft wrote to Sloat on 12 July, dealing chiefly with the seizure of other Californian ports, reached California, the ports in question were already in American hands. Other subjects covered in the letter were the establishment of civil government in the newly won territory; the dispatch of Stevenson's volunteers and of the artillery in the *Lexington*; and, most important, orders for the seizure and occupation of the Mexican harbors along the Gulf of California, once Alta California had been secured.

Although civil government had been established by the time that letter arrived, no one knew which service should be responsible for administering it, and while Bancroft said: "The government relies on the land and naval forces to cooperate with each other in the most friendly and effective manner," he failed to state which branch had primary responsibility. This oversight was, before long, to cause grave concern in both California and Washington.

On the morning of 15 July a large vessel stood in to Monterey Bay and, at noon, she was identified as the *Congress*, which had left Hampton Roads on 30 October 1845 with Commodore Stockton on board. As soon as she had dropped anchor, Stockton called on his superior officer and, at that first meeting between the two commodores, Sloat told Stockton that he was not well and intended to transfer his command to Stockton at an early date. Stockton, it will be remembered, had been sent as second-in-command of the squadron, but he carried with him orders permitting Sloat to transfer the command if his health so dictated.

The day after the *Congress* arrived, another large ship put in to Monterey. She was HMS *Collingwood*, flying the flag of Admiral Seymour, commander of the British Pacific Squadron, whose mission was to gauge the strength of Californian sentiment for a British protectorate over the area. Although there was no longer any point to that mission, the *Collingwood* stayed at Monterey for a week, during which time she fitted new spars that had been cut on the nearby hills.

News of the fall of Monterey caught up with Frémont on 10 July, and two days later he and 160 men, including Gillespie, left their camp on the Sacramento River and set out for Monterey. Gillespie and a small advance party went on ahead, and Frémont reached San Juan Bautista on 16 July, about half an hour before Purser Fauntleroy, who was on one of his patrols of the hinterland of Monterey, rode into town with a detachment of his dragoons. Frémont's men and the dragoons spent two days at San Juan gathering up munitions—nine cannon, two hundred old muskets, twenty kegs of powder, and sixty thousand pounds of cannon shot—before departing for Monterey.

As the little army entered Monterey on 19 July, it presented quite a spectacle. Walter Colton, a chaplain in the U.S. Navy, who witnessed the

ROBERT F. STOCKTON
U. S. Naval Academy Museum

scene, described it: ". . . two hundred strong, all well mounted, and have some 300 extra horses in their train. They defiled, two abreast, through the principal street of the town. The ground seemed to tremble under their heavy tramp. The citizens glanced at them through their grated windows. Their rifles, revolving pistols, and long knives glittered over dusky buckskin which enveloped their sinewy limbs, while their untrimmed locks, flowing out from under their foraging caps, and their black beards, with white teeth glittering through, gave them a wild savage aspect."

It was not long before the hesitant naval officer and the impetuous army officer met. Each hoped to have his position strengthened by the other. Sloat, whose old fear that he had acted too hastily in seizing Monterey and San Francisco was beginning to gnaw at him again, was anxious to hear under what instructions Frémont had joined the rebels. Frémont wanted approval of

JOHN C. FRÉMONT

what he had done thus far and agreement that the campaign on land would continue. Neither man got what he wanted. Sloat was horrified to hear that Frémont had acted without orders and even without knowing that war had broken out: Frémont, who had been led by Larkin's letters to believe that the land campaign would continue, was shocked to hear from the Commodore that it would not and, moreover, that Sloat would not support him.

Sloat's reaction to Frémont's revelation that he had operated without written orders was not surprising. "He was so discouraged and offended," reported Frémont, "that he terminated the interview abruptly, quitting the cabin, and leaving me!" Thirty years of peacetime service had instilled in him—as it had in others—the idea that to act on one's own initiative was to invite censure. As justification for his seizure of Monterey and San Francisco, he had apparently come to rely in his own mind on the instructions he imagined Frémont had. It is no wonder, then, that when he found there were no such instructions and that he had, in fact, been operating on his own initiative, he was nonplussed and more determined than ever to relinquish his command and go home as soon as possible. He was tired, sick, and old, and such a course would allow him to escape the burden of having to make any more decisions about operations along the coasts of California and Mexico. It would also free him from a headstrong second-in-command, whose

The Frigate *Congress*

strategic thinking was diametrically opposed to his own. He may also have deemed it wise not to risk antagonizing Stockton, whose political importance was considerable.

After his rejection by Sloat, Frémont spent several days trying to make up his mind what his next move should be. On 22 July he visited Commodore Stockton on board the *Congress* and came away with his mind made up. Stockton was not opposed to a land campaign and had told him that, when he took over command of the squadron, he would gladly accept the explorer's offer of his services.

The very day after the meeting between Stockton and Frémont, Sloat transferred to Stockton the command of operations ashore. It is difficult to understand why he made this move six days before he transferred the whole command, and neither he nor Stockton ever offered any explanation for the preliminary step. There is some evidence, but it is by no means conclusive, that it was done because Stockton considered it necessary to take action against General Castro before Sloat left California.

As soon as he took command of operations ashore, Stockton issued orders transforming Frémont's force into "the California battalion of United States troops." Frémont was given the rank of major and put in command of the battalion, and Gillespie was made a captain and became second-in-command. However, the California Battalion did not meet the legal requirements either for a volunteer or a militia organization and, ultimately, a special act of Congress had to be passed so that the expenses it incurred before General Kearny arrived in California and regularized the situation could be paid. Kearny discharged the men of the battalion and made them re-enlist in conformity with the law governing volunteer organizations. Even though it was a land force, the California Battalion should be regarded as an organization of naval supernumeraries, since it was organized by Stockton and operated as part of his command. The California Battalion operated as a field force and provided garrisons at Sonoma, San Juan Bautista, Santa Clara, and Sutter's Fort to supplement those that had already been established at San Francisco and Monterey.

Stockton's plan of operations against General Castro was to cut off his retreat southwards from Los Angeles by having a force advance inland from San Diego, then to land another force at San Pedro for the 25-mile march on Los Angeles. If this plan worked, Castro would be trapped between two strong forces, and there would be reasonable hope that the only active resistance to the American occupation could be crushed. As soon as he took over command of operations ashore, Stockton began to implement the first part of his plan by sending Frémont's battalion to San Diego on board the *Cyane*, which Sloat had put under Stockton's command. Frémont's orders were to secure at San Diego what horses and cattle he would need, then move inland.

On Wednesday morning, 29 July, Commodore Sloat transferred the complete command of the Pacific Squadron and all its operations to Stockton and, within the hour, boarded the *Levant* and sailed for home.

Two days after his departure, he wrote Bancroft that he had "determined to return to the United States via Panama . . . believing that no further opposition would be made to our taking possession of the whole of the Californias . . . and that I could render much more important service by returning to the United States with the least possible delay, to explain to the government the situation and wants of that country, than I could remaining in command in my infirm state of health."

Secretary Bancroft had not received the above-quoted letter nor did he know that Monterey and San Francisco were in American hands when, on 13 August, in exasperation, he wrote to Sloat directing that his orders of 24 June 1845 be executed "at once," and relieving Sloat of his command.

By his timidity, Sloat had jeopardized the plans of the United States in the

Pacific. If he had had strong opposition to contend with, or if Britain had been interested in the acquisition of California, his vacillation at Mazatlán and at Monterey would probably have had disastrous consequences. That it did not, does not excuse him. Nor can he be excused for his reluctance to act without express orders from Washington, inasmuch as, in those days, a commander on a distant station was expected to use his own initiative when he could not easily communicate with his government.

Nevertheless, his accomplishments in California cannot be overlooked. Under his command, Monterey and San Francisco had been occupied and the framework for the conquest of the rest of the territory had been laid. And, in his proclamation at Monterey, he had, with uncharacteristic temerity, claimed California for the United States.

XIV

REVERSALS AT LOS ANGELES

Soon after dawn on 30 July 1846, as she lay at anchor in the harbor of Monterey, California, the frigate *Congress* hoisted the blue pennant of a squadron commander, thereby announcing that Commodore Robert Field Stockton had taken command of the U.S. Pacific Squadron.

The new commander, fifty-one years old, small, and rather underjawed, had the reputation of being a thorough seaman and an energetic officer. Five years earlier, he had been instrumental in getting the administration of President John Tyler to fit the steam sloop *Princeton* with John Ericsson's revolutionary screw propeller. In 1845, although he was one of the junior commodores in the Navy, he had been selected to carry the annexation resolution to Texas. His personal characteristics, however, were less admirable than his professional ones: he was vain, overbearing, tactless, and glory-seeking. It would have been difficult to find a man less suited to deal with the proud and sensitive Californians.

The proclamation that Stockton issued when he took command was the antithesis of the one Sloat had issued. It covered much the same ground as Sloat's, but castigated General Castro for expelling Frémont and accused him of perpetrating serious crimes against the people of California, particularly the American settlers. It vowed to drive the General from the country, and demanded that the Mexican officials recognize his—Stockton's—authority. It concluded with the promise that, as soon as civil government was functioning, he would withdraw his forces. Though Larkin had done what he could to soften the wording of the proclamation, the attack on Castro and the demand that the Mexican officials recognize Stockton's authority, were blunders of the first order that scarcely endeared the Commodore to the Californians.

Stockton was not one to make idle threats. He had vowed to drive Castro

Sketch of the Sloop *Cyane*
Franklin D. Roosevelt Library, Hyde Park, New York

out of California, and so he would. The *Cyane*, carrying Frémont and his men with orders to put into effect one phase of his two-pronged drive on Castro and Los Angeles, had left Monterey on 25 July and anchored off San Diego four days later. Shortly after she had dropped anchor, the *Cyane* seized a Mexican hermaphrodite brig, the *Juanita*, in the harbor and found she was loaded with forty thousand percussion caps.

When the excitement of seizing the *Juanita* was over, Lieutenant Stephen C. Rowan and a small landing party left the *Cyane* and went ashore to test the opposition and to raise the American flag. They met no opposition and, about twenty minutes after they had landed, Frémont led his men ashore, made camp, and set about trying to collect horses and cattle. Although Frémont was warned that his camp might be attacked on the night of 31 July and, as a precaution, one hundred more men were landed from the *Cyane*, no such attack came, nor was any other attempt made to contest the seizure of San Diego.

By the time Frémont left the area on 8 August to march northward to Los Angeles, instead of eastward to block Castro, he had not managed to get any cattle and had only eighty-three of the two hundred horses he needed. The *Cyane* remained at San Diego for two days after his departure, then sailed for San Pedro and, on her way, captured the Mexican brig *Primavera*.

Leaving the *Savannah*, now under the command of Captain Mervine, at Monterey and the *Portsmouth* at San Francisco to protect northern California, Stockton, accompanied by Consul Larkin, sailed from Monterey on board the *Congress* on 1 August. He was bound for San Pedro, where he would implement the second phase of his plan. During the afternoon of 4 August, the *Congress* put in to Santa Barbara and a landing party went ashore. The little town offered no resistance—nor did it have a flagstaff, so a studding-sail boom was landed and before long the American flag fluttered from its peak. When the *Congress* sailed from Santa Barbara to continue her journey, Midshipman William Mitchell and sixteen men were left behind as a garrison. Shortly after the big frigate arrived at San Pedro on the morning of 6 August, First Lieutenant Jacob Zeilin, U.S. Marine Corps, led his Marines ashore and when the American flag had been hoisted over the town, the rest of the landing party joined them.

Stockton now found himself in a situation never before faced by an American naval officer: he had to conduct an extensive land campaign with a force composed almost exclusively of sailors. Only 90 of his 360 men carried muskets: the others carried carbines, pistols, swords, and boarding pikes—a sorry collection of weapons with which to fight the Californians' favorite weapon, the cavalry lance. This motley "army" had a small artillery train of three 6-pounders taken from a Hawaiian bark, the *Don Quixote*, found at San Pedro, and a 32-pounder taken from the *Congress*.

Being under the impression that his force was greatly outnumbered by the Californians, Stockton was anxious to strike before the latter could organize a strong defense. Yet, he could not advance without giving his sailors some drill in land fighting. He knew better than to try to teach them more than the most rudimentary military commands—"halt," "march," "form in line," "form in square," and "charge"—and he made a point of drilling them always to keep the same men on either side of them.

While he was preparing for a military conquest, Larkin, still not convinced that war had broken out, was working for a peaceful one and hoping that he could talk the leaders of California into making a settlement. Before leaving Monterey, Larkin had suggested to Governor Pico that, in order to prevent the country from falling into chaos, to protect the lives and property of the local officials, and to ensure prosperity for the area, he should declare California independent under American protection.

Larkin's suggestion did not go unheeded, for on 7 August Captain José María Flores and Pablo de la Guerra arrived in San Pedro with a message from General Castro, and Stockton received them aboard his flagship. The General wanted to know what the policy of the Commodore was, and proposed that, since there was still no news of war, a truce should be called while the two sides held a conference. He may have been merely playing for time, but he had little, if anything, to gain by doing so because his army was melting away and he needed more than time to build it up again. In any case, Stockton's answer was that he would not negotiate unless California declared her independence under American protection.

On 9 August when the messengers arrived back at Campo en la Mesa (on what is now Boyle Heights in downtown Los Angeles) with word of Stockton's senseless condition, whose acceptance would have left Castro nothing to negotiate, the Californians held a council of war. Overestimating the American force, and realizing that he had little support around him and little money, and that his army had dwindled to one hundred men, Castro decided to flee California. Under the circumstances, there was little else he could have done but, to cover his flight, on 10 August he wrote Stockton a letter announcing that, in view of Stockton's "insidious" response to his request for a conference, he would fight.

On 11 August, Stockton considered his "army" was ready to move and, that afternoon, set out for Los Angeles. The men marched in a square formed around the cattle, the baggage, and the four guns, which had been mounted on cartwheels and had to be pulled by the men because horses were in such short supply. They spent the night of the eleventh encamped at Rancho Los Carritos, in the area that is now North Long Beach, and the next day Consul Larkin, Passed Midshipman Charles H. Baldwin, and one servant went on ahead of the main body, and reached Los Angeles that same day.

When word that the Americans were advancing on Los Angeles reached Castro at La Mesa, he broke camp. A few of his soldiers, among them ex-governor Juan B. Alvarado, fled north, but most of them retired to Rancho San Pasqual (in present-day South Pasadena). Castro and Governor Pico fled south to the state of Sonora, and the Mexican government in California ceased to exist.

Larkin, Baldwin, and their servant were on hand to greet Stockton and his sailors when, with the brass band from the *Congress* at their head, they marched into the sleepy little town that stretched along the bank of the Rio Los Angeles on 13 August. About an hour after Stockton arrived, Frémont and his men marched into town. Since they had come up the coastal road, they had missed the escaping Castro and Pico.

The remnants of Castro's army, now under the command of Captain Flores and Captain Andrés Pico, a brother of Governor Pío Pico and one of the ablest of the Californian leaders, surrendered on 14 August and were released on parole. Ten pieces of artillery abandoned at La Mesa by Castro fell into American hands, and six of them were found to be in good condition. Later that day, Stockton sent Lieutenant William A. T. Maddox, U.S. Marine Corps, and some of Frémont's men in pursuit of ex-governor Alvarado and the soldiers who had escaped with him. Maddox caught up with his quarry near San Luis Obispo, and after a skirmish, seized Alvarado and several other prominent Californians.

Meanwhile, at Monterey, there was a flurry of excitement on 12 August when the *Warren*, which had been waiting at Mazatlán since June for word on the state of affairs between the United States and Mexico, came in with official notice that war had broken out. Captain Mervine, the senior naval officer in the port, immediately sent the sloop south with her news, and she put in to San Pedro on 17 August.

Two days after writing his exasperated letter of 13 August to Commodore Sloat, Secretary Bancroft wrote a long dispatch repeating his earlier instructions about the operations that were to be undertaken. He stressed the importance of occupying San Francisco, Monterey, and San Diego, so that a peace based on the fact of possession would give Alta California to the United States. He also ordered the seizure of Guaymas on the Gulf of California, which he had suggested in May, and empowered the commander of the Pacific Squadron to make agreements temporarily neutralizing any Mexican province that was willing to revolt against Mexico and to grant American vessels free access to its ports.

After the occupation of Los Angeles, Stockton took steps to organize the conquered territory. He imposed an *ad valorem* import tax of fifteen per cent and a port tax of fifty cents per ton. On 17 August he promised that civilian territorial government would soon be established and elections would be held. Within a week thereafter, he issued a proclamation establishing a civil government that provided for an appointive governor who would hold office for four years, unless removed earlier by the President of the United States, and would be the chief executive of the territory: legislative power would reside in the governor and a council of seven. The first legislative council would be appointed by the governor, but thereafter would be elected by the people. Existing local offices and Mexican laws would continue until changed by the legislative council. Thus, except as it was modified on the local level by Mexican practice, the form of government of California would be the same as that in any other territory of the United States. On 22 August Stockton set 15 September as election day.

Clearly, in establishing a civil government, Stockton exceeded his authority. The action he took is unique in American history. Had he followed tradition, he would have established military rule, as Sloat had done at Monterey. Neither American nor international law sanctions the formation of a civil government by the fiat of a military officer. Indeed, the Constitution of the United States specifically entrusts that power to Congress.

In February 1848, when Stockton made an over-all report on operations in California, he set forth the thinking that had led him to act as he did: a functioning civil government would provide undeniable evidence of conquest, and would make opposition to occupation a civil, rather than a military, crime; civil government could protect property and civil rights better than could military government; and he had to be free to conduct an expedition he then intended to lead to Acapulco. Furthermore, he argued, he had restored tranquillity to California.

When it seemed that Alta California was safe in American hands, Commodore Stockton prepared to move against the Mexican ports in the Gulf of California and farther south. On 19 August he proclaimed a blockade of the entire west coast of Mexico, but since he did not have enough ships to enforce such an extensive operation, it was only a paper blockade, which ran counter to both the laws of war and the policy of the United States. Quite unconcerned about the troubles his illegal proclamation would create, Stockton ordered the *Cyane* (Commander Samuel F. Du Pont) to blockade San Blas and the *Warren* to blockade Mazatlán, and the two sloops, representing merely the advance guard of a much larger expedition, left to take up their new assignments on 23 and 28 August, respectively.

Reasoning that Acapulco would be the main base for the privateers that the Mexicans would undoubtedly send to attack American commerce in the Pacific, Stockton decided to seize it. To do so would not only deprive the Mexicans of a base for their privateers, but would give him a point from which to attack Mexico City from the rear. Since the whole naval force in California would be needed for this undertaking, all sailors on garrison duty would have to be withdrawn and returned to their ships. Consequently, in order to replace them in the garrisons at San Francisco, Monterey, Los Angeles, Santa Barbara, and San Diego, and to provide a mobile field force to be left in California, Frémont was authorized to enlarge the California Battalion from 160 to 300 men. Stockton divided the territory of California into three military districts and named Frémont over-all military commandant, but told him that when he—Stockton—left for Acapulco, Frémont would

SAMUEL F. DU PONT
U. S. Naval Academy Museum

become governor of California and Gillespie, then at Los Angeles in command of the southern district, would become its secretary.

The *Cyane* rounded Cape San Lucas, the southern tip of Baja California, on the last day of August and two days later stood in to San Blas. Her captain, Commander Du Pont, immediately proclaimed the blockade, and a landing party commanded by Lieutenant Stephen C. Rowan went ashore and spiked twenty-four cannon, twelve of which were 32-pounders. In the course of 2 and 3 September, the *Cyane* seized the Mexican sloop *Solita* and the brigantine *Susana*, but the latter was considered unseaworthy and was scuttled. Du Pont then decided to go to Mazatlán to confer with Commander Hull of the *Warren* and, having been told by his prisoners that the Mexican brig *Malek Adhel* was at Mazatlán, to cut her out if Hull had not yet arrived.

However, when the *Cyane* arrived at Mazatlán, Du Pont found that Hull had been there since 6 September. That same day, soon after the *Warren* had dropped anchor, a Mr. Bolton came out in one of the boats of HMS *Frolic* to report that the *Malek Adhel*, with sails unbent and running rigging unreeved, was lying within one hundred and fifty yards of the mole of the inner harbor. Hull decided to cut her out before the Mexicans could unship her rudder and tow her up the creek for safekeeping, and to attack her next day while the Mexicans were at siesta. Accordingly, the morning of 7 September was spent preparing the *Warren* for the attack—her boats were hoisted out and a three-hundred-fathom line was put in her launch. Shortly after noon, she made sail and stood in towards the town, and when she came abreast of it and was a quarter of a mile from the *Malek Adhel*, she dropped anchor again.

At 2:30, after swinging ship to bring the *Warren*'s starboard battery to bear on Mazatlán, Hull directed Lieutenant William Radford and sixty-nine men to embark in four boats and pull for the *Malek Adhel*. Radford's men had boarded the brig and fastened her hatches before her snoozing crew realized what was going on. Caught below decks in the defenseless brig, the Mexicans dove overboard and swam for shore. After raising the American flag, the boarding party weighed one of the brig's anchors and unshackled the other, then, using the *Warren*'s boats to head their prize towards the open sea, kedged her out of the harbor.

Belatedly, a large body of Mexican soldiers marched to the mole, while others dragged a field piece to the top of a hill commanding the harbor channel, but, probably out of respect for the long range of the *Warren*'s 32-pounders, neither group opened fire, and by early evening the undamaged *Malek Adhel* was alongside the *Warren*. Commander Hull had the prize brig fitted out as a cruiser, and assigned Lieutenant William B. Renshaw to command her. Eighty feet long on deck and mounting two iron 9-pounders and ten brass 6-pounders, she was a fine sailer and a good sea boat.

The day after the capture of the *Malek Adhel*, the *Warren* captured another Mexican brig, the *Carmelita*, inbound for Mazatlán, and on 9 September Hull proclaimed the port under blockade.

When the *Cyane* left Mazatlán, after Commanders Du Pont and Hull had discussed their plans, she sailed across the Gulf of California to proclaim the blockade at La Paz, Baja California, where she arrived on 14 September. Although the governor of Baja California, Colonel Francisco Palacios Miranda, had chosen to collaborate with the United States and had agreed to neutralize the peninsula, the *Cyane* seized the merchant ships she found in La Paz Harbor—the brigantines *Correo*, *La Paz*, and *Manuela*, the schooners *Julia*, *Mazolea*, *Eliza*, *Victoria*, and *Adelaide*, and the sloop *San José*. The schooner *Julia* was a fast Baltimore clipper and Du Pont manned her as a tender under the command of Lieutenant George L. Selden. Colonel Miranda protested the seizures and was informed by Du Pont:

> The persons and property of the people of Lower California will be respected; the supplies which this ship or any other of the United States may require will be scrupulously paid for at fair prices. But the munitions of war, and vessels sailing under Mexican colors, or the property of Mexicans, must form an exception.

All such therefore, as are now in the harbor of La Paz must be considered as prizes to the United States.

While he was at La Paz, Du Pont learned that a Mexican gunboat had recently sailed from Mulejé, some two hundred miles to the north, bound for Guaymas. Following up the report, the *Cyane* left La Paz on 28 September with the intention of seizing the gunboat and any other shipping that might be found at Guaymas, and of instituting the blockade of that port.

At San Pedro, Commodore Stockton re-embarked his sailors in the *Congress*, now under the command of Lieutenant John W. Livingston, and on 5 September set sail for Monterey. On her way, the flagship put in to Santa Barbara to take aboard Midshipman Mitchell's garrison, which would be needed for the expedition to Acapulco, and there Stockton found Passed Midshipman Archibald McRae, who was carrying Secretary Bancroft's comprehensive instructions of 15 May addressed to Commodore Sloat.

Arriving at Monterey on 15 September, Stockton heard a rumor that one thousand Walla Walla Indians were about to attack the settlements around Sutter's Fort, and sent the *Savannah* to investigate. Not only would such an Indian invasion threaten the American occupation of California and require all of Stockton's force to meet and defeat it, but it would delay, at the very least, his operation against Acapulco. Not content to await the findings of Captain Mervine in the *Savannah*, the Commodore left Monterey on 24 September aboard the *Congress* and followed him to San Francisco. He arrived there late in the afternoon of 27 September—the same afternoon the much slower *Savannah* came in—and was told there was no truth in the rumor: the Indians had come south to trade and to see the "white men" about the murder of one of their chiefs by an American the year before. That news meant that the Commodore was free to continue planning his expedition to Acapulco.

It was Stockton's intention, once he had taken Acapulco, to march on Mexico City—an operation that would require a large number of men. Even if he had enough sailors in his ships, they were not well enough trained to undertake a land campaign of that magnitude. Consequently, on 28 September, he wrote Frémont, who had left Los Angeles for the Sacramento Valley on 11 September to try to recruit men for the California Battalion, asking him to raise seven hundred men to go to Acapulco.

Assuming that Frémont would be successful and that he would, therefore, not have to denude his ships of their crews in order to accomplish the second phase of his plan, he told Captain Mervine, in a letter dated 30 September, that he was arranging to rotate two sets of vessels to maintain the blockade off the coast of Mexico. The next day, he commented to Bancroft that he had no doubt that "an effort will be made by the Mexicans to recover the territory . . . but I'll make them fight their first battle at Acapulco, or between that and the City of Mexico." He further reported that the *Savannah* would sail for the coast of Mexico the following day, the *Portsmouth* in a few days, and the *Congress* as soon as possible.

However, his sanguine hopes of implementing his plan against Acapulco and Mexico City were dashed when Frémont reported that it was almost impossible to recruit men for foreign service. That news seems to have caused Stockton to postpone his expedition.

Be that as it may, Stockton was not yet aware of the turmoil in Los Angeles that ended all thoughts of attacking Acapulco.

Los Angeles was the center of pro-Mexican, anti-American feeling in California, and Gillespie's garrison of forty-eight men from the California Battalion was too small to overawe its turbulent population of some 1,500: in fact, it provoked, rather than deterred, unrest. Gillespie's own description of the men under his command explains why that was so:

> Some very good men but many bad & discontented from having been obliged to remain in the South until a relief could arrive. They were men unaccustomed to control, perfect drunkards whilst in the ciudad of wine & Aguardiente, but serviceable Riflemen in the field. They were men for whom the Californians could have no respect, & whom, from the spirit of insubordination they constantly evinced, the Californians thought they could overcome—Every means in my power were tried to enforce discipline, but the men whom I depended upon would not do the Soldier's duty . . .

If the garrison did not merit the confidence of its commander, it can be said that he, in turn, did not inspire the confidence of the Californians. The tall, red-headed commander, with a stiff, pointed beard, was thirty-three years old and spoke Spanish fluently, but he had a quick temper, an intense dislike of the Californians, and an overriding lack of tact.

There had been rumors of an impending uprising even before Frémont left Los Angeles on 11 September, and about the middle of the month they became so persistent that Gillespie sent his ten most undisciplined men to garrison an outpost at Warner's Ranch, on the road to the Mexican state of Sonora, and sent Ezekial Merritt and a small band of men to San Diego. On 20 September he sent word to Frémont and to Stockton that he needed reinforcements, but his messages fell into the hands of the California conspirators. Three days later, the American garrison at Los Angeles was awakened at 3:00 a.m. by the sound of firing in front and in the rear of Government House on Main Street, where they were quartered. A band of about twenty outlaws were attacking, but when the Americans returned their fire, they "retired percipitately," and a search party sent out at daybreak found no trace of them.

Although a few men described by Gillespie as "foreigners" joined the garrison that day, bringing it up to fifty-nine men, the situation deteriorated rapidly and, by nightfall, the people of Los Angeles were up in arms against the Americans.

In the course of 24 September, some 150 Californians gathered near General Castro's old camp at La Mesa, about a mile and a quarter from Government House, and Servulo Varela, the leader of the band that had attacked the American garrison the day before, proclaimed rebellion. However, he soon lost the leadership of the insurrection to Captain Flores, an intelligent and well-educated Mexican who—like most of the other leaders of the revolt— broke parole by taking part in the uprising. Gillespie did what he could to stem the open revolt. He seized all the powder he could find in Los Angeles, both to keep it from the Californians and because he needed it. He provided himself with artillery by having one of the four old, spiked, and unmounted guns that Stockton and Frémont had left behind, cleared and mounted on a pair of ox-cart wheels. Then he secured one thousand pounds of pipe lead to make projectiles for his cannon, but just what use he intended to make of it is not certain.

That night, he sent a messenger, Juan "Flaco" Brown, to report the situation to Stockton.

After noon the next day, Flores proposed an armistice preparatory to the surrender of the Americans, but Gillespie had no intention of even discussing surrender. Two days later, the garrison that Gillespie had sent to Warner's Ranch was captured by the Californians. Each side waited and watched the other. Then, on 28 September, Gillespie moved his men to what he thought would be a more defensible position on Fort Hill, a quarter of a mile from Government House. Unfortunately, there was no water at the new position and the next day, 29 September, thirst forced the Americans to surrender.

The terms of surrender called for the Americans to evacuate Los Angeles but allowed them to keep their small arms, and they were allowed to keep their cannon until they reached San Pedro. They marched out of Los Angeles on the last day of September and arrived at San Pedro that evening. An American merchantman, the *Vandalia*, was anchored in San Pedro Harbor, and Gillespie and his men boarded her on 4 October, but not before they had violated the surrender agreement by spiking their cannon.

Soon after the Americans had left Los Angeles, Flores sent detachments to clean out the other American garrisons in southern California. Manuel Garfias and a few men moved against Lieutenant Theodore Talbot's small garrison of men from the California Battalion, who had replaced Midshipman Mitchell's naval garrison at Santa Barbara, but Talbot heard of the impending attack and he and his nine men escaped across the mountains to Monterey. Francisco Rico led a detachment to San Diego and forced the garrison there to take refuge on an American whaler, the *Stonington*, that was in the harbor, but a few days later, on 9 October, the garrison went ashore again and reoccupied the town.

In spite of his extensive campaign in August, on 1 October Stockton held no more of California than he did when he took command of the squadron at the end of July. He had only himself to blame, for it was his insistence on dealing General Castro a crushing defeat that had ruined any chance of arranging a peaceful settlement. His overbearing manner and unconcealed contempt for the native Californians did nothing to ease the transition from one government to the other, and his policy of stationing small garrisons in the midst of highly inflammable, recently conquered, and disgruntled populations was as unwise psychologically as it was militarily. Furthermore, it was as inexcusable to choose the tactless Gillespie to command the tinderbox that was Los Angeles as it was to garrison men of the California Battalion there. Had Stockton garrisoned Los Angeles with Marines or sailors, however poorly they might have been suited to the task, there would not have been the friction that the strutting and drunken Bear Flaggers created.

XV

REVERSALS CONTINUE

Juan "Flaco" Brown, who was carrying Gillespie's report to Stockton, arrived at Monterey on 30 September, having made the journey from Los Angeles in the record time of five days, only to find that the Commodore was at San Francisco. Without delay, he continued north and, the next day, delivered his message aboard the *Congress*.

Thrown into a panic by Brown's news, Stockton's first reaction was that he must immediately send the *Congress*, the *Savannah*, and the *Portsmouth* to San Pedro. However, upon more mature consideration and before the above plan had been put into effect, he decided to make a two-pronged drive on Los Angeles, as he had done in August: Frémont and the California Battalion would be transported by sea to Santa Barbara, a three-day march from Los Angeles, while he—Stockton—would head for San Pedro in the *Congress*.

Since it would take a few days to complete his arrangements, he canceled the orders for Captain William Mervine to take the *Savannah* to a blockade station in the Gulf of California, and ordered him to San Pedro to hold the Californians in check until he himself could get there.

Frémont, who was still in the Sacramento Valley, was ordered to come to San Francisco and to bring with him as many men and saddles as he could. In the meantime, Stockton chartered an American merchant ship, the *Sterling*, to carry the California Battalion to Santa Barbara.

Fog delayed the departure of the *Savannah* from San Francisco until 4 October, and she did not reach San Pedro until the early morning of 6 October. The *Vandalia*, with Gillespie and his men aboard, was still at anchor in the harbor, and when the frigate anchored near her, Gillespie boarded her to confer with Mervine. After hearing Gillespie's report, Mervine decided to lose no time in trying to recapture Los Angeles.

Twenty-four hours after the *Savannah* had arrived, her boats began landing 225 of her men and Gillespie's detachment. When all were ashore, they set out for Los Angeles. The operation was hastily conceived, inadequately planned, and poorly executed. The men had no supply train, no ambulances, and no artillery. Mervine was a competent naval officer but he knew nothing about conducting operations on land. With foolhardy courage, he assumed that his untrained sailor-infantry, unsupported by artillery, would be able to fight off the fast-striking, lightly armed, irregular Californian cavalry, get through to Los Angeles, and, once there, hold out in the midst of a hostile population until Stockton came to their relief.

The line of march formed with Gillespie's riflemen in the lead followed by Captain Ward Marston, U.S. Marine Corps, and his Marines and, a short distance behind them, the main body of sailors. Soon after leaving the beach, Gillespie's men ran into a band of Californians at Rancho Palos Verdes, but had no trouble chasing them away. All morning, the column of Americans marched across a plain covered with dry, wild mustard, six to eight feet high, and early in the afternoon, reached Rancho Dominguez—in present-day North Long Beach, and about fifteen miles from their starting point—and camped there for the night. The Californians gathered nearby and after nightfall began firing harassing shots into the American camp. Apparently fearing that this was the prelude to an attack, Mervine roused his sleeping men. No attack came, but at two o'clock, the Californians began intermittently shelling the camp with a 4-pounder cannon that had been buried in a garden in Los Angeles when the town was captured by the Americans.

At daylight, 8 October, Mervine's men broke camp and set out again towards Los Angeles. When they had been on the march for about an hour, they sighted the main body of Californians, which was under the command of José Antonio Carrillo and was formed into three groups: some forty horsemen on either wing, and ten in the center with the 4-pounder, which was mounted on a pair of wagon wheels.

Foreseeing that if his men remained in a column, Carrillo would try to throw them into confusion by shelling them with the cannon, then follow up with a cavalry charge, Mervine formed them into a square. As the Americans began to charge, the Californians fired their cannon into the closely packed square, then, with *reatas*, dragged it back out of reach of Mervine's approaching men. Three times the Americans charged, and three times the gun took its toll before being pulled back. Then, Mervine took counsel with his subordinates, and it was decided that, with the Americans on foot and the Californians on horseback, it was impossible to capture the gun, and it would be foolhardy to try to fight through to Los Angeles as

The 4-pounder cannon that was buried
in Los Angeles when that town was
captured by the Americans. It is now
in the U.S. Naval Academy Museum.
U. S. Naval Academy Museum

long as the Californians had it. Consequently, the only course open to the
Americans, was to retreat.

The march back to San Pedro was slow and dreary: it was five hours
before the men were back in their ships. Four of the ten men who had been
wounded, died, and the island in San Pedro Harbor on which they were
buried, became known as Isla de los Muertos, or Deadmen's Island.

From its inception, the odds had been against the expedition being anything but a fiasco. Had Mervine known that the Californians had almost
exhausted their supply of powder for the gun, he might have been able to
hold on long enough for his expedition to accomplish something. As it was,
the main achievement of the expedition was to point up the hazards of attempting to fight a land campaign with an army of sailors.

Aboard the *Savannah*, Mervine again took counsel with his subordinates
and it was decided not to take any further action until Stockton arrived.
Gillespie and his men were taken off the *Vandalia* and given quarters in the

Savannah, and Mervine chartered the merchant ship and sent her to San Francisco to inform Stockton of what had happened.

While he was waiting for Stockton to arrive, Mervine received an appeal for reinforcement from Ezekial Merritt, who with his small garrison, had reoccupied San Diego on 9 October. Lieutenant George Minor and fifty-two men were sent by sea to San Diego, where they found the garrison effectively restricted to the barracks at the west end of the town. The barracks were protected from assault by a marsh, and the garrison provided itself with added protection by salvaging six brass 9-pounders from the old Spanish fort overlooking the harbor. Despite the reinforcements, the Americans could not drive off the Californians who hung about the outskirts of the town and prevented the garrison from enlarging its territory.

Frémont and 160 men, embarked in a fleet of boats commanded by Midshipman Edward F. Beale, reached San Francisco on 12 October and immediately boarded the waiting *Sterling*. Later that day, the merchantman and the *Congress*, with Stockton embarked, sailed out of San Francisco. The *Sterling* was bound for Santa Barbara, where Frémont was to supply his force with horses for his march to Los Angeles, and the *Congress* was taking the Commodore to San Pedro. A fair wind drove the two vessels down the coast in company, and on 15 October, they fell in with an American merchant vessel, the *Barnstable*, carrying dispatches from Lieutenant Maddox, the commandant at Monterey. The dispatches reported that an attack was threatened and Maddox needed reinforcements, so Stockton ordered the *Sterling* to go on to Santa Barbara, and the *Congress* headed for Monterey, where she arrived the following day.

Stockton sent fifty-two men and three guns ashore to help Maddox and, three days later, on 19 October, the *Congress* weighed anchor and ran on down the coast. She made one more stop—at Santa Barbara—before reaching San Pedro. Stockton, assuming that Frémont would have arrived at Santa Barbara some days previously, was anxious to find out what success he was having in buying horses. Surprised not to find either Frémont or the *Sterling*, he went on to San Pedro.

After parting company with the *Congress*, the *Sterling* met the *Vandalia* bringing Stockton the news that Los Angeles had fallen and that Mervine's effort to recapture it had failed. When Frémont heard this, he concluded that he would not be able to get horses and supplies at Santa Barbara, and that Monterey would be the best place for him to prepare for his advance on Los Angeles. Consequently, he directed the *Sterling* to turn back. On the way back, she was becalmed for several days and did not reach Monterey until 28 October, nine days after Stockton had left.

The *Congress* arrived at San Pedro in the late afternoon of 25 October and, after sizing up the situation, Stockton directed that a landing be made on the morning of 27 October. At daybreak that morning, Gillespie's riflemen clambered into five of the *Savannah*'s boats and cast off. As they drew near the shore, they caught sight of a few Californians and, thinking that their landing was to be opposed, they hesitated. A landing party of sailors and Marines, prepared for any contingency, were waiting in their boats alongside the ships, and as soon as Stockton saw the riflemen waver, he sent in the naval party. A few shots were fired at the approaching boats, but the defenders soon withdrew, and, within an hour, the sailors and Marines were ashore. The riflemen followed them, and when the town had been secured, entrenchments were thrown up to defend it against an anticipated attack. Several skirmishes, which the Californians called the Battle of La Mesa, proved that a large enemy force was in the area, but no attack came.

Stockton, impatient to conclude the recapture of Los Angeles, soon decided that San Pedro was not the best base for the operation. For one thing, the harbor offered little protection for large vessels; and, for another, he would not be able to get the transport he needed, because the great number of Californians encamped at Rancho Los Carritos had driven off all the livestock in the neighborhood. He decided to make San Diego his base, and on 23 November explained the move to Bancroft: "I resolved therefore to embark the troops, and waste no more time there [San Pedro], but to go down South, and, if possible, to get animals somewhere along the coast before the enemy could know or prevent it, and to march to the city [Los Angeles] by the Southern route."

Leaving the *Savannah* to watch for Frémont, the Commodore departed San Pedro in the *Congress* on 29 October. The flagship arrived off San Diego the next day and, as she attempted to cross the bar at the mouth of the harbor, she ran aground. Without making a second attempt to get into the harbor, she dropped anchor outside, and the next day her Marines and forty Bear Flaggers went ashore to relieve the pressure on Lieutenant George Minor and the garrison.

The *Stonington*, the whaler that had sheltered the garrison of San Diego when it was forced out of town at the beginning of October, was still in port and Stockton sent her to Ensenada in Baja California with a detachment of volunteers under the command of Captain Samuel Gibson of the California Battalion to secure horses and cattle. They returned in mid-November bringing with them sixty horses, two hundred cattle, and five hundred sheep.

Towards the end of October, Lieutenant Renshaw left Mazatlán in the prize brig *Malek Adhel* and arrived at Monterey on the 27th. When the *Sterling* came in the next day and Renshaw heard about Frémont's change of plans, he decided that the Commodore should be apprised of it, so he sailed south again and arrived at San Pedro late on 31 October, only to hear from Mervine that Stockton had left two days previously for San Diego. Renshaw caught up with him on the first of November.

Two days after Renshaw's arrival, Stockton sailed for San Pedro in the *Congress*. When he got there on 4 November, he told Mervine to take the *Savannah* to Monterey and give what assistance he could to Frémont. Hoping that Renshaw had been given incorrect information or that, if he had not, Frémont might be on his way south again, Stockton in the *Congress* went with Mervine in the *Savannah* as far as Santa Barbara. However, Frémont was not there, so the *Savannah* went on her way to Monterey, while the *Congress* headed back to San Diego, where she arrived on 15 November.

The Commodore, not wanting to leave his flagship outside the harbor where she would be at the mercy of the winter storms, determined that she try again to cross the bar. This time, she succeeded but ran aground inside the harbor and, as the tide was ebbing, the big ship threatened to heel over. As her crew struggled to shore her up with spars, a force of almost one hundred Californians, taking advantage of the commotion, attacked the town. Thereupon, Stockton sent ashore as many men as he could spare to reinforce the garrison, and the attackers were beaten back. When the tide turned, the *Congress* floated free and anchored off San Diego, where her guns guaranteed that the attack would not be resumed.

With the *Congress* safe in the harbor and the town secure from attack, Stockton turned his attention to the security of his base and to preparations for his advance on Los Angeles. He had a fort built on a hill to the east of town, drilled his sailors, and set them to making saddles, shoes, and gun carriages.

Commodore Stockton's withdrawal from San Pedro to San Diego gave Captain Flores an opportunity to organize resistance, but he found it difficult to stir up enthusiasm for the cause. The fact that he was a Mexican and, thus, automatically suspect in the eyes of the Californians, proved a great handicap to his endeavors. Moreover, he had little material with which to work: he had hardly any money, only forty rounds of ammunition for his cannon and a thousand rounds for his muskets—and only four hundred men. His strategy was to keep the Americans from penetrating inland by harassing them with guerrilla tactics and, for that purpose, he divided his men into three forces: about one hundred men under Manuel Castro operated near San Luis Obispo and watched Frémont; about the same number under Captain Andrés Pico covered San Diego; and Flores stayed in the area of Los Angeles with the largest body of men ready to counter whichever column—Frémont's or Stockton's—seemed most menacing. On 16 November Castro inflicted heavy losses on a detachment of volunteers on their way to join Frémont, but shortly afterwards, considering that he had too few men to accomplish anything worthwhile, he went south to Los Angeles.

Meanwhile, at Monterey, Frémont was gathering what reinforcements he could. American immigrants were pressured into joining the army and, all told, 428 men were recruited, but the scarcity of horses remained a problem and Frémont was reduced to seizing any he could find and giving their owners receipts to be honored by the government after the war. On 17 November, having cut the garrisons to minimum strength, he left Monterey with 300 men and headed south. They got to San Juan Bautista on 21 November and stayed there until the end of the month, completing their preparations.

On the first day of October, the *Cyane* having left La Paz on 28 September bound for Guaymas in search of enemy shipping, put in to Loreto, on the west coast of the Gulf of California, and seized two schooners, the *Libertad* and the *Fortuna*, that were in port. In the next several days, before proceeding across the Gulf to Guaymas, where she arrived on 6 October, she captured the schooner *Rosita* at Loreto, and the sloops *Chapita* and *Alerto* at Mulejé.

At Guaymas, Commander Du Pont demanded that the ships in the port, which included two gunboats, the *Anahuac* and the *Sonorense*, and the merchant brig *Condor*, be surrendered. When Colonel Antonio Campuzano refused to comply, Du Pont gave him until 2 o'clock the following afternoon, 7 October, to evacuate the town. Again, Campuzano failed to comply and, at the expiration of Du Pont's ultimatum, the *Cyane* began to bombard the town and the two gunboats. Either her shots or the Mexicans set fires in the two warships which destroyed them.

While the period of grace was in effect, Campuzano had had the *Condor*, the most important vessel in the harbor, warped into a cove near his barracks and anchored within pistol shot of the shore. Under cover of the cannonade on the town and the harbor, Lieutenant George W. Harrison and forty-two men boarded her and, as they began to work her out of the cove, the Mexicans fired on her. Counterfire from the brig and from the *Cyane*'s launch, which was providing cover for the boarding party, silenced the Mexicans for a while. Then, cross fire from the sides of the cove began pocking the *Condor*'s bulwarks and masts with musket balls and breaking the water around her with grapeshot. This time, the *Cyane* silenced the Mexican guns for good. Harrison brought the *Condor* out of the cove, but when inspection showed her to be worthless, she was burned.

After Du Pont had proclaimed the blockade at Guaymas, the *Cyane* left on 10 October to replace the *Warren*, which had gone north to San Francisco for supplies, in maintaining the blockade of Mazatlán. However, by the first of November, the same need forced the *Cyane* to return to San Francisco, where she arrived on 1 December, and her departure left no American vessel in the Gulf of California. Stockton had ordered the *Portsmouth* from San Francisco to blockade Mazatlán and San Blas, on 7 October, but her orders were changed to San Diego, and her departure was held up until Los Angeles could be retaken.

Much of Stockton's difficulty in keeping up the blockade was caused by lack of vessels: he did not have enough warships to carry on the campaign in California and, at the same time, enforce a blockade of the ports on the west coast of Mexico. However, towards the end of 1846 there was hope that the situation would soon be alleviated. The razee *Independence*, the sloop *Dale*, and the brig *Preble* had left the east coast of the United States during the summer and early fall. The storeship *Erie*, which had arrived at Monterey on 4 September and had there been fitted out as a cruiser, was carrying dispatches to Panama, but she would be available when she returned. And there was one other vessel on which Stockton could count—the schooner *Shark* which had left Mazatlán in April on a cruise to Oregon, and was expected off California shortly. That expectation was not to be fulfilled, for on 10 September the *Shark* was wrecked by breakers at the mouth of the Columbia River.

While Stockton was struggling to regain his hold over southern California, General Kearny was advancing towards it. With 300 men of the First Dragoons under Major Edwin V. Sumner, he left Santa Fe, New Mexico, for Los Angeles on 25 September. The route he was to take was, roughly, the long and difficult Gila Trail: after following the Rio Grande for more than 200 miles from Santa Fe, he would cross to the Gila River, follow it to its confluence with the Colorado River, then drop down along the banks of the Colorado for about 40 miles before crossing the Desert of California (now the Imperial Valley) to the frontier of settled California.

On 6 October when Kearny was near Socorro, New Mexico, on the Rio Grande, he met the famed "Mountain Man," Kit Carson, who was on his way to Washington with dispatches from Commodore Stockton announcing the occupation of California. Carson had set out on his journey before the uprising in Los Angeles and consequently thought the Americans were firmly in control of the country. When Kearny heard that, he naturally assumed that he would not need a large force to garrison the area and, keeping only Captain Benjamin D. Moore and 100 men to serve as an escort, he sent Major Sumner and the rest of the men back to Santa Fe. He also prevailed upon Carson to turn his dispatches over to another "Mountain Man," Thomas Fitzpatrick, and to return to California as a guide for Kearny and his men.

Kearny first learned of the revolt in California from a Mexican courier

STEPHEN W. KEARNY

captured on 23 November. After nine more days of marching, the last three of which were across the Desert of California and were so punishing that many of the already exhausted horses died, he and his dragoons came to Warner's Ranch, the first habitation on their route beyond the desert, on 2 December. The inhabitants of the isolated ranch confirmed that there had been a revolt and told Kearny that Stockton was at San Diego but, apart from that, they could tell him little about the state of affairs. Consequently, he decided to let Stockton know where he was and to ask for an escort to lead him and his men to San Diego.

Thomas Stokes, an Englishman, who was entrusted with the mission of carrying Kearny's letter, delivered it to Stockton on the evening of 3 December, while the Commodore was interrogating two Californian deserters. Taking one of the deserters as a guide, Gillespie and thirty-nine men, with a brass 4-pounder, left San Diego one and a half hours after Stokes' arrival to meet Kearny and to suggest to him that he try to make a surprise attack on the 150 Californians watching San Diego.

After spending 3 December resting at Warner's Ranch and rounding up about one hundred horses and mules, most of which were too wild to be of much use, Kearny and his men set forth again. On the fifth, they met Gillespie's detachment, and, as both forces were preparing to encamp for the night at Rancho Santa María, they heard that Captain Andrés Pico, who had recently taken command of the forces around San Diego, and a troop of Californians were near the village of San Pasqual, some nine miles away, blocking the road to San Diego. Kearny ordered Lieutenant Thomas C. Hammond to take a scouting party and reconnoiter Pico's position.

Pico knew nothing about Kearny's arrival, and when he heard that Gillespie had left San Diego, he assumed that he had gone on a foraging expedition and it would, therefore, be some time before he returned. Intending to intercept him when he did return, Pico posted his seventy-two men at San Pasqual and directed them to let their horses out to graze while waiting for the foragers. However, it was not long before the sounds of Hammond's scouting party moving about were picked up by Pico's alert sentinels, and the Californians immediately set about rounding up their horses, which had already wandered off in all directions.

Hammond returned to camp shortly before midnight, and when Kearny heard his report and realized that the element of surprise had been lost, he decided to wait until morning to attack. Unless it was simply that he still wanted to carry out Stockton's suggestion that he try to surprise the Californians, or that he wanted their horses, it is difficult to see why he chose to attack at all. From a purely military point of view, an attack was unnecessary: Kearny, whose force outnumbered the Californians by almost two to one and was well equipped with artillery, could undoubtedly have forced his way through to San Diego; and even if Pico had been foolhardy enough to attack him, he would probably have had little difficulty in beating off the attackers.

Whatever the reasoning, it must have been compelling, for Kearny was a competent officer and he was aware that his men were in no condition to fight: they had not recovered from the effects of the long and arduous march from Santa Fe, and their mounts were either weary or uncontrollable. Moreover, neither he nor his men had any experience in fighting horsemen armed with lances.

At 2:00 a.m. on 6 December, Kearny roused his men and they mounted on their motley collection of horses and mules. Captain Abraham R. Johnston, with twelve dragoons mounted on the best horses, led the little army. Close behind them came Kearny with a personal bodyguard of six or seven dragoons. Following the General, was Captain Moore with the main body of dragoons, about fifty in number, most of them riding tired mules; then Gillespie and twenty-one Bear Flaggers. After them came Lieutenant John W. Davidson, two howitzers, and a few more dragoons. Bringing up the rear, were Major Thomas Swords and fifty to sixty men, with Gillespie's gun, guarding the baggage. The night was moonlit, but it was cold and damp, and as the column rode along a ridge road, the cold numbed the men's minds and limbs, while the dampness wet down the powder in the Hall carbines carried by the dragoons.

When the advance guard was about three-quarters of a mile from Pico's camp, Kearny ordered an advance at a trot. Apparently, Captain Johnston misunderstood the order. He sent his men forward at a charge, which put so much distance between them and the main body, which was moving at a trot, that they were engaging the Californians before the rest of the force was in position to support them. Johnston's charge caught the Californians in the process of mounting their retrieved horses, and threw them into confusion. Nevertheless, they held their ground and forced the out-numbered American advance guard to withdraw.

When Pico saw Captain Moore and the main force of dragoons approaching, he hastily moved back half a mile or so to where the ground was more even. Seeing this, Moore gave the order to charge. Mounted as they were on a poor assortment of horses and mules, the Americans could not even advance in ordered ranks, and when they charged, their disarray increased and they became widely separated from one another and from the men coming up behind them. Pico countercharged, and in the melee that ensued, the saber-wielding Americans were outmarched by the well-mounted Californian lancers. The fight had been joined for about fifteen minutes before Gillespie's men and the artillery reached the battlefield and, when they did, the mules pulling one of the howitzers bolted and dragged the gun into the enemy's lines.

Pico and his men then withdrew, but they had wrought havoc among the 150 Americans: almost a score of men, including Captains Moore and Johnston and Lieutenant Hammond, were dead, and thirteen, including Kearny and Gillespie, were wounded. One of Pico's seventy-two men was captured and probably no more than twelve were wounded. The Americans, obviously, were in no condition to pursue the retreating Californians, and Pico was content not to re-engage until he received the reinforcements and artillery that Captain Flores had promised to send him.

The little American army was in a pitiable condition: provisions were almost exhausted, horses and mules were worn out, the men were tired and hungry—and their commander was too badly hurt to exercise command. Captain Henry S. Turner, the next senior officer, sent Alexis Godey, one of Frémont's "Mountain Men," to get help from Stockton. Until such help arrived or until the injured recovered enough to move, there was little the stranded men could do but make camp, bury their dead, and treat their wounded companions.

Thomas Stokes, who had carried the word to Stockton when General Kearny arrived at Warner's Ranch, had been with the General when the battle started and when he saw that it was going badly, had ridden off to

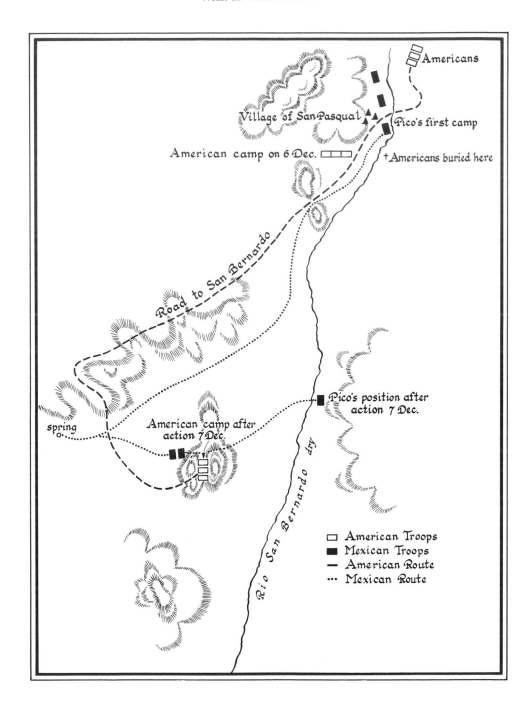

PLAN OF THE ACTION AT SAN PASQUAL

San Diego. He arrived there that same evening, 6 December, and told what he knew, but he could give no information on the final outcome. Some details were supplied the following morning, when Godey came in with Turner's letter, but that document failed to mention how strong a force Pico had, and neither Stokes nor Godey could estimate it. To be on the safe side, Stockton decided to send every available man to Kearny's relief. Accordingly, he ordered the preparation of two days' rations, and made ready to send Acting Lieutenant John Guest with an advance guard and two guns to Mission San Diego, just north of present-day San Diego. But before Guest left, an Indian came in with a report indicating that although Pico's force was not great, Kearny's supplies were almost exhausted and it was essential that he be relieved as quickly as possible. Thereupon, Stockton changed his plans and began to prepare a small but highly mobile force to go to the General's assistance.

On the evening of 7 December, still another messenger arrived from Kearny's camp—Edward F. Beale, now an Acting Lieutenant. On the basis of Beale's report, Stockton increased the relief force, and the next day Lieutenant Andrew V. F. Gray and 215 men, with instructions to move only at night, set out to relieve the stranded army.

Meanwhile, Kearny's men built travois to carry the wounded and on 7 December started out on a slow and painful march towards San Diego. No opposition was encountered until they reached a small hill near Rancho San Bernardo that same day and found it occupied by some of Pico's men. Although they succeeded in dislodging the Californians, in the process of doing so they lost what few cattle they had left. They made camp on the hill and, intending to spend a few days there to give the wounded a chance to rest, they dug a well. However, three days later, on 10 December, the peace of the camp was shattered when Pico drove a herd of wild horses against it. The horses were turned back by gunfire before they could do any damage, but one was killed and made into soup.

That same day, Kearny estimated that the wounded had recovered sufficiently to ride, and decided to resume the march after daybreak the next morning. Before they left, Gray and the relief column arrived and the combined force set out on what, for Kearny and his men, was the last leg of a long and eventful journey. When they limped into San Diego on the afternoon of 12 December, they received a warm welcome.

XVI

LOS ANGELES REGAINED

Immediately upon arrival in San Diego on 12 December 1846, General Kearny conferred with Commodore Stockton. What took place at that meeting is as uncertain as is the exact relationship between the two commanders during the campaign that followed. Later, both men claimed to have been in command, just as they both claimed to be governor of California. The reports that they dispatched to Washington were self-justifications and, therefore, of little use to the historian, who must base his conclusions on the realities of the command structure that are apparent. Stockton was in command, and whether he was in command because he was governor of California, or because he was commander-in-chief of the expedition, or simply because he supplied most of the troops, is not important.

At the time the General and the Commodore had their first conference, all was not in readiness for the drive to recapture Los Angeles. One of the Bear Flaggers, Captain Samuel J. Hensley, was away on a foraging expedition along the coast of Mexico, Frémont was still in the Salinas Valley on his way to Santa Barbara, and Kearny's weary dragoons needed time to recuperate.

Although he rejected Kearny's recommendation that the operation should begin as early as 22 December, Stockton did not intend to delay long. His plan was to march north to Mission San Luis Rey and, thereafter, to be governed by the movements of Frémont and by what action the Californians took: he was evidently afraid that, if he got too far from San Diego, the enemy would cut his communications with that base. His original intention seems to have been to create a diversion to the south, while Frémont's much smaller force took Los Angeles. Apparently, however, Kearny convinced him—and he probably did not need much convincing—that it would be better to have the main force fight its way through to the city.

When Captain Hensley returned to San Diego with 140 horses and 300 cattle, Stockton had all the horses and cattle he could reasonably expect to acquire. He offered the horses Hensley had brought to Captain Turner, but Turner declined the offer, on the grounds that they were not good enough for the dragoons.

Two days before Christmas, the Commodore finally issued the orders that would set in motion the advance on Los Angeles: the dismounted dragoons, Companies A and B of the California Battalion, detachments from the *Congress*, the *Savannah*, and the *Portsmouth*, and the artillery under Lieutenant R. Lloyd Tilghman, were to march out of San Diego on the morning of 28 December. Everything went according to plan, and by the end of 29 December the entire expedition was on its way. Commander Montgomery was left in command at San Diego, where the *Congress*, the *Portsmouth*, and the *Cyane*, which had arrived on the 27th, swung at anchor.

The army that Stockton led was large—607 men—but it was not well equipped: only 200 of the men were armed with muskets, and most of the others carried carbines or boarding pikes; the emaciated horses and oxen were too weak to work for long as draft animals, and the men had to help pull the artillery, as well as the ammunition and store carts; about the only fresh provisions were some cattle and, during the march, they had to be surrounded by men to prevent them from straying or being stolen by the Californians. The route of the 140-mile march was roughly the same as the modern U.S. Highway 101.

On New Year's Day 1847, the leader of the Californian insurgents, Captain José María Flores, relayed to Stockton a rumor that peace had been concluded between Mexico and the United States, and suggested that operations be suspended at least until it could be ascertained whether the *Shark*, which was due back from her cruise to Oregon at any moment, carried any definite information. Flores advised that the bearers of his message, Julian Workman and Charles Fluge, had volunteered to act as mediators, in the event Stockton agreed to a truce, but, he warned, if Stockton refused, the responsibility for the consequences would rest with the Americans for, in that case, he, Flores, would fight to the bitter end. Stockton haughtily refused even to read the letter, and informed the emissaries that if he caught Flores, he would shoot him as a parole violator. On 5 January, as a countermeasure to Flores' message, he issued a proclamation that offered amnesty to any Californian, except Flores, who would surrender.

Flores expected that Frémont coming down from Santa Barbara would reach the area of Los Angeles before Stockton did, and laid plans to meet that threat first. However, before the end of the first week in January, he realized that Stockton's force was the more immediate threat, and moved his army south from San Fernando to La Jaboneria Ford on the San Gabriel

Crossing the San Gabriel River
Franklin D. Roosevelt Library, Hyde Park, New York

River. He had some 450 men, but they were not well armed and did not
have enough powder to allow them to engage in a prolonged battle.

In the meantime, Stockton was approaching the San Gabriel River, and
La Jaboneria was the ford by which he intended to cross it. On 7 January,
for the first time, his men saw enemy horsemen in front of them, which
Stockton took as an indication that the main body of Flores' army was in
the vicinity. Late that day, when he reached the Coyote River—the lower
stretch of the San Gabriel, no longer having a separate name—he sent out
scouts, and under cover of darkness they discovered that his surmise was
correct and that Flores had laid an ambush at the ford.

To the right of the American position, there was another crossing, the
Bartolo Ford, which was some fifty yards wide, with knee-deep water and
quicksand on the bottom. In the area of the ford, fringes of underbrush ran
along both banks of the river and beyond that, on the south side where
Stockton was, the terrain was level; but, on the north side, where Flores
was, there was a range of hills, about fifty feet high, jutting up some 600
yards back from the river.

On the morning of 8 January after Kearny had addressed the men,
Stockton led them towards the Bartolo Ford and, thus, away from the left

193

Captain Flores attacks the American left wing.
Franklin D. Roosevelt Library, Hyde Park, New York

flank of Flores' army. As soon as Flores realized where the Americans were heading, he shifted his forces in the same direction and, reaching Bartolo before Stockton did, posted his men along the hills, from which their artillery covered the ford.

Before moving across the plain on their side of the river, the Americans halted and formed into a square. With their baggage carts, spare oxen, and beef cattle inside the square, they moved on again and, when they were about two miles from the ford, they were able to discern flashing lances decorated with red pennons across the river. A quarter of a mile from the ford, they halted again, while Stockton rearranged their order. As they began to move on, a hundred horsemen driving a herd of horses came thundering across the river and tried to break up their formation, but the square held, and the Californians went back across the river.

Keeping his main force and two guns to cover the ford, Flores sent a detachment of some 100 to 150 men about 300 yards to the right of that position and a similar detachment an equal distance to the left. His artillery fired round shot and grapeshot at the advancing Americans, but neither had much effect because most of the powder was poor and the makeshift cannonballs did not fit the guns properly.

At the riverbank, the American square stopped and, apparently at Kearny's

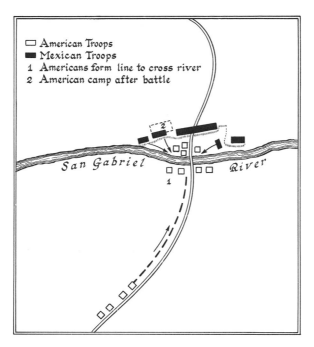

PLAN OF THE BATTLE OF SAN GABRIEL

command, the artillerymen began to unlimber their pieces. When Stockton saw what they were doing, he countermanded the instruction and ordered the whole force to cross the river before opening fire. The guns were dragged across first, an operation that required hard labor on the part of both officers and men, including the Commodore. While the artillerymen were preparing to answer Californian fire, the center crossed and, under cover of the four-foot-high riverbank, deployed to support the guns. The flank columns followed the center across and took up their positions on the left and right ends of the line. For the rear of the square, burdened as it was with baggage carts and livestock, the crossing was slow.

While his troops formed along the crest behind the underbrush on the north bank, Stockton supervised the artillery, personally aiming and firing the guns with great accuracy. His third shot disabled one of Flores' guns, and a later shot silenced the other. With the Californian artillery temporarily out of action, Stockton seized the opportunity to order Captain Hensley and his Bear Flaggers to attack. They charged forward and drove the Californian left flank from the hill it was occupying. No sooner had the Bear Flaggers reached their new position than Stockton realized that his right flank was dangerously exposed and called them back. Seeing Hensley pull back, Flores gave the order for his left wing to counterattack but, as it began to advance, one of Flores' aides apparently panicked and shouted "Halt," whereupon it turned back in confusion. Flores then ordered his right wing against the American left, but it was beaten back by artillery fire.

With the enemy attacks turned back, Stockton straightened out his lines and ordered his men to charge and to cry "New Orleans," in remembrance of Andrew Jackson's victory at that city on 8 January thirty-two years before. As the Californian center and left fell back in good order, but without offering any resistance, Flores sent his right wing to make a wide sweep around the left flank of the American line and attack it from the rear. This tactic was no more successful than the previous ones. Beaten off by a curtain of fire thrown up by Gillespie's men, the attackers returned to their own lines.

Pushed back by the American charge, Flores took up a new position, half a mile beyond his original one, where a ravine protected one of his flanks, and reopened fire with his artillery. During the artillery duel that ensued, accurate American fire several times drove the Californian gunners from their pieces. Flores finally abandoned the fight and retired in the direction of Los Angeles. Since he had no cavalry, Stockton made no attempt to pursue the fleeing Californian horsemen.

In the ninety-minute battle, two Americans were killed and nine wounded: Californian losses were about the same. The sailor army had acquitted itself very well—it had not flinched under either the cannonade or the cavalry charges—and Stockton had proved his courage in battle. His tactics, however, were questionable, particularly forcing the ford in the face of enemy guns when his own artillery support was out of action. Had the Californians been able to deliver accurate fire, they could have wrought havoc among the American infantry as it forded the river. Apparently, Stockton's contempt for the Californians led him to believe that Flores' men would flee at the sight of one American.

After the battle, the Americans camped near the place where Flores' right wing had first been positioned, and their band celebrated the victory by playing "Hail Columbia" and "Yankee Doodle."

As Flores retreated, many of his men ran away but those who remained with him halted at the Cañada de los Alisos, near the main road to Los Angeles—and near what is now the site of Union Stockyards—to await the Americans. During the night, some of the men returned to the battlefield and around midnight exchanged fire with the American pickets. Stockton roused his men and prepared for an attack, but when none was forthcoming, he sent them back to their blankets.

About three-quarters of a mile from the American camp there was a ranch where Stockton thought there might be some Californians, so at daylight on 9 January he sent Lieutenant Zeilin and thirty Marines to investigate. When the party returned from the ranch, having found nothing of concern,

Battle of La Mesa
Franklin D. Roosevelt Library, Hyde Park, New York

Stockton set out again for Los Angeles. As he crossed the wide plain that lies between the San Gabriel and Los Angeles rivers and is called simply La Mesa, he turned his army off the main road and traveled a short distance to the left before turning again and marching parallel with it. After going some six miles, they sighted the Californians at Cañada de los Alisos. There were, perhaps, 300 of them deployed in a long line that extended from the *cañada*, or ravine, on their left and on the edge of which Flores posted his artillery, almost to the American line of march.

In order to open the range, Stockton turned slightly farther to the left. As his men, advancing in their usual square formation, came within range, the Californian guns opened on them. Except that it killed one ox and one mule in the center of the square, the fire was as ineffectual as ever, but this may have been because Stockton told his men to throw themselves to the ground when they saw a puff of smoke that announced the advent of a cannonball, rather than because the gunnery was poor. As the Americans kept moving forward, while answering with fire from the field pieces at the front corners of their square, Flores moved his men across their path and brought up two more guns. About six hundred yards from the enemy, Stockton halted his command and had the four guns at the leading corners of his square collected in a single battery. That battery and the 6-pounder

197

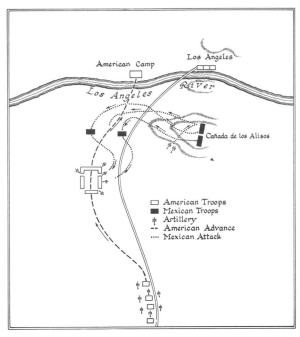

PLAN OF THE BATTLE OF LA MESA

at the rear of the right flank poured concentrated fire on the Californian guns and, after about fifteen minutes, drove them out of range.

The futile cannonade had used up nearly all the powder Flores' artillery had so, as a last resort, he threw in his reserves and ordered a charge against the left flank of the American formation. The onrushing cavalry got to within eighty yards of the American square before being forced back by heavy fire. Disheartened by their inability to break the square or to halt the advancing Americans, late that afternoon Flores and the remnants of his army retired to the area that is, today, Pasadena.

The fighting had lasted two and a half hours, in the course of which Stockton had destroyed the Californian army. One of his men and one of Flores' men had been killed; five Americans and an unknown number of the enemy had been wounded.

Stockton's force crossed the Los Angeles River about three miles below Los Angeles. They could have entered the town that evening, but the Commodore was afraid that, at that time of day, the men would be more apt to get drunk than they would be in daylight, and decided to camp outside for the night.

Early next morning, 10 January, under a flag of truce, a deputation from the town appeared at the American camp and offered to surrender the town in return for a promise that property would be respected. The promise was given and, about noon, the little army, with its band playing, marched into Los Angeles. In spite of the surrender, they remained watchful and ready to fight for, according to Lieutenant William H. Emory, the streets were full of "desperate and drunken fellows, who brandished their arms and saluted us with every term of reproach." Riflemen and Marines chased away a few horsemen who could be seen on the ridge overlooking the town, and, with his own hands, Gillespie raised over Government House, the flag he had hauled down when he surrendered almost four months previously. In a house that stands to this day, Avila Adobe on Olvera Street, Stockton set up his headquarters.

It had been expected that Frémont and his force would play a large part in the campaign to retake Los Angeles. Now it had been retaken, the Californian army had been scattered, and where was Frémont?

He had left San Juan Bautista at the end of November, and on 14 December had reached San Luis Obispo, expecting to find it garrisoned. He surrounded it with his men and, in the rainy darkness of that night, made a surprise attack. It was undefended and succumbed easily. However, at nearby Wilson's Ranch, Frémont discovered and captured Jesus Pico, a cousin of Pío and Andrés Pico, and, at this time, the Californian commander in the area, and thirty-five of his men. In taking this command, Pico had broken his parole and, apparently with the intention of making him an example for other parole-breakers, Frémont called a court-martial the next day to try him. The court found Pico guilty and sentenced him to death, but some of Frémont's officers had earlier been befriended by Pico, and they and Pico's wife pressed Frémont to pardon him, and he relented. The action turned out to be very sagacious, for Pico, feeling that he owed his life to Frémont, accompanied the expedition south and rendered considerable service.

Frémont left San Luis Obispo on 17 December and, after crossing the San Rafael Mountains in a bad storm, reached Santa Barbara on 27 December. There, he found the prize schooner *Julia* waiting to lend him any possible assistance. He took one of her guns, then sent her on down the coast to prevent the Californians from setting an ambush for him and his men in the Rincon Pass, where the road they would have to travel ran between high hills and the coast. After spending a week at Santa Barbara, he proceeded south again, got safely past Rincon, and on 5 January 1847 reached the Mission of San Buenaventura (now Ventura), where his men skirmished with a small group of Californian horsemen. The following day, a larger force of Californians—sixty or seventy of them—appeared up ahead, but although another brief skirmish took place, they did not attempt to impede Frémont's progress.

On 9 January a letter from Stockton, dated 3 January, was delivered to

Frémont. In it Stockton advised the explorer that he and his army had left San Diego and expected to reach Los Angeles on 8 or 9 January. He ordered Frémont to avoid battle, if possible, and if he had to fight, to do so only from a closely packed formation, and he warned him against attempting to pursue the Californians, lest he suffer the same fate Kearny did. Two days later, when he was near the Mission San Fernando (now a suburb of Los Angeles), and had already heard of the fall of Los Angeles, Frémont received a letter from Kearny, dated 10 January. After giving him the news about Los Angeles, offering to send him assistance, if he needed it, and, just as Stockton had done, cautioning him about the Californian cavalry, the General instructed him to join the main American force at Los Angeles, and requested immediate acknowledgement of his letter.

Late on the day he received Kearny's letter, 11 January, Frémont came upon Flores and the remnants of his army encamped at the nearby Rancho Los Verdugos, and sent Jesus Pico to try to talk the one hundred or so men into discussing the terms under which they would surrender. After conferring among themselves, the Californians agreed to a discussion but, either because he thought his presence would complicate the negotiations or because he was afraid of Stockton's declared intention to hang him for parole violation, Flores turned over command of his men to Andrés Pico and left for Sonora during the night.

Andrés Pico chose Francisco de la Guerra and Francisco Rico as his negotiators, and sent them to the meeting along with Jesus Pico. When Frémont learned that the Californians were willing to talk terms, he granted a twenty-four-hour truce, and allowed the Californians to move to the Mission San Fernando. Articles of capitulation were drawn up on 12 January and, the next morning, at the Rancho Cahuenga, Agustín Olvera signed them for the Californians, and Major P. B. Reading, Major William H. Russell, and Captain Louis McLane signed for the Americans.

The Articles provided for the Californians to return home on parole, and for any who wished to do so, to leave the country after the war; they guaranteed that those who surrendered would be protected, that none would be required to take an oath of allegiance during the war, and that all the inhabitants of California would enjoy equal rights. An additional article in the document voided all previous paroles.

The Treaty, or Capitulation, of Cahuenga, in effect, ended the war in Alta California. It cannot be denied that its terms were statesmanlike and were as generous as any the Californians could have asked—they were, in fact, almost the same as those they had earlier proposed to Commodore Stockton. Nevertheless, Frémont erred in entering into any agreement at all, for he had no authority to do so and he was within communicating distance of his superior. Technically, the agreement required ratification by Stockton to make it effective, but by the time Stockton received the text, its terms were already being applied and he had no choice but to accept them.

Events leading up to the signing of the articles of capitulation and the signing itself are instances of Frémont's insubordination. Another example of this attitude was his failure to comply with Kearny's request for immediate acknowledgment of his instructions of 10 January, or with similar requests attached to letters Kearny wrote him several days later. The first word that either the General or the Commodore had of Frémont was when an officer carrying the surrender document rode in to Los Angeles.

Frémont led his 400 men and six guns into Los Angeles on 14 January, in the midst of a heavy rainstorm. As a sign of their acceptance of the new course of events, the inhabitants of Los Angeles gave a ball in honor of Kearny, Stockton, and Frémont.

In a little more than six months, U.S. naval forces in the Pacific Ocean, aided by the California Battalion and two understrength companies of dragoons, had seized and pacified the whole of the area that is, today, the state of California. Appreciation of the magnitude of this accomplishment increases when one remembers that the land operations involved had to be conducted for the most part by a naval force, usually at a considerable distance from the sea. Commodore Stockton deserves credit for planning and executing most of the campaigns. But whether the campaigns would have been necessary anyway, or whether they were made necessary by his stupidity—for example, the revolt in September 1846 was primarily the result of his poor judgment and high-handed treatment of the natives—is another question.

If Stockton's strategy was good, its execution was poor: he planned an operation that involved Frémont, then kept hardly any check on where he was or what he was doing, and made little effort to coordinate action with that dilatory officer. Some of his tactics were good, some bad: he made excellent use of the square, both on the march and in action, and he handled his artillery well. Yet, he took an unnecessary risk when he forced his army to cross the San Gabriel River, in the face of heavy artillery fire, without the support of their own artillery.

While the campaign to recapture Los Angeles was in progress, a revolt, which seems to have had no connection with the one in the south, arose in the north. It grew out of the harsh and arbitrary treatment that the men of the California Battalion meted out to the natives of the area around San Francisco. Particularly guilty in the eyes of the rebels was Captain Charles Weber, so when, on 8 December 1846, they captured Lieutenant Washington

A. Bartlett, the acting *alcalde* of San Francisco, when he and some men from the *Warren* were on a foraging expedition, they tried to barter his freedom for that of Weber.

On 29 December Captain Ward Marston, U.S. Marine Corps, left San Francisco with 101 Marines and mounted volunteers and one gun, on a punitive expedition to Santa Clara to put down the rebellion. Marston and his men were about seven miles from the Mission Santa Clara on 2 January 1847 when they came upon Francisco Sanchez, the erstwhile military commandant of San Francisco who was leading the rebels, and about 120 men. In the brief engagement that followed, two Americans were wounded, and four Californians were killed and five wounded. The insurgents then withdrew into the Santa Cruz Mountains. The next morning, in the presence of the British Vice Consul, James A. Forbes, Marston and Sanchez met and agreed to an armistice while the former inquired of his superiors what terms for a permanent cessation of hostilities would be acceptable.

Three days later, on 6 January, Marston informed Sanchez that his superiors would accept nothing less than unconditional surrender, but gave his verbal promise that no further abuses would be committed against the natives. Sanchez accepted the arrangement, and the war in northern California came to a close.

A dispute had been brewing between General Kearny and Commodore Stockton over the control of California. Stockton claimed that since he had prior possession of the territory and had established a functioning government, he had exclusive control over it. Kearny claimed that his orders from Washington gave him control. The quarrel came to a head on 16 January, when Stockton issued a commission making Frémont governor of California. Kearny countered by demanding that Stockton cease meddling in civil government. In a caustic reply to that demand, Stockton wrote that he governed by right of prior conquest, did not recognize that Kearny had any authority, and would ask for the army officer's recall. The following day, 17 January, Frémont wrote Kearny that he did not recognize his authority and would take orders only from Stockton.

Kearny was in an impossible situation. Not having enough men to back up his claim to authority by force, he had no choice but to withdraw and await reinforcements. On 18 January he and his dragoons set out on a five-day journey to San Diego.

The day before Kearny reached San Diego, the *Independence* carrying Commodore W. Branford Shubrick had anchored at Monterey, and Shubrick had assumed command of the Pacific Squadron. On her way from Boston to the Pacific coast, the *Independence* had put in at Valparaiso, where on 2 December Shubrick had met with Commodore James Biddle. In compliance with Secretary Bancroft's order of 13 May 1846, the latter was on his way from the Orient to assume temporary command of the Pacific Squadron but, since he could not immediately move north, he instructed Shubrick to go ahead and take command in the interim. Those were, in fact, the instructions with which Shubrick had left the United States on 22 August.

When Kearny heard of the arrival of the new Commodore, he decided to lose no time in conferring with him about the command relationship. Consequently, on the last day of January, in company with Consul Larkin, he boarded the *Cyane* and set sail for Monterey. After comparing their instructions, the two commanders arrived at a mutually agreeable division of authority and settled on Monterey as the temporary capital of California. Kearny then sailed for San Francisco, where he arrived on 13 February and met Colonel Robert B. Mason, who had arrived the day before in the *Erie* and was the bearer of new orders from Washington.

Colonel Mason carried orders dated 3 November 1846 from General Winfield Scott to General Kearny directing that civil government in California was to be headed by the senior Army officer and that the naval commander was to be responsible for drawing up port regulations, controlling imports, and collecting duties. On 20 February Lieutenant James M. Watson arrived carrying orders dated 5 November from John Y. Mason, who in September had replaced Bancroft as Secretary of the Navy, to Commodore Stockton. This set of orders gave Stockton the same instructions about the administration of California as Kearny received from General Scott, but advised him further that, any time Kearny was absent, command ashore would be assumed by Colonel Mason. Stockton was also informed that when Commodore Shubrick arrived in California, Stockton could either hoist a red pennant and stay with the squadron as second-in-command, or he could return to the United States in the *Savannah*.

Kearny arrived back in Monterey aboard the *Savannah* on 26 February, and he and Shubrick began drafting proclamations on the official delineation of authority as set forth in the newly arrived directives from Washington. While these proclamations were completed by 1 March and bore that date, they were not issued until 4 March. Historians have wondered why there was that delay, but it probably was simply that on 2 March Commodore James Biddle arrived to take command of the squadron, and Shubrick wanted to be sure that the joint statements had the approval of his superior officer. That explanation seems to be confirmed by a remark Kearny made in a report dated 15 March 1847 to Colonel Roger Jones, Adjutant General of the U.S. Army: "Upon Commodore Biddle's arrival I had a full understanding with him relating to our duties."

The first of the ante-dated proclamations defined the areas of responsibility of the two services: the Army had charge of the civil government and activities on land, while the Navy assumed authority over port and customs operations. The second announced that Kearny had taken control of the civil government.

Thus, the problem of who controlled the government of California was finally settled.

Reinforcements for General Kearny's army began arriving in California in the latter part of January 1847. The storeship *Lexington*, carrying Company F, Third Artillery, with cannon, small arms, and munitions arrived at Monterey on 26 January, and three days later Major Philip St. George Cooke and the Mormon Battalion reached San Diego. Between 6 and 26 March, Stevenson's First New York Volunteers, who had sailed from the east coast of the United States around Cape Horn, came in to San Francisco, and before long were scattered throughout California on garrison duty.

XVII

OCCUPYING BAJA CALIFORNIA

In the middle of January 1847, active campaigning in Alta California was at an end, troops to take over garrison duties were due to arrive momentarily, and the Navy was turning its attention to Baja California and the west coast of Mexico.

Commodore Stockton and his sailors left Los Angeles for San Diego aboard the whaler *Stonington* on 19 January. Three days later, he wrote to advise the Secretary of the Navy that he was about to depart for Mexico, but the very day he wrote that letter, Commodore Shubrick arrived at Monterey to assume command of the Pacific Squadron. Nevertheless, Stockton did undertake one more operation before Shubrick relieved him.

When the Mormon Battalion arrived at San Diego on 29 January, Major Cooke brought the news that General Anastasio Bustamante was planning to lead an attack on Alta California. In an attempt to head it off, Stockton landed a small force about 120 miles below San Diego, but there was no sign of any Mexican army because, as it was later learned, revolts preceding Santa Anna's return to power in Mexico prevented Bustamante from getting any farther north than Guanajuato.

On the way from Washington, at this time, were new sets of orders for both the naval commander and the army commander in the Pacific. Included in the first set was an order, dated 24 December 1846, that reflected Secretary of the Navy Mason's horror at the unenforceable and, therefore, illegal blockade that Commodore Stockton had proclaimed on 19 August, and went on to direct that no port on the west coast of Mexico "be regarded as blockaded, unless there is a sufficient American force to maintain it actually present, or temporarily driven from actual presence by stress of weather, intending to return."

In an order that was dated 11 January 1847, Mason defined Stockton's rights and powers in California, but by the time that letter reached California the dispute between the Commodore and General Kearny had long since been settled.

The second set of orders was also dated 11 January and was from Secretary of War William L. Marcy to General Kearny. It instructed the General to occupy at least one port in Baja California so that there should be no question about American possession of both Alta and Baja California.

One of the drawbacks of operating on the Pacific coast was that, although some supplies could be purchased in Hawaii and a few in California, most of them had to come all the way from the east coast of the United States. By late January, the naval squadron had less than a two-weeks' supply of salt provisions, and Walter Colton observed that the sailors "can hardly muster a shirt apiece, and one pair of shoes among half a dozen is becoming a rare sight." A month later, he reported: "We are eagerly looking for the arrival of stores-ships from the United States. Our squadron is without provisions, except fresh grub from the shore. Our ships, as far as sea-service is concerned, are of about as much use as so many nautical pictures. They look stately and brave, as they ride at anchor in our bay; but let them go to sea, and they would carry famine with them."

Until the storeship *Southampton* (Lieutenant Robert D. Thorburn) arrived during the summer, the squadron could not undertake any operations that would involve all its ships. It could scrape together from among the various vessels enough supplies to keep one or two of their number cruising on blockade in the Gulf of California, but that was all that could be done.

Another source of concern to the American commanders in the Pacific was the fact that the nearest Admiralty Courts were on the Atlantic coast and, besides being almost impossible to send prizes around Cape Horn to have their legality adjudicated, it was not worthwhile to do so. In an attempt to solve this problem, General Kearny, in his capacity of governor of California, established the Admiralty Court of the Territory of California on 24 March 1847, and appointed Chaplain Walter Colton as judge. Later, however, the Supreme Court of the United States ruled that, not having been established by act of Congress, the court was not legally constituted.

Since the beginning of November, when Commander Du Pont had been forced to sail the *Cyane* to San Francisco for supplies, the demands of the Los Angeles campaign had made it impossible to send any American naval vessel to the Gulf of California. On 14 November, while on her way north from Callao, the sloop *Dale* had touched at Mazatlán, but when her captain found that there were then no American warships in the Gulf, he went on to San Francisco.

Unaware that his replacement, Commodore Shubrick, had arrived in California, on 2 February Stockton ordered Commander Montgomery in the *Portsmouth* to re-establish the blockade at Mazatlán and, when that had been accomplished, to raise the American flag at San José del Cabo, La Paz, Pichilinque, and Loreto, all in Baja California. The *Portsmouth* rounded Cape San Lucas, Baja California, on 14 February, and three days later appeared off Mazatlán. When Montgomery notified the Mexican authorities there that the port was under blockade, Commander Sir Baldwin Walker, captain of the British sloop *Constance*, lodged a strong protest: he claimed, with considerable justification, that the blockade was a paper one and, moreover, had been interrupted. Montgomery rejected the protest, and set about enforcing the blockade. While the *Portsmouth* was on station off Mazatlán, her tender, the *Loben Eliza*, captured the Mexican schooner *Magdalena*.

When the ship-of-the-line *Columbus*, wearing the pennant of the new commander of the Pacific Squadron, anchored at Monterey on 2 March, Commodore Biddle immediately took over from Commodore Shubrick. One of his first acts as commander was to withdraw Stockton's blockade proclamation, except as it applied to Mazatlán and Guaymas, and to order the *Cyane* to the Gulf of California with new blockade instructions. She left San Francisco on 7 March and, ten days later, in accordance with earlier instructions, Biddle ordered Captain Mervine to take the *Savannah* home, but to stop first at San Diego and offer passage to Commodore Stockton. The offer was declined and Stockton stayed in California until 20 June, when he went home by an overland route.

After maintaining the blockade of Mazatlán for more than a month, Commander Montgomery prepared to carry out his mission across the Gulf of California in Baja California. On 25 March the *Portsmouth* headed for San José del Cabo, at the tip of the peninsula, and at noon, four days later, anchored in the roadstead off that port. Montgomery promptly sent his executive officer, Lieutenant John S. Missroon, ashore to deliver a demand for the surrender of both the town and district. Although the Council of San José refused to accede to the demand, Lieutenant Benjamin F. B. Hunter and 140 men, who were landed the next morning, 30 March, met with no resistance and, shortly after noon, while a twenty-one-gun salute was fired by the *Portsmouth*, the American flag was run up over the town. By daybreak next morning, the entire landing party was re-embarked, Montgomery having decided not to leave a garrison in town.

The *Portsmouth* stayed off San José until 2 April, when she stood down the peninsula for the little village of San Lucas. The following afternoon, the Marine detachment in the *Portsmouth* went ashore and hoisted the American flag, while Montgomery announced by proclamation that he was taking possession of the village and the district. Again deciding not to leave a garrison, Montgomery returned to San José where, on 7 April, the *Portsmouth* encountered the American ship *Admittance*, and seized her on the grounds that she was trading with the enemy.

Heading back up the Gulf coast of the peninsula, the *Portsmouth* arrived about midmorning on 13 April off La Paz, the capital of the state of Baja California and the only place on the peninsula that qualified as a town. Following what had become his standard procedure, Commander Montgomery sent Lieutenant Missroon ashore to demand the town's surrender. Colonel Miranda, the collaborationist governor of the state who, in September, had protested Commander Du Pont's seizure of ships in the harbor of La Paz, complied with the demand, and the following day the American flag was hoisted to the reverberations of a twenty-one-gun salute.

The articles of capitulation that were signed at La Paz followed closely those of the Treaty of Cahuenga drawn up by Frémont, but they went further in providing for the continuance in office of the civil officials and in granting to the *Bajacalifornios* the rights and privileges of U.S. citizens. Together with a proclamation issued later by Commodore Shubrick announcing that Baja California would be annexed to the United States, the articles of capitulation were responsible for a number of *Bajacalifornios* collaborating with the United States.

During the night of 22 April, the sloop *Cyane*, sailing for the Gulf on Commodore Biddle's orders, rounded Cape San Lucas, and on the morning of the twenty-third joined the *Portsmouth* off San José. Commander Du Pont conferred with Montgomery, then headed the *Cyane* for Mazatlán, where she arrived on 27 April. Two days later, Commodore Shubrick also arrived there in the *Independence*. He came specifically to issue the new blockade notice necessitated by the proclamation Biddle had made in March. On 30 April two armed boats from the *Independence* caused quite a commotion ashore when they set out to reconnoiter Mazatlán's old harbor. A passenger in one of the boats described what happened: "Not perceiving any bustle or stir pervading the town, we pulled warily in, until, on passing out from the cover of the corvette's [*Cyane*'s] guns, we unconsciously raised the most infernal din imaginable. Drums rattled incessantly, dirty soldiers formed into companies; the Governor and suite attended by a guard of cavalry galloped up and down the beach. Consuls ran up their flags, women and children ran up the hills, all evidently . . . at the anticipation of a hostile invasion." So real was the alarm that the Mexicans brought artillery to bear on the American boats, which then discreetly returned to their mother ship.

Shubrick left Mazatlán for San Francisco in the *Independence* on 3 June and, since the *Portsmouth* had gone to Monterey, the *Cyane* was then the only American warship left in the Gulf. Apparently in an effort to maintain the blockade at both Mazatlán and San José, Du Pont sailed her back and forth between the two ports. Meanwhile, on 8 June, Biddle sent the *Portsmouth* back to the Gulf and when she arrived at San José on the morning of 20 June, Montgomery was suprised to find the *Cyane* in port, and ordered her to return immediately to Mazatlán. However, her departure was delayed until 22 June, and the *Portsmouth* got there before she did.

Disturbed that the blockade of Mazatlán had been interrupted by the *Cyane*'s absence at San José, Montgomery discussed the matter with Du Pont, and it was decided that the former should return to San Francisco for instructions. He sailed in the *Portsmouth* on 28 June and, since the status of the blockade was in doubt, the *Cyane* left on the same day to resupply in Hawaii.

In May 1847, when General Kearny was at Monterey preparing to turn over his command in California to Colonel Robert B. Mason and to return to the United States, he received Secretary Marcy's instruction of 11 January directing that at least one port in Baja California should be occupied. Consequently, he ordered Lieutenant Colonel Henry S. Burton and two companies of the New York Volunteers to establish garrisons at either La Paz or San José, or at both. He completed the transfer of his command and of the governorship of California to Colonel Mason on 31 May and, by the time Companies A and B of the New York Volunteers, embarked in the storeship *Lexington,* sailed from Santa Barbara on 4 July, he had left the territory.

Kearny went home by an overland route. In company with Frémont, he set out from Sutter's Fort on 16 June, but it was not until they reached St. Louis on 25 August that he informed his companion of his intention to prefer charges against him. Frémont found himself summoned before a court-martial that convened in Washington, and convicted, among other things, of failing to obey the orders of a superior officer—General Kearny. Although extenuating circumstances can be argued in his defense, there can be no question of Frémont's guilt, nor can there be any question that Kearny gained no stature by not telling Frémont what he intended to do until they reached St. Louis. Even in 1846, Frémont undoubtedly had aspirations beyond a career in the Army, and his actions in California were characteristic of a man who has carefully canvassed the field, then backed the commander— the politically powerful Commodore Stockton—whose later support and appreciation would be most advantageous.

Commodore Shubrick was extremely unhappy with his assignment to the Pacific, as well he might have been. Less than six weeks after he had taken command of the squadron, Biddle had arrived to replace him, and he had been relegated to the role of a junior commodore. On 7 May, Secretary Mason had written to tell him that he would be relieved by Commodore Thomas ap Catesby Jones but, not in receipt of that letter, on 1 June Shubrick wrote Mason asking to be relieved. However, Commodore Biddle's orders gave him the authority to return home when, in his opinion, his presence in California was no longer needed. By July, Biddle had come to the conclusion that such was the case and, there being little need in California for a vessel the size of the *Columbus*, on the 19th of the month he returned command of the Pacific Squadron to Shubrick.

Biddle sailed for home six days later, leaving Shubrick free to carry out the operations he had outlined to Secretary Mason on 15 June: leaving the now unseaworthy *Warren* and one of the other sloops or the *Congress* to protect California, about 1 November he would sail in the *Independence* to the Gulf of California, where he would extend the blockade to Guaymas— he did not then know about the *Cyane* breaking the blockade at Mazatlán— then go south and seize Mazatlán, San Blas, and Acapulco.

On 21 July the *Lexington* anchored about two miles off La Paz, and Colonel Burton and the New York Volunteers embarked in the ship's boats and were rowed towards the shore. About three-quarters of a mile from the beach, they jumped into the four-foot-deep water and, carrying their arms and equipment over their shoulders, waded the rest of the way. Once on land, they formed for the march to the barracks but, either because they were given wrong directions or because they misunderstood the directions they were given, they found themselves in the cemetery instead. That was the only mishap encountered, and the post that Burton established without any opposition from the 500 to 600 inhabitants of the town of flat-roofed, adobe houses remained the chief American post in the area until the end of the war.

Three days after Montgomery arrived at San Francisco in the *Portsmouth* on 3 August with the news of the interruption of the blockade at Mazatlán, Shubrick issued a new proclamation announcing the forthcoming blockade of that port, Guaymas, and San Blas. There would be no need to station ships on blockade duty at those three ports, however, until the fall because during the summer months they were effectively closed, anyway, by hurricanes. So, when Captain Elie A. F. La Vallette, the new captain of the *Congress*, was ordered on 10 August to proceed to the coast of Mexico with his ship, the *Portsmouth*, and the *Dale* (Commander Thomas O. Selfridge), his mission was commerce destruction. By 10 October, the Commodore promised, he would leave San Francisco in the *Independence* (Lieutenant

The sloop *Dale* bombards Mulejé.
Franklin D. Roosevelt Library, Hyde Park, New York

Richard L. Page) and, with the rest of the squadron, would sail south and join La Vallette's fleet off Cape San Lucas.

On their way south from San Francisco, the vessels under Captain La Vallette's command put in to Monterey and, from there, proceeded to the coast of Mexico. The *Portsmouth* left Monterey on 4 September, and the *Congress* and the *Dale* left four days later, but they all arrived at San José on the same day, 19 September. While the *Congress* stayed at San José, the *Portsmouth* headed for Mazatlán, and the *Dale* for La Paz. When Commander Selfridge reached his destination, Colonel Burton told him that sentiment at Loreto and Mulejé was strongly pro-Mexican and asked him to investigate. Selfridge sailed the *Dale* up the coast and she anchored off Loreto on the evening of 28 September. All was quiet there, but when it was learned that two hundred men, arms, and ammunition had recently been sent from Guaymas to Mulejé, Selfridge went on up the coast.

Hoping it would help him to learn the true state of affairs at Mulejé, he decided to run in under English colors, and that he did on 30 September. Soon after midday, Lieutenant Tunis Augustus Macdonough Craven tried to go ashore but a party of Mexicans threatened to fire if his boat attempted to enter the creek that led to the village. Forced to return to the *Dale*, he then suggested that several boats go in and seize the schooner *Magdalen*, which he had seen lying aground about half a mile up the creek. Selfridge agreed to the proposal, and swung the *Dale* around to cover the creek. Craven and fifty men embarked in four boats, and rowed to the schooner. After some difficulty, they managed to get her afloat, then towed her out to the *Dale*, but when it was found that she had been stripped and was useless, she was burned.

On the morning of 1 October, Commander Selfridge sent a messenger ashore with a demand that the village preserve neutrality and abstain from intercourse with Mexico during the war and surrender all arms and other public property. While waiting for a reply, Selfridge worked the *Dale* closer inshore to a point from which she could command the creek and the valley through which it ran for two miles and, on the recommendation of a council of war, ordered seventeen Marines and fifty-seven sailors to prepare boats and be ready to land. He also ordered Passed Midshipman James M. Duncan to prepare the launch and her 9-pounder. Shortly after noon, the reply was delivered: Captain Manuel Pineda, the local commander, said that not only did the *Bajacalifornios* refuse to remain neutral but, before long, they would recapture La Paz. "This port," boasted Pineda, "with its valiant soldiers who have their instructions, will defend itself, and they will maintain their arms until the last drop of blood has been shed."

As soon as this message was received, Craven, the waiting landing party, and Duncan clambered into their boats and pulled for the creek. As they entered it, at about two o'clock, the *Dale* opened fire. She fired sporadically at long range for about ninety minutes, then had to cease because the boats got into her line of fire. In those ninety minutes, however, she had forced Pineda to abandon his defenses before the town, as well as a strong position atop a hill on the right bank of the creek, about 3,000 yards from the ship.

While Duncan stayed in the launch to lend gun support, Craven and his men landed on the right bank of the creek and began advancing up the valley. Before they had gone far, they were fired upon from a house and thicket on their left, and Craven promptly ordered the house burned. They made for the hill which the *Dale*'s fire had forced the Mexicans to abandon and just after they reached it, the Mexicans opened fire from the left bank, and two men were wounded. Counterfire from the landing party soon put the Mexicans to flight. Leaving a few men to hold the hill, Craven and the rest of the men pushed ahead for another half-mile, where they came to a bridge across the creek. There, Craven called a halt and decided to go no farther because the creek threatened to get shallower and the launch, having already grounded several times, was having a hard time keeping up with the men ashore. Furthermore, it was getting late and the men were exhausted from the 90-degree heat. They marched back to their boats and, by early evening, all were back in the *Dale*. Little had been accomplished

Sailors and Marines from the *Dale* go ashore at Loreto.
Franklin D. Roosevelt Library, Hyde Park, New York

by this expedition, which was not successful even in setting fire to a small, rotten, abandoned sloop it found up the creek.

The next morning Selfridge decided that, in view of the threatening weather, it would be risky to renew the attack, and he headed the *Dale* down the Gulf for Loreto and La Paz.

Both sides claimed victory at Mulejé, but the Mexican claim probably had more substance because Selfridge had not achieved his purpose in going there—to cut communications between that village and Guaymas. More-over, the fighting spirit of the *Bajacalifornios* had been aroused.

When the *Dale* put in to Loreto on 5 October Selfridge landed Marines and a company of sailors to make a show of strength, and they returned to the ship with two brass 4-pounders, a swivel gun, a musket, and three lances. Four days later, she was back at La Paz where a similar show was made, the object apparently being to strengthen the position of Colonel Burton's small garrison.

Selfridge and Burton decided that communications between Mulejé and Guaymas must be severed, so the naval commander chartered the schooner *Libertad* for seven dollars a day, placed one of the *Dale*'s 9-pounder launch guns aboard her, and sent her north under Lieutenant Craven.

On 17 October, as the *Congress*, up from San José, lay in the outer roads at Guaymas, the *Portsmouth* came up from Mazatlán and dropped anchor near her and the *Argo*, a Chilean-flag brigantine that had been seized by the *Portsmouth*. The following afternoon, Captain La Vallette of the *Congress* sent Lieutenant Fabius Stanly and John Robinson, erstwhile American Consul at Guaymas, ashore to suggest to Colonel Antonio Campuzano, commander of the 400-man garrison, that he surrender. When the Colonel refused even to consider such a suggestion, preparations were made for action in the event that a formal demand for surrender would be likewise refused. In the evening, one of the *Congress'* 32-pounders was landed on Isla Almagre Grande, a position from which it controlled the harbor, and the *Argo* was stationed off the island to protect the gun.

Before daylight next morning, the preparations were resumed. The *Portsmouth* was towed into position in the inner harbor by her own boats, and five hours later at 10:30, the *Congress* was on her assigned station. About noontime, Montgomery was rowed ashore from the *Congress* to deliver the formal demand for the surrender of "all the forts and fortified places in and about the town of Guaymas, together with all the cannon, small arms, munitions of war, and other public property contained therein."

As he had done the day before with the informal demand, Campuzano promptly turned down the formal one. Whereupon Montgomery, having been empowered to do so, told him that no action would be taken against the town for two hours, so that women and children could be evacuated. Campuzano countered with the request that he be allowed five hours' grace, and Montgomery granted the extension because he did not think it could be used for any significant strengthening of the town's defenses. At the expiration of the time, Campuzano delivered his final statement of refusal, but by then it was 5:20 in the afternoon and La Vallette decided to delay action until the next morning.

At 6:15 on the morning of 20 October, preparatory to putting the landing party ashore, the *Congress* began bombarding the port, and within a few minutes the *Portsmouth* followed suit. The cannonade from the two vessels set fire to several houses and killed one person. When it had been going on for more than an hour and almost five hundred rounds had been fired, a white flag appeared on shore. The *Congress* responded with a signal for the captain of the port to come out to her. Within the hour, that official came on board carrying a letter signed by J. V. Sandoval, a member of the *ayuntamiento*, and informing La Vallette that Guaymas had been evacuated by the military during the night. Campuzano had no heavy artillery with which to oppose the landing, and the Americans later discovered that he had withdrawn to the barracks at Bocachicacampo, four miles up the coast, where he had fourteen guns.

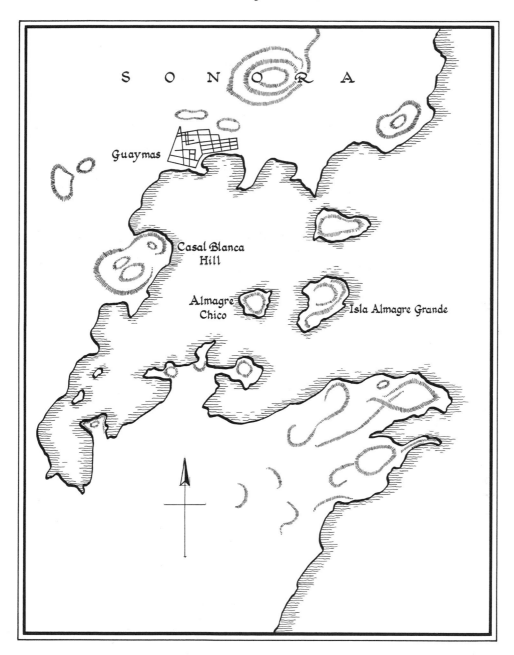

GUAYMAS AND ITS HARBOR

Commander Selfridge is wounded at
Casal Blanca Hill, Guaymas.
Franklin D. Roosevelt Library, Hyde Park, New York

By early afternoon Marines from the two American vessels had landed and the American flag was flying over the fort on Casal Blanca Hill, near the pier. La Vallette then proclaimed the conquest of Guaymas and its precincts, and the removal from office of all federal officials. However, he invited local authorities to continue in office on condition that they agreed to warn the Americans if Mexican troops should approach, and to report daily to the American commander: should they fail in either of these requirements, the penalty would be bombardment. In return, the port of Guaymas was opened for trade under the supervision of a collector appointed by the Americans. Duties were established at five cents per ton and fifteen per cent *ad valorem*. After issuing the proclamation and making a search for munitions, the landing party hauled down the flag and re-embarked.

Most of the several thousand townspeople had fled inland from Guaymas before the landing, and the foreign traders and others who had stayed in town were allowed, after the landing, to move up the coast because Campuzano had cut off Guaymas' water and food supplies. The day after the landing, 21 October, a party of Marines and sailors went ashore again to destroy the town's fortifications, and the day after that, a party from the

216

Portsmouth landed to make another search for arms, and returned with sixteen pistols. After noon on 23 October, La Vallette, having instructed Montgomery in the *Portsmouth* to keep watch over the port until the *Dale* came up from La Paz to relieve him, departed in the *Congress*. On 27 October, the *Portsmouth* captured a Mexican schooner, the *Caroline*, off Guaymas.

Guaymas presented the Americans with an unusual situation. As Commodore Shubrick reported on 27 November, the vessel stationed there "can do nothing more than keep the flag flying on an island under the cover of her guns." Because the town was open on the land side to the infiltrating type of attack at which the Mexicans were so adept, the Americans never did attempt to garrison it. A large garrison could, undoubtedly, have handled any attack the Mexicans might have launched, but men to provide such a garrison could not be spared. On the other hand, an American vessel lying in the harbor and an American gun on Isla Almagre Grande were sufficient to guarantee that the town could not be used by the Mexicans. By the end of the war, there was not a house in Guaymas that had not been damaged by the struggles for possession of the town.

The *Dale* arrived at Guaymas on 8 November, having left La Paz five days earlier, and on the ninth the *Portsmouth* left to return to Mazatlán. No sooner had Commander Selfridge arrived on his new station than he was faced with Mexican efforts to reoccupy the town. The very day the *Portsmouth* left, he learned that large numbers of Mexican troops had infiltrated the town during the preceding night, apparently in hopes of taking by surprise any Americans who might land. However, four cannonballs fired into the town by the *Dale* drove them away and later attempts at infiltration were similarly dealt with.

Intending to make a show of force before issuing a new proclamation extolling the advantages of American occupation, Selfridge, with seventeen Marines, fifty seamen, and a 6-pounder boat gun, went ashore on the afternoon of 17 November. They got as far as the fort on Casal Blanca Hill, when they were fired on by a force of Mexicans estimated to be 250 strong. In the first exchange of fire, Selfridge was seriously wounded and the command of the shore party devolved on Lieutenant William Taylor Smith. Until they succeeded in getting a message through to the *Dale* and she opened fire, the Americans were pinned down in the fort, but the sloop's fire soon drove the Mexicans out of town and the landing party returned to the ship without further loss. American claims to have inflicted thirty to forty casualties upon the Mexicans were undoubtedly exaggerated.

Soon after that incident, the threat to Guaymas eased, as desertions and a lack of supplies took their toll of Campuzano's force. The *Dale* remained off Guaymas until 23 December, when the *Southampton* came in to replace

A launch from the *Dale* fires on the
Mexican camp at Bocachicacampo.
Franklin D. Roosevelt Library, Hyde Park, New York

her, but hardly more than a month later, on 27 January 1848, she was back
at her accustomed anchorage.

Two days after the *Dale* returned to Guaymas, Lieutenant Edward M.
Yard, who had replaced the wounded Selfridge as her captain, heard that a
Mexican detachment at Cochori, about eight miles east of the town, on a
large shallow bay called La Laguna, was threatening the Indians from whom
the Americans were getting fresh provisions. He decided to make a surprise
descent on the village. Before dawn on the morning of 30 January, Lieutenant Craven, who in October had taken the *Libertad* on a fruitless mission to
Mulejé, two companies of seamen, and a detachment of twelve Marines
embarked in the *Dale*'s boats and stealthily made their way across La Laguna.
About three miles south of Cochori, they landed.

Craven's plan was to attack from three sides simultaneously: Lieutenant
Stanly and one company of seamen would circle round the hamlet and
attack it from the north; Sergeant D. D. Ramsdell and the Marines would
attack from the eastern, or inland, side; and Craven and the other company
of seamen would attack from the south; the launch with her 6-pounder
would lie off the waterfront to provide support, if needed.

As Stanly's men entered the hamlet, they were discovered by a sentinel and he fired at them. At the sound of the shot, all three groups of Americans charged, and the defenders were routed. Fifteen Mexicans, including the commander, Captain Mendoza, the captain of the port, Lieutenant Zaavidra, and their mistresses were captured: three were killed, and five wounded. A bugle, twenty muskets, five hundred ball cartridges, a stand of colors, and other equipment fell into American hands. As the morning watch ended, Craven and his men re-embarked in their boats, and two hours later were back on board the *Dale*.

On 12 February Lieutenant Yard sent a similar expedition under Lieutenant Stanly to break up what was left of Colonel Campuzano's camp at Bocachicacampo. Because the barracks there stood on a stony mountain spur facing west and the terrain offered no cover for an attacking force, Stanly decided that the only thing to do was to creep as close as possible without being detected, then rush the barracks at the first challenge.

Shortly after midnight on 13 February, he and about sixty seamen and Marines went ashore at Guaymas and, after separating into three groups, they all headed for Bocachicacampo. They converged on their target from the northwest, southwest, and west, and as soon as a challenge rang out, they charged from all three directions. Under the pressure of the attack, the Mexicans, abandoning most of their arms and equipment, fled. A week later, Lieutenant Stanly returned with nineteen men from the *Libertad* and demolished the barracks.

The last of the fighting in the area of Guaymas took place on 9 April. On that date, Lieutenant Stanly and a small detachment landed at the estuary of the Soldado River and marched inland for twelve miles to spike three guns. On their way back to their boats, they were engaged in a brief skirmish with some Mexicans, and claimed to have killed one and wounded three of them: two Americans were wounded.

Late that month, the armistice preceding the Treaty of Guadalupe Hidalgo went into effect in the Gulf of California and on 24 June 1848, Guaymas was returned to Mexican control.

XVIII

MAZATLÁN AND BAJA CALIFORNIA

Early in August 1847, when Commodore W. Branford Shubrick had ordered the *Congress*, the *Portsmouth*, and the *Dale* to the coast of Mexico, he had promised Captain La Vallette that he and the rest of the squadron would leave San Francisco by 10 October and would join La Vallette off Cape San Lucas. He left on 9 September and the next day, at Monterey, he notified Colonel Robert B. Mason, who at the end of May had replaced General Kearny as Army commander in California, that he intended to go south to conduct an active campaign in the Gulf of California during the fall and winter of 1847, and asked the Colonel if he would need any naval vessels for the defense of Alta California. Mason replied that he thought it would be wise to leave one vessel in Californian waters, and reciprocated by offering Shubrick the use of any of the garrison at La Paz that could be spared by Lieutenant Colonel Henry Burton, Army commander in Baja California.

After issuing orders for the *Southampton* to take on stores at San Francisco, Shubrick embarked in the *Independence* and, with the *Cyane* and the *Erie*, left Monterey on 16 October to keep his rendezvous with La Vallette. On the way, the *Erie* became separated from her companions and was not with them when they arrived off Cape San Lucas on 27 October, only to find that the *Congress* was not there. A calm that lasted two days prevented them from immediately going in search of her. However, they got under way and made San José del Cabo on 29 October, falling in with the *Congress* that same day.

San José, according to Henry A. Wise, a lieutenant in the *Independence*, "stands in a pretty valley, with red, sterile mountains topping around it. One broad street courses between two rows of cane and mud-built dwellings, thatched with straws. . . . At the upper end of the avenue, standing on a slight, though abrupt, elevation from the valley behind, was the cuartel [barracks]. . . ."

The Commodore had hardly arrived at San José when he learned from a spy that "some revolutionary movements" were going on near Todos Santos on the Pacific coast of the peninsula. Late on 1 November Lieutenant Montgomery Lewis and twenty-eight men left San José to investigate the report and, after a hard march, reached Todos Santos the next morning, but the Mexicans had been warned of what was afoot and had disappeared by the time Lewis got there. After being entertained by Padre Gabriel González, one of the Mexican leaders, Lewis and his men returned to San José on 7 November. The "revolutionary movements" were, in fact, preparations for an attack that was to be made on La Paz.

While Lewis was away, Shubrick issued a proclamation, dated 4 November, announcing that active operations were about to begin in Baja California and that the United States intended to retain possession of the territory when the war was over. He hoped that the prospect of their country belonging to the United States would encourage the *Bajacalifornios* to support the American cause, and many of them, accepting the truth of the statement, did lend assistance to the Americans. At the end of the war, many of those who had so collaborated, had to leave with the American forces, in order to escape the wrath of their more patriotic neighbors.

There seems to have been a difference of opinion between Colonel Burton, on the one hand, and Shubrick and La Vallette, on the other, both as to the gravity of the threat of revolution and as to how to handle it. At a meeting between Shubrick and Burton, held at San José, the latter said that although a large-scale uprising appeared to be imminent, he hoped his one hundred and ten men would be able to cope with it. He pointed out, however, that under the circumstances, he would not be able to spare any of his men for Shubrick's operations at Guaymas and Mazatlán. Furthermore, he protested, if the *Dale* were to be sent to Guaymas, his forces would be left without any close naval support.

Shubrick and La Vallette took a less serious view of the threat: the former did not think the *Bajacalifornios* would be able to take either La Paz or San José del Cabo, and the latter was of the opinion that the "organization of an insurrection in that quarter [Baja California] had been broken up." Even so, there was, in the opinion of the two naval officers, little the *Dale* could do either at La Paz or San José to stamp out the revolutionary movement, whereas if its supply base, Guaymas, were effectively blockaded, its forces could be eliminated. The detachment of the *Dale* to support Burton's force would weaken the blockade.

There was validity in both positions. The presence of the *Dale* would, undoubtedly, have shortened the sieges of La Paz and San José, but in retrospect,

W. BRANFORD SHUBRICK

it must be concluded that, since both ports withstood siege anyway, Commodore Shubrick made the correct decision when he sent the *Dale* to Guaymas.

Shubrick assigned four officers and twenty Marines under Lieutenant Charles Heywood to garrison San José, and instructed Heywood to preserve order and discipline, and to keep his men confined to quarters as much as possible, in order to avoid friction with the populace. The garrison, with supplies for thirty days, seventy-five muskets, with which to arm friendly natives, and a 9-pounder carronade, was landed on 8 November and took up its quarters in the small cuartel, an old mission building, situated as described above by Henry Wise. Having landed the garrison, the *Independence*, the *Congress*, and the *Cyane* left San José late in the day, and sailed for Mazatlán.

The most thriving port on the west coast of Mexico and second only to Veracruz in the republic, Mazatlán is situated in the triangular space formed by three hills. To the south, bluffs and islands provide protection for the anchorage called Puerto Nuevo (New Harbor), while to the north there is safe anchorage for small vessels in Puerto Viejo (Old Harbor). East and west of the town, the shoreline consists of curving, sandy beaches, and some of the best buildings in a town of good houses stood on a patch of sand to the west known as Olas Altas (High Waves), because of the surf breaking

THE HARBOR AT MAZATLÁN

there. When the three American warships arrived off Mazatlán on the evening of 10 November, the town's garrison of 560 men was commanded by Colonel Rafael Telles, whom Justin H. Smith called "a happy-go-lucky insurgent of convivial tastes, oriental convictions on the subject of seraglios, and aboriginal ideas touching honor."

The *Congress* anchored in Puerto Viejo which, though a hazardous shelter for a vessel of her size, commanded the roads leading into the town as well as a beach behind the town that might be used for landings; the *Cyane* worked her way into Puerto Nuevo where, because of her light draft, she was able to anchor within range of the wharf; and the *Independence* dropped anchor so close to Olas Altas that her stern nearly rested in the surf. Telles realized that he would not be able to defend the port against this imposing force and, during the night, he withdrew inland to Palos Prietos. While he was evacuating the town, the American squadron was busy launching its boats, readying its guns, and bringing ammunition up on deck.

Early next morning, 11 November, the *Independence* hoisted her colors with a white flag at the fore, and Captain La Vallette, Lieutenant Henry H. Lewis, Lieutenant Henry W. Halleck, U.S. Army Corps of Engineers, who had been loaned by Colonel Mason and had accompanied the Commodore from California, and the Commodore's secretary, Henri la Reintrie, left the flagship and went ashore to deliver a surrender demand. The civil officials of Mazatlán replied that they had no voice in decisions on surrender and, since the town and port had been evacuated by the military, requested that the four-hour limit attached to the demand be extended to allow them time to intercede with the military to prevent hostilities. Taking the president of the *ayuntamiento* with them, the Americans returned to the *Independence*, and some two hours later, at ten o'clock, Telles, by then safely encamped at Palos Prietos, sent word that he had no intention of surrendering.

At noon, the period of grace having expired, the *Independence* hauled down the flag of truce, and the ships prepared a landing party. During the morning, the *Erie*, which had become separated from the flagship and the *Cyane* on the way to Cape San Lucas, had come in, and her men took part in the landing. La Vallette and 730 men embarked in 29 boats, and less than two hours after the flag of truce had been hauled down, they had landed in three divisions and hoisted the American flag over the port of Mazatlán to the accompaniment of a twenty-one-gun salute from the *Independence*. One hundred rifles and muskets, some saddles, and a few pieces of artillery were found in the barracks and seized.

The regulations which Shubrick promptly laid down for the handling of relations between his military government and the townspeople were substantially the same as the clauses of the articles of capitulation. They imposed a moderate tariff, allowed all goods to be freely exported, and mercury to be freely imported; they promised freedom of religion; and forbade the sale of liquor to American personnel; they gave assurance that, so long as the laws were respected, there would be no interference with the normal life of the town, but cautioned the Mexicans that any insurrection would be punished according to the laws of war.

Commodore Shubrick appointed Captain La Vallette military governor of Mazatlán and gave him command of a 400-man garrison. Lieutenant Halleck laid out fortifications: a circular redoubt on a steep hill overlooking the harbor; a battery on La Garita, a hill to the north of the town, guarding the main land approach; and a barracks north of the town. Telles hovered about the neighborhood but, having only from 500 to 800 men, he did not dare attack the town. On 14 November, he shifted his base from Palos Prietos to the Presidio of Mazatlán, about 12 miles due west of town, and from there he sent out cavalry patrols to intimidate the natives and keep them from supplying the American forces. Two days after Telles moved his camp, Shubrick asked Major General Winfield Scott in Mexico City for between 500 and 1,000 men to garrison Mazatlán. Scott replied on 2 December that he had none to spare but that, if and when he received enough reinforcements to allow him to do so, he would send a garrison. That did not happen.

When La Vallette heard that Telles had sent a 90-man advance force under a Swiss lieutenant, Carlos Horn, to Urias, about ten miles from Mazatlán, on the road to San Sebastián, he sent Lieutenant George L. Selden and ninety-four sailors to clear the road. Lieutenant Halleck, the Army engineer, went with Selden. A second force under Lieutenant Stephen C. Rowan embarked in boats and ascended the *estero*, or large, shallow bay, that ran inland beyond Puerto Nuevo, in the hopes of cutting the Mexicans' line of retreat.

Selden and his men left Mazatlán shortly after midnight on 20 November. Except for a brief skirmish with a Mexican outpost about one mile from Urias, their march was uneventful and they took their assigned position near the village. Rowan's men, having failed to find the road, disembarked slightly east of Urias and, at dawn, opened fire on the Mexicans. As the latter formed to answer the threat, Selden's men fell upon their flank and threw them into confusion. Rowan pursued the fleeing enemy but could not intercept them, and the Americans had to be content with capturing the Mexican baggage. One American was killed and twenty were wounded, while four Mexicans were killed and it is not known how many were wounded.

After that, only two more skirmishes of any significance took place in the area of Mazatlán. On the night of 12 December, Lieutenant Montgomery Lewis and a party of forty-three men, who were scouting for Telles' cavalry patrols, surprised a group of Mexicans about ten miles from town and put them to flight, and the following night Lieutenant William W. Russell, U.S. Marine Corps, and twenty Marines had a similar experience with some Mexicans they found at Palos Prietos.

By 21 February 1848, the fortifications that Lieutenant Halleck had laid out at Mazatlán the previous November had been completed and a garrison of 400 or 500 men behind them could withstand any attack the Mexicans might launch. But the Mexican force in the area was continually dwindling and, aside from making harassing raids intended to cut off American supplies, it made no attempt to attack Mazatlán.

While Commodore Shubrick was consolidating his position at Mazatlán, an anti-American movement was gathering strength in Baja California. A revolt in Mulejé overthrew the state's collaborationist governor, Colonel Miranda, and replaced him with Mauricio Castro. Captain Manuel Pineda, who at the beginning of October had defied Commander Selfridge when he went in to Mulejé in the *Dale*, had trained an army to dispute the American hold on Baja California. He was an able organizer and, by 1 November, having received a fresh supply of arms from Sonora, he was ready to take the offensive. His headquarters were at San Antonio, some thirty miles south of La Paz and, from there, he planned to attack both the capital city, La Paz, and San José del Cabo.

His first attempt to take La Paz began before daylight on 11 November. He and some 120 of his men forced their way into the town, but were repulsed by the American artillery. A second attempt was made on 17 November, but it was no more successful than the first, and Pineda withdrew to La Laguna, about six miles away. During the attacks, one American was killed and two wounded, while four or five Mexicans were killed and as many wounded.

Two days later, Pineda made his move on San José. About 150 men under Vicente Mejía, José Matías Moreno, and Lieutenant José Antonio Mijares of the Mexican Navy, moved into town and presented Lieutenant Heywood, commander of the small American garrison, with a demand for surrender. When the demand was refused, they encamped on La Somita, a small hill about 350 yards behind the old mission building where the garrison was quartered. The building was in a good defensive position on high ground at the north end of San José, but it was falling apart: when Lieutenant Heywood and his men had moved into it, they had had to prop up the roof with timbers to keep it from falling in and, except for the main entrance, they had had to fill in the doors and windows with masonry, in which they had made loopholes. However, some of Heywood's officers and Marines, along with twenty friendly *Bajacalifornios* who had come in for protection during the siege, were posted in a well-built house that stood in front of the mission and guarded that approach to it.

That night, 19 November, the Mexicans attempted to rush both the mission and the house in front of it, but were beaten off, and two of them were killed and "a number" wounded: three Americans were wounded. The next night they tried again, this time attacking from the front and the rear, but a few musket shots, one of which killed Lieutenant Mijares, dispersed them. On the morning of 21 November, they saw two vessels on the horizon standing in for San José and, assuming them to be warships coming to the relief of the American garrison, they abandoned the siege and withdrew. Later in the day, the vessels anchored off the town and proved to be two whalers, the *Magnolia* and the *Edward*.

The whalers stayed a while at San José and their captains did everything in their power to help Heywood and the garrison. They agreed to take the women and children of the town aboard their vessels, should the Mexicans make another attack, and, on one occasion, when it looked as though an attack was imminent, they landed their crews to strengthen the garrison. There were not enough firearms to go around, so some of the men from the whalers were prepared to use their harpoons.

During the evening of 24 November, a launch bearing news of what had happened at San José reached Mazatlán. Within an hour, Commodore Shubrick had the storeship *Southampton* loaded with men, ammunition, and provisions, and towed out of the harbor on her way to San José with orders to stay there as long as she was needed. When she got there on 26 November and landed two guns, twenty-six men, and provisions, the *Magnolia* and the *Edward* went on their way.

After being forced to withdraw from San José, the Mexican force under Mejía and Moreno rejoined Pineda, bringing his army up to 350 men, as against Colonel Burton's garrison at La Paz of 112, so he decided to attack that town once again. On the afternoon of 27 November, his troops rushed the town, but were severely mauled by Burton's New Yorkers. That was the last attempt Pineda made to recapture the capital, but he remained in the offing until 8 December, when the *Cyane* arrived off the port and he withdrew to San Antonio. Rumors of his return persisted for a month, however, and several times the *Cyane* landed detachments to reinforce the garrison.

On 1 December, the *Portsmouth*, which was scheduled to return to the United States, was ordered, first, to join the *Southhampton* at San José. She came in two days later and, so long as there was a naval vessel in port, the town was safe from further attack.

Shubrick's plans for the deployment of his vessels were disrupted by the uprising in Baja California. Instead of sending the *Cyane* to blockade San Blas, as he had intended to do, he had to send her to La Paz and leave the *Whiton*, a bark and tender to the *Independence*, to keep up the semblance of a blockade off San Blas until the *Lexington* arrived from California. Even so, the substitution of the storeship *Lexington* for the *Cyane* was not wholly satisfactory, for although the former was armed, she was not a regular warship.

Not until 11 January 1848 did the *Lexington* join the *Whiton* off San Blas, but the very next morning Lieutenant Frederick Chatard of the *Whiton* set about the mission with which he had been entrusted—to dismantle Mexican defenses along the Pacific coast. With forty-seven men from the two vessels, he went ashore and, after landing at the customhouse, led thirty of the men to the fortress Castillo de la Entrada, about a mile away. They removed the fortress' guns and carried them down to the shore, only to find that all but two of them were useless. They did, however, manage to seize a boat belonging to the customhouse and they cut two schooners out of the harbor. Six days later, Chatard sailed in the *Whiton* for Manzanillo, where he and a small group of men went ashore and spiked three guns. Thereafter, the only guns the Mexicans had left along the whole Pacific coast were the ones in the dilapidated fort at Acapulco.

Captain Pineda correctly surmised that so long as the American posts in Baja California had naval support, he had no chance of retaking them: the landing parties that the ships could provide, as well as the heavy artillery of the vessels, gave the Americans too big an advantage. Thus, his only chance for success lay in picking out an American post whose naval support was absent, and throwing his whole force against it. San José soon became just such a target. The *Southampton* had returned to Mazatlán soon after the *Portsmouth* joined her on 3 December 1847, and the latter stayed at San José only a month.

Heywood's garrison, which had been increased from twenty to twenty-seven Marines, fifteen sailors, and twenty *Bajacalifornio* volunteers, was short of supplies and when, after the *Portsmouth* left and Pineda moved his entire force into the area, fifty women and children took refuge with the garrison, the shortages became serious. Before long, there was no bread at all, and the command was reduced to half-rations of salt provisions. It was Pineda's capture of a foraging party on 22 January 1848 that signaled the opening of the second siege of San José, but before the garrison was cut off from all communication with other American posts, Heywood sent a messenger in a boat to Mazatlán to tell Shubrick of the attack.

From 22 January until 4 February, when they occupied the town, the Mexicans were constantly in sight from the American post, yet in all that time they made no attempt to rush it, apparently because they were waiting for their powder supply to be replenished. After two days of being penned in their quarters by sniper fire, Heywood and his men broke out on the 6th and drove the Mexicans from the village, but they were not numerous enough to retain control, and the Mexicans returned. In spite of Mexican bullets sent in their direction, the Americans managed to make two more sorties into the town on 7 February in search of rice and tobacco; they did not return empty-handed, even though one of their number was killed. The next afternoon, a schooner from La Paz, trying to deliver supplies to the garrison, was driven off by the Mexicans and, two days later, all of San José was once again under Mexican occupation.

Heavy fire directed at the American post on 11 February took the life of Passed Midshipman Tenant McLanahan, and that night, the Mexicans threw up a breastwork about one hundred and fifty yards northwest of the mission house where the Americans were penned and commanding the well that supplied the garrison with water. The defenders shelled the work but failed to destroy it. Then, when they made a night sortie for water and drew heavy fire, Heywood realized that the only thing to do was to dig a new well closer to the mission. Digging began, but there was no water at the new site.

Towards the end of the afternoon watch on 14 February, the Americans sighted a vessel standing in to the town. She was the *Cyane* from La Paz. After sundown, she dropped anchor, and at daylight the next morning Commander Du Pont with 102 officers and men landed about three miles from San José. At San Vicente, between the landing place and the town, they ran into some Mexicans, but fought them off and continued on their way to the beleaguered garrison. However, about the time Du Pont and his men were landing, Heywood and thirty of his men sortied from their quarters. The Mexicans in town, probably discouraged by the arrival of the warship, did little to deter them and, by the time Heywood and Du Pont joined forces, they had been dislodged from San José.

Naval support for his enemy was the factor Pineda knew he could not cope with, so when the Mexicans were forced out of the town, they withdrew to San José Viejo, but later moved to Santa Anita. On 24 March, Du Pont and Heywood with one hundred men tried to make a surprise descent on Santa Anita, but Pineda had been forewarned and the Mexicans escaped to Santiago. Thus ended the threat to San José.

While San José was under siege, Colonel Burton at La Paz was preparing a campaign to wipe out resistance in Baja California. As early as 13 February, he began collecting horses and saddles so that some of his men could be mounted, and during the last days of February, he seized two Mexican observation points near La Paz. But his campaign did not really get under way until another company of New York Volunteers and 115 recruits landed at La Paz on 22 March. Three days after the arrival of those reinforcements, Captain Seymour G. Steele and a party of thirty-three Volunteers swooped down on Pineda's main camp at San Antonio. They took three prisoners, captured Pineda's correspondence, and released Passed Midshipmen Alexander F. Warley and James M. Duncan, and three men of the San José garrison, all of whom had been with the foraging party whose capture in January had been the prelude to the siege of San José. During the fight, Pineda was wounded so severely that he had to turn over command of the Mexican forces in Baja California to the governor, Mauricio Castro.

The day after that success, Colonel Burton, bent on dealing the deathblow at Mexican resistance, personally led three companies of New Yorkers, totaling 217 men, out of La Paz and headed for Todos Santos. On the last day of the month, the Americans fell upon the Mexican camp in that village and, after a thirty-minute fight, in which ten of his men were killed, Castro and the remnants of his army broke up in confusion, and fled. At Santiago, some twenty-five miles to the east, the fleeing Mexicans, including Castro, were captured by two detachments of Americans from San José, one landed from the *Cyane* and the other under Lieutenant George L. Selden.

On 8 April 1848, Commodore Shubrick reported to Secretary of the Navy Mason that the Mexican forces in Baja California had been dispersed.

At Guadalupe Hidalgo on 2 February 1848, a treaty between the United States and Mexico had been signed, and General William O. Butler, who had succeeded General Winfield Scott as Army commander, had subsequently agreed to an armistice in the Valley of Mexico. Shubrick received Butler's

THOMAS AP CATESBY JONES

order promulgating that armistice on 30 March and although, technically, it was binding around Mexico City only, Shubrick believed he should abide by its terms, and he undertook no further hostile action. He did, however, strengthen the garrison at San José by replacing Heywood and his men with a company of New York Volunteers.

The armistice put an end to all hopes for the implementation of a plan that the commander of the Home Squadron in the Gulf of Mexico, Commodore Matthew C. Perry, had proposed the year before, and in which the Pacific Squadron had been ordered to cooperate—a joint Army-Navy expedition across the Isthmus of Tehuantepec, which would isolate the states of Tabasco and Chiapas from the rest of Mexico.

The idleness that came with the armistice made the New York Volunteers so restive that a mutiny developed and, in April, the *Cyane* had to be sent to San José to bring off the ringleaders. Captain Steele at La Paz had similar trouble in June and had to send to Mazatlán for help in dealing with the Volunteers of his garrison. The *Independence* responded to his plea and during the week of 18 June took off thirteen leaders of the disturbance.

Almost six months after Secretary of the Navy Mason had responded to Commodore Shubrick's request to be relieved of his Pacific command by advising him that Commodore Thomas ap Catesby Jones would be sent to replace him, Jones sailed from Norfolk in the *Cumberland* on 30 October 1847. The *Cumberland* took him as far as Jamaica, and from there he made his way to Chagres, then to Panama and Callao, where he boarded the ship-of-the-line *Ohio* (Captain William V. Taylor) bound for Mazatlán. He arrived at Mazatlán on 6 May 1848. Thus, the "goat" of 1842, described by a member of the *Ohio's* crew as "a spare-built man, with a kink in his back," returned to the scene of his misadventures.

As soon as news of the ratification of the Treaty of Guadalupe Hidalgo reached Commodore Jones on 13 June 1848, he began issuing orders for the withdrawal of American naval forces from Mexican territory. He ordered Captain La Vallette, military government of Mazatlán, to have the embarkation of men and material completed and all prisoners released so that control of the town could be returned to the Mexicans on 17 June. To the accompaniment of a twenty-one-gun salute late in the afternoon of that day, General Manuel de la Canal y Castillo Negrete of the Mexican Army accepted from La Vallette control of Mazatlán.

On the evening of 19 June, Jones in the *Ohio* with the *Congress* left Mazatlán to join the *Dale* at Guaymas. They arrived there four days later and, at noon on 24 June, that port was returned to the Mexicans. The three American warships stayed at Guaymas until 5 July, when they stood out for La Paz, across the Gulf, where the *Independence* and the *Lexington* were already at anchor. Preparations for the evacuation of La Paz took six weeks, and that capital of Baja California was not returned to Mexican control until the last day of August. That day the *Ohio* embarked the garrison and three hundred *Bajacalifornios* who had collaborated with the Americans and were afraid of retaliation by their countrymen. She then dropped down the coast to San José del Cabo, where, on 6 September, she picked up what was undoubtedly the last American unit to leave Mexico—a company of New York Volunteers—and sailed for Monterey.

Commodore Shubrick stayed at La Paz only two days. On 11 July he sailed in the *Independence* for a cruise to Hawaii and the South Seas. The operations that he, in conjunction with Lieutenant Colonel Burton, conducted along the west coast of Mexico were well handled. Although he was short of men and vessels, he managed to occupy or neutralize all of Baja California and the Mexican coast north of Acapulco. Had the war continued and had he been able to acquire the manpower he needed, there is no doubt that the customhouse at Acapulco would have been among those that contributed to the American war effort.

Of the three men who had held command of the Pacific Squadron for a long period, Shubrick was the only one who demonstrated effective leadership in wartime. He did not have the flamboyance—or the blind egocentricity—of Stockton, nor, although he exercised restrained caution, did he suffer from

Sloat's pathological fear of making a misstep. History has not treated Commodore Shubrick generously, in that the two major operations he conducted, the war in the Gulf of California and a delicate mission to Paraguay in the late 1850s to obtain satisfaction after a U.S. steamer had been fired on, are scarcely mentioned by historians.

XIX

OPENING THE WAY WEST

Naval operations are one part, and only one part, of a war. Frequently, naval supremacy is necessary to success in a war, but it is rarely sufficient alone. According to Karl von Clausewitz, the renowned author of *On War*, the aim of war is "to disarm the enemy," and the combination necessary to achieve that aim is destruction of the enemy's military forces, occupation of his country, and destruction of his will to resist.

Under normal conditions, so long as there is a capacity to resist, there will be the will to resist and, in the last analysis, destruction of enemy military forces and occupation of enemy country, must rest with foot soldiers and their supporting arms. The job of a navy is to ensure that the land forces can get to wherever they can best do those things, and to see to it that seaborne reinforcements of men and munitions do not increase the enemy's capacity to resist. Thus, as Alfred T. Mahan wrote, the prime objective of a navy is to achieve "that overbearing power on the sea which drives the enemy's flag from it, or allows it to appear only as a fugitive; and which, by controlling the great common, closes the highways by which commerce moves to and from the enemy's shores."

Once command of the sea has been established, the naval mission is to protect army lines of communication on or near the sea, and to prevent outside help from reaching the enemy by establishing a blockade of his ports. Any other aid to an army, for example, seizing and garrisoning enemy territory, or making harassing raids on his coast, is secondary and additional to a navy's principal task of denying the sea to the enemy and securing it for friendly vessels.

Matthew F. Steele, an army historian, was generous in his appraisal of how, in the Mexican War, the U.S. Navy carried out the basic naval mission: "The cooperation of the American navy throughout the Mexican War was most effective. Not only did it escort the transports of the armies of both Taylor and Scott, guard their bases from the side of the sea, put Scott's army ashore at Vera Cruz and join in the siege of that city; but it also maintained an effectual blockade of the Mexican coasts on the Gulf and on the Pacific sides, and besides Tampico, captured several other important coast towns."

In contrast to that army judgment, Commodore Perry's biographer, Edward M. Barrows, saw the operations in the Gulf of Mexico as "a campaign in which fever and the elements furnished the only casualty list of consequence," and attributed little more importance to the operations in the Pacific. Even if he was justified in making those appraisals, he was not correct in stating that the "war itself was mostly burlesque in a tropical setting . . . ," for the operations on both coasts provided striking illustrations of the Navy achieving its prime objective of sea power, as outlined by Mahan: it was eminently successful in preventing Mexican interference with American trade or with supply and reinforcement of American land forces, and in denying those facilities to the enemy. In fact, the American Navy in the Mexican War performed its primary function so successfully that it was able to undertake its secondary one of seizing points on the coast of Mexico. On the west coast it did even more than that: before land forces were available, it occupied California. Commodore Dudley W. Knox, on the other hand, undoubtedly overstates the case when he argues that the conquest of California "was an enterprise wholly impossible without the employment of the Navy, which deserves almost exclusive credit for its success."

Since Mexico never really threatened American command of the sea, the most important task of the Navy was establishing and maintaining the blockade. Duty on the blockade was exacting and tiring. It had to be performed in the sweltering heat of summer when, in the Gulf of Mexico, yellow fever raged, as well as during the vicious northers of winter, and, accurate charts being few and far between, it called for constant vigilance. It is a tribute to the Home Squadron in the Gulf that during the entire war, bad weather and poor charts caused the loss of only four vessels.

There is no complete listing of the number of blockade-runners taken, but there is every reason to believe that the blockade was effective—to exactly what degree, it is impossible to determine. Some blockade-runners got through—at least six of them ran in to Veracruz in the five months before it fell—but it is not likely that their contribution to the Mexican war effort was significant. The Gulf ports that remained in Mexican hands after Tampico and Veracruz had fallen were too small and too inaccessible to large vessels to have allowed important quantities of war material to be landed. Nor is there anything to indicate that sizable importations went through the Pacific ports either before or after they were closed.

Out of the operations along the Gulf of Mexico came the first development of an amphibious body within the Navy. The Naval Brigade established by Commodore Conner and exploited by Commodore Perry differed in both concept and makeup from earlier naval landing parties which, in effect, were boarding parties transferred ashore. There was never any thought of the latter undertaking operations on the scale of those conducted by the Naval Brigade, nor were they self-contained, as was the Naval Brigade with its own artillery, engineers, medical parties, and so forth. Before the war, there was hardly any such thing as doctrine for amphibious operations, and little seems to have developed during the war: except for the one at Veracruz, all the landings give every indication of having been played by ear. Not much effort was made to land the men in waves, and no arrangements were made for their logistic support when they were ashore. Both commodores realized that troops ashore needed overwhelming fire support, but neither ordnance nor gunnery had progressed to a point where close fire support could be supplied.

In the operations along the Pacific coast, Commodores Sloat, Stockton, and Shubrick all used the traditional type of landing parties. Stockton was not averse to having his sailors perform as soldiers, but he did not use them in the same way as the men of the Naval Brigade in the Gulf of Mexico were used.

Shortages in two major areas hampered the operations on both coasts. The first, and probably the most serious, was the shortage of men which, because it prevented the Navy from manning all the vessels that it wanted to send to the combat zones, led to both squadrons being smaller than they should have been. Not only did the shortage of vessels make it impossible satisfactorily to rotate them between the war fronts and home bases, but, as was seen in the account of its operations, the Home Squadron was so short of vessels, particularly steamers, that it was frequently hard put to maintain the blockade.

The second area of critical shortage was supplies and, although the Home Squadron suffered from it throughout Commodore Conner's tenure of command, it was the Pacific Squadron's biggest handicap. Certainly, in the case of the Pacific Squadron, the distances over which supplies had to be shipped were mainly responsible for creating the problem, but there were other factors. One of these factors was the failure of the supply bureaus in the Navy Department to develop a satisfactory procedure for anticipating the demands of the service and being prepared to fill them from nearby depots. Another factor was the laxity of the squadron commanders themselves in keeping the Department apprised of what was going to be needed. At the root of both squadrons' logistic problems lay the inability of their commanders and of the Navy Department to recognize that peacetime operating procedures cannot be applied effectively to wartime. In extenuation, however, it must be pointed out that except during the relatively small operations against France fifty years previously, and against the Barbary pirates forty years previously, the Navy had had no experience in maintaining squadrons of vessels at sea during hostilities.

The men who held the top commands during the Mexican War had received their training as junior officers during the War of 1812, and had risen to command during the thirty years of peace that followed it. If, along with gunnery and seamanship, the War of 1812 taught caution—and it did—the subsequent thirty years taught overcaution. In Sloat and Conner, that characteristic was as much a result of their training as it was a personal trait. Alonzo C. Jackson, who served as a midshipman aboard the *Savannah* when Commodore Sloat was in command of the Pacific Squadron, wrote that the war "proves that although our old officers have not for many years had that experience without which none can be perfect in the art of war they have not forgotten what they thoroughly learned during the War of 1812." One is tempted to agree with Jackson's words, even if one does not interpret them as he intended.

There was a strange anomaly about the commanders who were first under fire during the War of 1812: they had a good grasp of how to handle single-ship operations in the face of a superior foe, but were excessively cautious when faced with a weak opponent. Yet, to those men belongs the credit for the maritime accomplishments of the Mexican War. The conquest of California began when Sloat seized Monterey and San Francisco, and there is every reason to believe that, had it not been for the foolish and high-handed actions of his successor, Stockton, it would have been concluded with little bloodshed. In his short term as commander of the Pacific Squadron, Shubrick conducted an eminently satisfactory campaign along the west coast of Mexico, in spite of a shortage of vessels and supplies. Although he also was hampered by a lack of suitable vessels, it was Conner who initiated the policy of occupying the smaller Mexican ports and, with General Winfield Scott, he directed the successful landings at Veracruz. The operations of his successor, Perry, were well planned, well executed, and colorful, but they were secondary to Conner's seizure of Tampico and Carmen.

Just as the War of 1812 had trained the men who held high naval command in the Mexican War, the latter trained many of the men who had important commands during the Civil War—David G. Farragut, David D. Porter, Samuel F. Du Pont, Louis Goldsborough, Franklin Buchanan, Josiah Tattnall, and Raphael Semmes, to name a few.

The Mexican War gave the United States a striking example of the advantages—indeed, the necessity—of command of the sea, but the strategic thinking of the Navy Department and of Congress continued to be based on *guerre de course*. The naval appropriations act of 3 March 1847 allowed the Navy to build four very effective steamers, but only because operations in the Gulf of Mexico had pointed up the Navy's woeful shortage of steamers, not because Congress envisioned any change in wartime strategy.

Many of the proponents of Manifest Destiny saw in the successful conclusion to the Mexican War, the beginning of their long-cherished dream of overspreading "the continent allotted by Providence for the free development of our yearly multiplying millions." The acquisition of California and the Southwest, as well as the coincident clearing of American title to Oregon, did implant the country firmly in the Pacific basin, but the westward rush of prospectors and settlers following the announcement, made in 1848, even before the war ended, that gold had been found in California, broke the hallowed Missouri Compromise and sowed the seeds of the Civil War.

In spite of the impetus that the gold rush gave to the growth of the new commonwealth on the Pacific coast, California was not closely tied to the eastern United States until a transcontinental telegraph line was completed in 1861. The problem of communications, which during the Mexican War had prevented serious coordination between the operations in the Gulf of Mexico and those in California, was intensified when the war ended, and a solution to it became ever more pressing. Coordinate steamship lines from New York to Panama and from Panama to San Francisco, and magnificent clipper ships beating around the Horn were, at best, expensive and time-consuming stopgaps, as were the Butterfield Overland Mail, established in 1858, and the colorful and speedy Pony Express, established two years later. The first transcontinental railroad was not completed until 1869.

Another, and perhaps an even more significant result of the Mexican War was the development of California as the great entrepôt for commerce with the Far East. That development created pressures to enrich trading opportunities by keeping the doors to China wide open for trade, and for prying ajar the doors to Japan and Korea.

If the impact of the Mexican War on American history in general was complex and long-lasting, its impact on the U.S. Navy was revolutionary. It left that relatively small force with the enormous task of defending a nation with two sea frontiers, 2,500 miles apart by land, but more than 14,000 miles apart by sea.

Fulfillment of that mission with the means at hand when the war ended was impossible, and the decade following the war became the second peacetime period of expansion that the Navy underwent in the first ninety years of its existence. In 1849, the Navy List contained only seven oceangoing steamers, four of them unfinished. Eleven years later, it contained twenty-six, all but one of which were in service.

Expanding commerce from the West Coast in the direction of the Far East also put new demands on the Navy, particularly the ill-equipped East India Squadron. The Navy moved more ships to the Pacific. The need for shore-based logistic support brought about the establishment in 1854 of a permanent naval station at Mare Island, California. The long-lived Pacific Squadron began showing the U.S. flag across the far reaches of the world's greatest ocean, and in less than a century the United States became the mightiest naval power that ocean had ever known.

APPENDIXES

CHRONOLOGY

1845

MARCH

1, Sat.   President John Tyler signed the joint resolution annexing Texas.

4, Tues.   James K. Polk inaugurated as President of the United States.

31, Mon.   Mexico broke diplomatic relations with the United States.

JUNE

15, Sun.   Major General Zachary Taylor ordered to move his army into Texas.

24, Tues.   Commodore John D. Sloat ordered to occupy San Francisco, should war develop with Mexico.

JULY

4, Fri.   Texas accepted annexation.

25, Fri.   General Taylor's army reached St. Joseph's Island, near Corpus Christi, Texas.

SEPTEMBER

16, Tues.   U.S. government decided to appoint John Slidell as minister to Mexico.

OCTOBER

15, Wed.   Mexican government agreed to receive U.S. minister.

17, Fri.   Thomas O. Larkin named confidential agent in California.

30, Thurs.   President Polk met with Lieutenant Archibald H. Gillespie, U.S. Marine Corps.

NOVEMBER

10, Mon.   John Slidell's appointment as U.S. minister to Mexico made formal.

30, Sun.   John Slidell reached Veracruz.

DECEMBER

9, Tues.   Captain John C. Frémont arrived at Sutter's Fort, California.

29, Mon.   Texas admitted to statehood.

31, Wed.   President José Joaquín Herrera of Mexico deposed, and replaced by Mariano Paredes y Arrillaga.

1846

JANUARY

13, Tues.   General Taylor ordered to move his army to the Rio Grande.

FEBRUARY

9, Mon.   Lieutenant Gillespie arrived at Mazatlán.

22, Sun.   Lieutenant Gillespie left Mazatlán in the *Cyane* for Monterey.

MARCH

5, Thurs.   Captain Frémont and his expedition entrenched themselves on Gavilan Peak, California.

9, Mon.   Captain Frémont and his men withdrew towards Oregon.
Thomas O. Larkin requested a warship be sent to California.

17, Tues.   Commodore Sloat asked to be relieved of command of Pacific Squadron.

23, Mon.   General Taylor's army reached Point Isabel, Texas.

30, Mon.   John Slidell left Veracruz for New Orleans.

APRIL

1, Wed.   The *Portsmouth* left Mazatlán for Monterey, California, in response to Larkin's request.

12, Sun.   General Pedro de Ampudia, Mexican commander at Matamoros, demanded that Taylor withdraw his army beyond the Nueces River.

17, Fri.   Lieutenant Gillespie arrived at Monterey in the *Cyane*.

23, Thurs.   President Paredes declared a defensive war.
The *Portsmouth* reached Monterey.

25, Sat.   American reconnaissance patrol (Captain Seth Thornton, U.S. Army) attacked by Mexicans north of the Rio Grande.

MAY

4, Mon.   Commodore David Conner and most of the Home Squadron left Antón Lizardo, Mexico, for Brazos Santiago on the Rio Grande.

8, Fri.   General Taylor defeated Mexicans at the Battle of Palo Alto.
Commodore Conner's squadron reached Brazos Santiago and landed 500 men (Captain Francis H. Gregory) to reinforce the army garrison at Point Isabel.

9, Sat.   News of the attack on Captain Thornton's patrol on 25 April reached Washington.
General Taylor defeated Mexicans at the Battle of Resaca de la Palma.
Lieutenant Gillespie met Frémont at Klamath Lake, Oregon.

10, Sun.   Surgeon William M. Wood and Consul John Parrott reached Guadalajara, Mexico, learned that there had been fighting, and sent the news to Sloat at Mazatlán.

11, Mon.   President Polk asked Congress to declare war.

13, Wed.   Declaration of war signed by Polk.
Secretary of the Navy George Bancroft notified Sloat and Conner that the war had begun.

14, Thurs.   Commodore Conner issued a blockade proclamation covering Veracruz, Alvarado, Tampico, and Matamoros.

17, Sun.   Commodore Sloat received Wood's report that fighting had begun.

1846

18, Mon.	Captain John H. Aulick led a boat expedition up the Rio Grande to assist the army.
	The Mexican steamers *Guadaloupe* and *Montezuma* put to sea from Alvarado and escaped.
19, Tues.	Revenue cutter squadron (Captain John A. Webster, U.S. Revenue Marine) ordered to the Gulf of Mexico.
20, Wed.	Captain Aulick's expedition returned to Brazos Santiago.
	The *St. Mary's* began the blockade of Tampico, and the *Mississippi* began the blockade of Veracruz.
24, Sun.	The *Falmouth* captured the Mexican schooner *Criolla,* and the *Somers* seized the schooner *Amada.*
30, Sat.	Decision reached by the Cabinet to send an expedition under Colonel Stephen Watts Kearny to seize California.

JUNE

2, Tues.	The *Portsmouth* arrived at San Francisco.
4, Thurs.	The *Somers* visited Campeche, Yucatán.
7, Sun.	Commodore Sloat received a letter from Wood in Mexico City confirming earlier reports of fighting along the Rio Grande.
8, Mon.	The *St. Mary's* bombarded the defenses of Tampico.
	Commodore Sloat in the *Savannah* left Mazatlán for Monterey
10, Wed.	Ezekial Merritt and other Americans seized horses belonging to the Californian authorities.
13, Sat.	The *Somers* returned from Yucatán.
14, Sun.	Night attack on the gunboats at Tampico attempted by the *St. Mary's.*
	Bear Flaggers seized Sonoma, California.
24, Wed.	Skirmish north of San Francisco Bay between California militia and Bear Flaggers.
25, Thurs.	Issuance of letters of marque and reprisal authorized by the Mexican Congress.
26, Fri.	President Paredes issued regulations on privateering.

JULY

2, Thurs.	Commodore Sloat, in the *Savannah,* reached Monterey.
4, Sat.	Bear Flag Republic proclaimed.
7, Tues.	Commander Alexander Slidell Mackenzie met with ex-President Antonio López de Santa Anna in Havana.
	A landing party (Captain William Mervine) from the *Savannah,* the *Cyane,* and the *Levant,* occupied Monterey.
9, Thurs.	Landing party from the *Portsmouth* (Commander John B. Montgomery) occupied San Francisco.
15, Wed.	Commodore Robert F. Stockton in the *Congress* arrived at Monterey.
19, Sun.	Captain Frémont reached Monterey.
21, Tues.	Commodore Conner extended the blockade to Tecoluto, Tuxpan, and Soto la Marina.
23, Thurs.	Commodore Sloat appointed Stockton commander of operations ashore, and the latter organized the California Battalion under Frémont.

1846

27, Mon.
The United States offered to send a representative to Mexico to discuss peace.

Commodore W. Branford Shubrick ordered to command the Pacific Squadron.

28, Tues.
The *Cumberland* ran aground on Chopas Reef, forcing cancelation of a scheduled attack on Alvarado.

29, Wed.
Commodore Sloat transferred command of the Pacific Squadron to Stockton.

Landing party (Lieutenant Stephen C. Rowan) from the *Cyane* seized San Diego, California, and the Mexican brig *Juanita* was captured in the harbor.

AUGUST

4, Tues.
The *Congress* landed a garrison (Midshipman William Mitchell) at Santa Barbara, California.

6, Thurs.
President Paredes overthrown; José Mariano Salas named to serve as acting president.

Landing party (Lieutenant Jacob Zeilin, U.S. Marine Corps) from the *Congress* seized San Pedro, California.

7, Fri.
Commodore Conner with the *Mississippi*, the *Princeton*, the *Potomac*, the *Reefer*, the *Petrel*, and the *Bonita* attacked Alvarado but did not succeed in taking it.

10, Mon.
The *Cyane* captured the Mexican brig *Primavera* off San Diego.

12, Wed.
Secretary Bancroft offered command of the *Mississippi* to Commodore Matthew C. Perry.

13, Thurs.
Commodore Stockton with a landing party from the *Congress* occupied Los Angeles, California.

14, Fri.
Mexican forces in Alta California surrendered.

The *Truxtun* wrecked near Tuxpan.

16, Sun.
Santa Anna landed at Veracruz.

17, Mon.
Commander Edward W. Carpender, captain of the *Truxtun*, surrendered the wreck of his ship.

20, Thurs.
Commodore Perry ordered to take charge of the outfitting of the *Spitfire* and the *Vixen*.

21, Fri.
The *Porpoise* (Lieutenant William E. Hunt) captured the Mexican schooner *Nonata* in the Gulf of Mexico.

22, Sat.
The *Princeton* burned the wreck of the *Truxtun*.

Commodore Stockton proclaimed 15 September as the day on which elections were to be held in California.

Commodore Shubrick in the *Independence* left Boston for the Pacific.

29, Sat.
The Cabinet decided that Veracruz and Tampico should be seized.

SEPTEMBER

2, Wed.
Commander Samuel F. Du Pont, captain of the *Cyane*, proclaimed the blockade and seized the Mexican sloop *Solita* off San Blas, Mexico; a landing party (Lieutenant Stephen C. Rowan) spiked 24 cannon.

3, Thurs.
The *Cyane* captured the Mexican sloop *Solita* and the brigantine *Susana* off San Blas.

1846

7, Mon.	Boat expedition (Lieutenant William Radford) from the *Warren* cut out the Mexican brig *Malek Adhel* at Mazatlán.
8, Tues.	The *Warren* captured the Mexican brig *Carmelita* off Mazatlán.
9, Wed.	Commander Joseph B. Hull of the *Warren* proclaimed the blockade of Mazatlán.
	John Y. Mason succeeded Bancroft as Secretary of the Navy.
10, Thurs.	The *Shark* wrecked at the mouth of the Columbia River.
14, Mon.	Santa Anna became Commander-in-Chief of the Mexican Army.
	The *Cyane* seized the Mexican brigantines *Correo*, *La Paz*, and *Manuela*, the schooners *Julia*, *Mazolea*, *Eliza*, *Victoria*, and *Adelaide*, and the sloop *San José* at La Paz, Baja California.
23, Wed.	Lieutenant Gillespie's garrison at Los Angeles attacked.
24, Thurs.	Servulo Varela proclaimed rebellion in California.
	Lieutenant Gillespie sent Juan "Flaco" Brown to carry news of the rebellion to Stockton.
25, Fri.	General Kearny, escorted by the First Dragoons, left Santa Fe bound for California.
29, Tues.	American garrison at Los Angeles surrendered.

OCTOBER

1, Thurs.	Juan "Flaco" Brown delivered news of the rebellion at Los Angeles to Stockton at San Francisco.
	The *Cyane* captured the Mexican schooners *Libertad* and *Fortuna* at Loreto, Baja California.
2, Fri.	The *Cyane* captured the Mexican schooner *Rosita* at Loreto, Baja California.
4, Sun.	The *Cyane* captured the Mexican sloops *Chapita* and *Alerto* at Mulejé, Baja California.
6, Tues.	Commodore Perry took command of the *Mississippi*.
	General Kearny met Kit Carson near Socorro, New Mexico.
7, Wed.	Boat expedition (Lieutenant George W. Harrison) from the *Cyane* cut out and burned the Mexican brig *Condor* in the harbor of Guaymas, Mexico. The gunboats *Anahuac* and *Sonorense* were also burned.
	Captain Mervine landed a detachment from the *Savannah* for a march on Los Angeles.
8, Thurs.	Captain Mervine's attempt to recapture Los Angeles failed.
15, Thurs.	Commodore Conner with two large steamers, two small steamers, and five schooner-gunboats made a second assault on Alvarado.
17, Sat.	Home Squadron under Perry seized the American bark *Coosa* off the bar of Alvarado.
23, Fri.	Commodore Perry with the *Vixen*, the *McLane*, the *Forward*, the *Bonita*, and the *Nonata* seized Frontera, Mexico, along with the steamers *Petrita* and *Tabasqueña* and the schooner *Laura Virginia*; the *Bonita* captured the schooner *Amado* in the Tabasco River.

1846

25, Sun.   Commodore Perry and the squadron captured Tabasco and the shipping there: the brigs *Yunaute* and *Rentville*, the schooners *Tobasco* and *Alvarado*, and the sloop *Desada*. The schooner *Telegraph*, the sloop *Campeche*, and a towboat were also seized by the expedition at unreported times and places.

30, Fri.   Commodore Stockton in the *Congress* arrived at San Diego.

NOVEMBER

14, Sat.   Commodore Conner with two small steamers, four schooner-gunboats and a 300-man landing party seized Tampico, along with the Mexican schooner-gunboats *Union*, *Pueblana*, and *Mahonese*, the merchant schooner *Ormigo*, and the Spanish schooner *Isabella*.

15, Sun.   The *Boston* wrecked on Eleuthera Island in the Bahamas.

16, Mon.   Commander Josiah Tattnall led an expedition up the Pánuco River.

17, Tues. Captain Frémont's force left Monterey for Los Angeles.

18, Wed.   Landing party under Tattnall left for town of Pánuco to destroy Mexican guns stored there.

19, Thurs. Major General Winfield Scott appointed to command expedition to Veracruz.

21, Sat.   Commander Tattnall's expedition left Pánuco to return to Tampico.

23, Mon.   General Scott left Washington.

24, Tues. Three prize vessels, the steamer *Tabasqueña*, the brig *Yunaute*, and the schooner *Tobasco*, foundered in a gale at Antón Lizardo.

26, Thurs. Boat party under Lieutenant James L. Parker from the *Somers* burned the Mexican schooner *Criolla* at Veracruz.

DECEMBER

5, Sat.   Midshipman R. Clay Rogers captured by the Mexicans.

6, Sun.   Santa Anna elected president of Mexico.
           Battle of San Pasqual.

8, Tues.   The *Somers* capsized off Isla Verde, near Veracruz.
           Lieutenant Washington A. Bartlett and foraging party from the *Warren* seized by Californian rebels.

11, Fri.   Relief column (Lieutenant Andrew F. V. Gray) reached Kearny's camp.

12, Sat.   General Kearny and his army arrived at San Diego.

14, Mon.   Captain Frémont captured San Luis Obispo.

21, Mon.   Commodore Perry with the *Vixen*, the *Bonita*, and the *Petrel* occupied Carmen.

27, Sun.   General Scott landed at Brazos Santiago.
           Commodore Perry's squadron captured the Mexican schooner *Amelia* and the Spanish schooner *Isabel* off Alvarado.
           Captain Frémont reached Santa Barbara.

29, Tues. Commodore Stockton departed San Diego with the main body of troops for the attack on Los Angeles.

1847

JANUARY

3, Sun.   General Scott ordered troops from Taylor's army to move to the mouth of the Rio Grande.

1847

6, Wed.	Francisco Sanchez and Californian rebels in northern California surrendered unconditionally.
8, Fri.	Battle of San Gabriel.
9, Sat.	Battle of La Mesa.
10, Sun.	Los Angeles reoccupied by Stockton's army.
11, Mon.	General Kearny ordered to occupy at least one post in Baja California.
13, Wed.	Treaty of Cahuenga signed.
14, Thurs.	Captain Frémont arrived in Los Angeles.
22, Fri.	Commodore Shubrick in the *Independence* reached Monterey and superseded Stockton as commander of the Pacific Squadron.

FEBRUARY

5, Fri.	The transport *Ondiaka* wrecked north of Cape Royo, Mexico.
17, Wed.	The *Portsmouth* re-established the blockade at Mazatlán.
18, Thurs.	General Scott reached Tampico.
21, Sun.	General Scott arrived at Lobos.

MARCH

2, Tues.	Expedition under General Scott departed Lobos.
	Commodore James Biddle in the *Columbus* arrived at Monterey and took command of the Pacific Squadron.
4, Thurs.	Commodore Shubrick and General Kearny issued a proclamation (dated 1 March) apportioning responsibilities in California.
	The vanguard of Scott's transports reached Antón Lizardo.
5, Fri.	The last of some forty transports arrived at Antón Lizardo.
6, Sat.	In the *Petrita*, Conner and Scott reconnoitered possible landing areas near Veracruz.
9, Tues.	Landing made at Veracruz.
10, Wed.	The *Spitfire* made a diversionary attack on San Juan de Ulloa.
	The *Loben Eliza* (tender to the *Portsmouth*) captured the Mexican schooner *Magdalena* off Mazatlán.
21, Sun.	Commodore Perry took over from Conner as commander of the Home Squadron.
22, Mon.	Army batteries opened the bombardment of Veracruz; two small steamers and five schooner-gunboats under Tattnall's command also bombarded the city.
23, Tues.	Commander Tattnall with two small steamers and four schooner-gunboats resumed bombardment of Veracruz.
24, Wed.	The Naval Battery before Veracruz opened fire.
27, Sat.	The American squadron at Mazatlán seized the British schooner *William*.
29, Mon.	Veracruz occupied.
30, Tues.	Landing party (Lieutenant Benjamin F. B. Hunter) from the *Portsmouth* seized San José del Cabo, Baja California.
31, Wed.	Lieutenant Charles G. Hunter in the *Scourge* captured the town of Alvarado, and seized the *Relampago* and three other schooners.

APRIL

1, Thurs.	Tlacotalpán surrendered to the *Scourge*.

1847

2, Fri.	Commodore Perry in the *Spitfire* led one steamer and five schooner-gunboats up the Alvarado River to Tlacotalpán.
3, Sat.	The *Portsmouth* seized San Lucas, Baja California.
7, Wed.	The *Portsmouth* seized the American ship *Admittance* off San José del Cabo.
13, Tues.	Landing party (Lieutenant John S. Missroon) from the *Portsmouth* seized La Paz, Baja California.
15, Thurs.	Nicholas P. Trist appointed commissioner to negotiate peace.
18, Sun.	Commodore Perry with three small steamers, three schooner-gunboats, and a 1,519-man landing force captured Tuxpan.
	General Scott defeated Santa Anna at the Battle of Cerro Gordo.
30, Fri.	The *Bonita* captured the Mexican schooner *Yucateca*.

MAY

9, Sun.	The *Independence* captured the Mexican ship *Correo* off Mazatlán.
12, Wed.	Commodore Perry with six vessels arrived at Coatzacoalcos, Mexico.
13, Thurs.	President Polk ordered that six companies of Marines be sent to serve with Scott's army.
	Commander Abraham Bigelow led an expedition up the Coatzacoalcos River.
17, Mon.	Commodore Perry took formal possession of Carmen.
19, Wed.	Commodore Perry with a fleet of ten vessels visited Frontera.
21, Fri.	On board the *Scorpion*, Perry steamed up the Coatzacoalcos River to take possession of several villages.
27, Thurs.	Captain Samuel L. Breese and Commander Alexander S. Mackenzie began a two-day conference with Yucatán officials at Campeche.
31, Mon.	General Kearny transferred his command and the government of California to Colonel Robert B. Mason.

JUNE

1, Tues.	Commodore Shubrick requested relief from his command.
14, Mon.	Commodore Perry with four small steamers, one schooner-gunboat, one brig, three bomb brigs, one merchant schooner, and a 1,173-man landing party departed from Frontera for Tabasco.
16, Wed.	Tabasco occupied.
	General Kearny and Captain Frémont left Sutter's Fort for St. Louis.
22, Tues.	The *Bonita* seized the Yucatán steamer *Montezuma* near Tabasco.
24, Thurs.	Mexican attack on Tabasco repulsed.
25, Fri.	Lieutenant David D. Porter and a landing party from the *Spitfire* attacked near Tabasco.
30, Wed.	A landing party under Commander Bigelow captured Tamulté.

JULY

16, Fri.	Mexicans made daylight attack on Tabasco.
19, Mon.	Commodore Perry ordered evacuation of Tabasco.
	Commodore Biddle transferred command of the Pacific Squadron to Shubrick.
21, Wed.	Lieutenant Colonel Henry S. Burton and the New York Volunteers occupied La Paz, Baja California.

1847

AUGUST

4, Wed.   Commodore Perry ordered not to seize any more Mexican ports.

6, Fri.   Commodore Shubrick issued a new blockade proclamation for Mazatlán, Guaymas, and San Blas.

14, Sat.   Ex-President Paredes arrived at Veracruz on board the *Teviot*, landed, and escaped without being recognized.

OCTOBER

1, Fri.   Landing party (Lieutenant Tunis A. M. Craven) from the *Dale* attacked Mexican force near Mulejé.

5, Tues.   Landing party (Lieutenant Craven) from the *Dale* seized arms at Loreto, Baja California.

10, Sun.   The *Vesuvius* seized the American schooner *Wasp* in the Gulf of Mexico. The *Portsmouth* seized the Chilean brig *Argo* off Guaymas.

17, Sun.   Commodore Perry proposed a joint Army-Navy expedition across the Isthmus of Tehuantepec.

20, Wed.   Guaymas surrendered to the *Congress* and the *Portsmouth*.

25, Mon.   Commodore Thomas ap C. Jones ordered to relieve Shubrick as commander of the Pacific Squadron.

27, Wed.   The *Portsmouth* captured the Mexican schooner *Caroline* off Guaymas.

30, Sat.   Commodore Jones left Norfolk in the *Cumberland*.

NOVEMBER

1, Mon.   Lieutenant Montgomery Lewis's expedition left San José for Todos Santos, Baja California.

4, Thurs.   Commodore Shubrick proclaimed the American intention to retain Baja California after the war.

6, Sat.   The *Scorpion* seized the Mexican schooner *Renaissance* in the Gulf of Mexico.

7, Sun.   Lieutenant Lewis and his expedition returned from Todos Santos.

9, Tues.   The *Bonita* captured the Mexican schooner *Gavilán* in the Rio los Brocas, a tributary of the Tabasco River.

11, Thurs.   Landing party (Captain Elie A. F. La Vallette) from the *Independence*, the *Congress*, and the *Cyane* seized Mazatlán.
Mexicans attacked La Paz.

17, Wed.   Landing party (Commander Thomas O. Selfridge) from the *Dale* attacked in Guaymas.
Mexicans again attacked La Paz.

19, Fri.   Mexicans began siege of San José del Cabo.

20, Sat.   Lieutenant George L. Selden attacked Urias, Mexico.

21, Sun.   Siege of San José del Cabo lifted.

27, Sat.   Third attack on La Paz.

DECEMBER

12, Sun.   Lieutenant Montgomery Lewis routed a Mexican force near Mazatlán.

13, Mon.   Lieutenant William W. Russell, U.S. Marine Corps, began attack on the Mexican camp at Palos Prietos, Mexico.

1848

JANUARY

12, Wed.   Landing party (Lieutenant Frederick Chatard) from the *Lexington* and the *Whiton* destroyed guns at San Blas and cut out two schooners.

1848

17, Mon.   Landing party (Lieutenant Chatard) from the *Whiton* spiked guns at Manzanillo, Mexico.

18, Tues.   The *Lexington* seized two schooners at San Blas.

22, Sat.   Second siege of San José del Cabo began.

30, Sun.   Landing party (Lieutenant Tunis A. M. Craven) from the *Dale* attacked Mexican camp at Cochori, Mexico.

FEBRUARY

2, Wed.   Treaty of Guadalupe Hidalgo signed.

13, Sun.   Landing party (Lieutenant Fabius Stanly) from the *Dale* attacked Mexican camp at Bocachicacampo.

15, Tues.   The *Cyane* lifted the siege of San José del Cabo.

18, Fri.   General Scott relieved as commander of the army in Mexico by Major General William O. Butler.

20, Sun.   Landing party (Lieutenant Fabius Stanly) from the *Libertad* destroyed the Mexican camp at Bocachicacampo.

29, Tues.   Armistice agreed upon for the Valley of Mexico.

MARCH

7, Tues.   The Cabinet in Washington granted Perry discretionary power to provide Yucatán with powder and muskets.

10, Fri.   U.S. Senate ratified the Treaty of Guadalupe Hidalgo.

13, Mon.   Commodore Perry with five vessels arrived off Campeche, Yucatán.

14, Tues.   The *Petrita* foundered in the Alvarado River.

24, Fri.   Commander Samuel F. Du Pont led an expedition to Santa Anita, Baja California.

25, Sat.   Captain Seymour G. Steele and a detachment of New York Volunteers attacked the Mexican camp at San Antonio, Baja California, and released Passed Midshipmen Alexander F. Warley and James M. Duncan and three seamen.

30, Thurs.   Commodore Shubrick received news of the armistice in the Valley of Mexico.

31, Fri.   Lieutenant Colonel Henry S. Burton attacked the Mexican camp at Todos Santos.

APRIL

5, Wed.   Santa Anna left Mexico for Havana in the Spanish brigantine *Pepita*.

9, Sun.   Lieutenant Fabius Stanly and a small detachment skirmished with Mexicans near the estuary of the Soldado River.

MAY

6, Sat.   Commodore Jones reached Mazatlán and relieved Shubrick as commander of the Pacific Squadron.

25, Thurs.   Treaty of Guadalupe Hidalgo ratified by the Mexican Congress.

JUNE

11, Sun.   Veracruz returned to Mexican authorities.

15, Thurs.   Commodore Perry in the *Cumberland* departed Veracruz for New York.

17, Sat.   Mazatlán returned to Mexican control.

24, Sat.   Guaymas returned to Mexican control.

AUGUST

31, Thurs.   La Paz returned to Mexican control.

VESSELS OF THE HOME SQUADRON AND THE PACIFIC SQUADRON, 1846–48

This list includes the revenue cutters that served in the war zone, and the characteristics given are, insofar as can be ascertained, those possessed by the ships during the years of the war.

In the case of vessels built for the Navy, tonnage is given in terms of old measurement, and registered tonnage is given for converted merchantmen. Dimensions given are: length x beam x draft; the length cited is the distance between perpendiculars, unless noted as (d) length on deck, or (oa) length over-all; the beam is the extreme breadth of the hull, unless indicated (m) molded, or (g) over the guards; where the amount of draft is not known, (h) depth of hold, is used. The date of building denotes date of completion.

The sources for this appendix are diverse, the most significant being: Howard I. Chapelle, *The History of the American Sailing Navy* (New York, 1949); Frank M. Bennett, *The Steam Navy of the United States* (Pittsburgh, 1896); Robert W. Neeser, *A Statistical and Chronological History of the United States Navy* (2 vols. New York, 1909); George Fox Emmons, *The Navy of the United States from the Commencement, 1775–1853, with a Brief History of each Vessel's Service and Fate as Appears upon Record* (Washington, 1853); *Niles National Register*; Senate Executive Document 4, 36th Congress, 2nd Session, . . . *Information upon Various Subjects Pertaining to the Naval Establishment*; "List of Vessels, United States Navy, 1795–1850," Record Group 45, National Archives; and "Register of Union and Confederate Vessels," Record Group 45, National Archives.

Albany—Home Squadron

First-class sloop of war. 1,042 tons, 147'11" x 38'6"(m) x 17'6", 4 8-inch shell guns, 18 32-pdrs., 210 men, ship rig, 13 kts. Built by New York Navy Yard, 1846. Lost at sea in the West Indies, 1854.

Bonita—Home Squadron

Schooner. 74 tons, 59' x 19' x 7', 1 32-pdr. carronade, 40 men, schooner rig. Built by Brown and Bell, New York, 1846. Purchased at New York, 25 May 1846. Sold at Norfolk, 11 Oct. 1848. Sister to the *Petrel* and the *Reefer*.

Boston—Lost en route to join the Home Squadron.

Second-class sloop of war. 700 tons, 127' x 34'9" x 16'6", 4 8-inch shell guns, 16 32-pdrs., 190 men, ship rig, 12 kts. Built by Boston Navy Yard, 1826. Wrecked on Eleuthera Island, 15 Nov. 1846. Sister to the *John Adams*.

Columbus—Pacific Squadron

Ship-of-the-line. 2,480 tons, 193'3" x 53'6" x 25'8", 8 8-inch shell guns, 56 32-pdrs., 22 32-pdr. carronades, 780 men, ship rig, 12.5 kts. Built by Washington Navy Yard, 1819. Burned to avoid capture at Norfolk Navy Yard, 20 April 1861.

Congress—Pacific Squadron

First-class frigate. 1,867 tons, 179' x 47'8"(m) x 22'6", 8 8-inch shell guns, 46 32-pdrs., 480 men, ship rig. Built by Portsmouth Navy Yard, 1842. Sunk by the CSS *Virginia* in Hampton Roads, 8 March 1862.

Cumberland—Home Squadron

First-class frigate. 1,708 tons, 175' x 45'(m) x 22'4", 8 8-inch shell guns, 42 32-pdrs., 480 men, ship rig, 13 kts. Built by Boston Navy Yard, 1843. Sunk by the CSS *Virginia* in Hampton Roads, 8 March 1862. Sister to the *Potomac*, the *Raritan*, and the *Savannah*.

Cyane—Pacific Squadron

Second-class sloop of war. 792 tons, 132'4" x 36'3" x 16'6", 20 32-pdrs., 200 men, ship rig, 12 kts. Built by Boston Navy Yard, 1838. Sold at Mare Island Navy Yard, 30 July 1887. Sister to the *Levant*.

Dale—Pacific Squadron

Third-class sloop of war. 566 tons, 117' x 32'(m) x 15'8", 16 32-pdrs., 150 men, ship rig, 13 kts. Built by Philadelphia Navy Yard, 1839. Sold at Baltimore, 30 Nov. 1904. Sister to the *Decatur* and the *Preble*.

Decatur—Home Squadron

Third-class sloop of war. *See* the *Dale* for characteristics. Built by New York Navy Yard, 1840. Sold at Mare Island Navy Yard, 17 Aug. 1865. Sister to the *Dale* and the *Preble*.

Electra—Home Squadron

Ordnance storeship. 248½ tons, ? x ? x 13', 2 18-pdr. gunnades, 21 men, bark rig. Built at Philadelphia, 1845. Purchased at New York, 14 Jan. 1847. Sold at New York, 17 Nov. 1849. Ex-*Rolla*.

Erie—Pacific Squadron

Storeship. 611 tons, 117'11" x 32'4" x 17'10", 4 9-pdrs., 43 men, ship rig, 12 kts. Built at Boston Navy Yard, 1842. Sold at New York, 26 Nov. 1850.

Etna—Home Squadron

Bomb brig. 182 tons, 84'3" (d) x 25'6" x 10'3", 1 10-inch columbiad, 47 men, brig rig. Built in Connecticut, 1841. Purchased at Boston, 9 Feb. 1847. Sold at Norfolk, 11 Oct. 1848. Ex-*Walcott*.

Ewing—Home Squadron

Revenue cutter. 170 tons, 6 12-pdrs. Built at Baltimore, 1841. Transferred to the Coast Survey, 1848.

Falcon—Home Squadron

Schooner. 74 tons, 68'6"(oa) x 19' x 6', 1 24-pdr., 40 men, schooner rig. Captured at Tampico, 14 Nov. 1846. Sold at New York, 18 Oct. 1848. Ex-*Isabel*. Probably sister to the *Bonita*, the *Petrel*, and the *Reefer*.

Falmouth—Home Squadron
Second-class sloop of war. 703 tons, 127′6″ x 35′11″ x 16′11″, 22 24-pdrs., 190 men, ship rig, 12 kts. Built by Boston Navy Yard, 1828. Sold at Aspinwall, Panama, 7 Nov. 1863.

Flirt—Home Squadron
Schooner. 150 tons, ? x ? x 7′6″, 2 18-pdr. carronades, 33 men, schooner rig, 10 kts. Built in 1839. Transferred from the War Department, 1840. Transferred to the Coast Survey, 1851.

Forward—Home Squadron
Revenue cutter. 150 tons, 6 12-pdrs., schooner rig. Built by William Easby, Georgetown, D.C., 1842. Sold at Baltimore, Oct. 1865.

Fredonia—Home Squadron
Storeship. 800 tons, 160′ x 32′11″ x 20′6″, 4 24-pdr. carronades, 37 men, ship rig. Built at Newbury, Mass., 1845. Purchased at Boston, 14 Dec. 1846. Wrecked at Arica, Peru, 13 Aug. 1868. Ex-*Fredonia*.

Germantown—Home Squadron
First-class sloop of war. 942 tons, 150′ x 36′ x 17′3″, 4 8-inch shell guns, 18 32-pdrs., 210 men, ship rig, 14 kts. Built by Philadelphia Navy Yard, 1846. Burned to avoid capture at Norfolk Navy Yard, 20 April 1861.

Hecla—Home Squadron
Bomb brig. 195 tons, ? x ? x 10′2″, 1 10-inch columbiad, 47 men, brig rig. Purchased at New York, 5 Feb. 1847. Sold at New York, 18 Oct. 1848. Ex-*I. L. Richardson*.

Hunter—Home Squadron
Steamer. 96 tons, 100′ x 18′, 50 men, Hunter wheels, iron hull, 10 kts. Built by Joseph Tomlinson, Pittsburgh, Pa., 1846. Chartered at New Orleans, Nov. 1846. Wrecked on Isla Verde, near Veracruz, 21 March 1847.

Independence—Pacific Squadron
Razee. 1,891 tons, 188′ x 51′6″ x 24′4″, 8 8-inch shell guns, 48 32-pdrs., 750 men, ship rig, 13 kts. Built by Edmund Hartt and Josiah Barker, Boston, 1815; razeed at Boston Navy Yard, 1836. Sold at Mare Island Navy Yard, 23 Nov. 1914.

Iris—Home Squadron
Third-class steamer. 388 tons, 153′1″ (d) x 26′4″ x 11′, 1 32-pdr. carronade, 48 men, 218 h.p. steeple engine, side wheels, 8 kts. Built by Bishop and Simonson, New York, 1847. Purchased at New York, 1 Nov. 1847. Sold at Norfolk, 8 March 1849. Ex-*Iris*.

John Adams—Home Squadron
Second-class sloop of war. *See the Boston for characteristics.* 22 24-pdrs. Built by Norfolk Navy Yard, 1831. Sold at Boston, 5 Oct. 1867. Sister to the *Boston*.

Julia—Pacific Squadron
Schooner. Built in Baltimore. Captured by the *Cyane* at La Paz, Baja California, 14 Sept. 1846. Sold at San Francisco, date uncertain, probably 1847.

Lawrence—Home Squadron
Brig. 364 tons, 109′9″ x 26′2″(m) x 13′3″ (h), 2 32-pdrs., 8 32-pdr. carronades, 80 men, brig rig. Built by Langley B. Culley, Baltimore, 1844. Sold at New York, 1846.

Legare—Home Squadron
Revenue steamer. 364 tons, 140′ (d) x 24′ x 6′5″, 1 18-pdr., 1 12-pdr., 1 9-pdr., 2 4-pdrs., 120 h.p. horizontal engines, 2 screws. Built by H. R. Dunham & Co., New York, 1844. Transferred to the Coast Survey, 12 Nov. 1847.

Levant—Pacific Squadron

Second-class sloop of war. *See* the *Cyane* for characteristics. 4 8-inch shell guns, 18 32-pdrs. Built by New York Navy Yard, 1838. Lost at sea off Hawaii, 1860. Sister to the *Cyane*.

Lexington—Pacific Squadron

Storeship. 691 tons, 127′ x 34′7″ x 16′6″, 4 9-pdrs., 2 32-pdr. carronades, 43 men, ship rig, 11.5 kts. Built by New York Navy Yard, 1826, as a sloop of war; converted by Norfolk Navy Yard, 1843. Sold at Boston, 1860. Sister to the *Warren*.

Libertad—Pacific Squadron

Schooner. 1 9-pdr. Chartered at La Paz, Baja California, Oct. 1847. Returned to owner.

McLane—Home Squadron

Revenue steamer. 369 tons, 161′ x 17′ x 9′9″, 6 12-pdrs., side wheels. Built by Cyrus Alger, Boston, 1844. Converted to lightship at New Orleans, 17 Dec. 1847.

Mahonese—Home Squadron

Schooner. 100 tons, ? x ? x 7′, 1 24-pdr., schooner rig. Captured at Tampico, 14 Nov. 1846. Sold at Norfolk, 15 Oct. 1848. Ex-*Mahonese*.

Malek Adhel—Pacific Squadron

Brig. 114 tons, 80′ (d) x 20′7″ (m) x 7′9″ (h), 2 9-pdrs., 10 6-pdrs., brig rig. Built by William H. Webb, New York, 1840. Captured by the *Warren* at Mazatlán, 7 Sept. 1846. Sold at San Francisco, Sept. 1847. Ex-*Malek Adhel*.

Mississippi—Home Squadron

First-class steamer. 1,732 tons, 220′ x 66′6″ (g) x 21′9″, 2 10-inch shell guns, 8 8-inch shell guns, 257 men, 650 h.p. side-lever engine, side wheels, 11 kts. Built by Philadelphia Navy Yard, 1841. Sunk by Confederate batteries at Port Hudson, La., 14 March 1863.

Morris—Home Squadron

Schooner. Captured at Frontera, 23 Oct. 1846. May have been built in Baltimore. Disposition uncertain. Ex-*Laura Virginia*.

Nonata—Home Squadron

Schooner. 122 tons, 4 42-pdr. carronades, schooner rig. Built in New York; captured by the *Porpoise* in the Gulf of Mexico, 21 Aug. 1846. Transferred to the Army at Tampico, March 1847. Ex-*Belle*, ex-Mexican *Nonata*.

Ohio—Home Squadron and Pacific Squadron

Ship-of-the-line. 2,757 tons, 197′2″ x 53′10″ x 26′6″, 12 8-inch shell guns, 28 42-pdrs., 44 32-pdrs., 820 men, ship rig, 13 kts. Built by New York Navy Yard, 1838. Sold at Boston, 27 Sept. 1883.

On-ka-hy-e—Home Squadron

Schooner. 200 tons, 96′ (oa) x 22′ x 12′9″, 2 guns, schooner rig. Built by William Capes, Williamsburg, N.Y., 1840; purchased by the Navy, 1843. Wrecked on Caicos Reef in the West Indies, 21 June 1848.

Perry—Home Squadron

Brig. 280 tons, 105′ x 25′6″ (m) x 13′2″, 2 32-pdrs., 6 32-pdr. carronades, 80 men, brig rig, 11 kts. Built by Norfolk Navy Yard, 1843. Sold at Philadelphia, 10 Aug. 1865.

Petrel—Home Squadron

Schooner. *See* the *Bonita* for characteristics. Built by Brown and Bell, New York, 1846. Purchased at New York, 25 May 1846. Sold at New York, 18 Oct. 1848. Sister to the *Bonita* and the *Reefer*.

Petrita—Home Squadron

Steamer. 200 tons, ? x ? x 7′6″, 1 24-pdr. carronade, side wheels. Built in New York, 1834. Captured at Frontera, 23 Oct. 1846. Foundered in the Alvarado River, 15 April 1848. Ex-*Champion*, ex-*Secretary*, ex-Mexican *Petrita*.

Porpoise—Home Squadron

Brig. 224 tons, 88′ x 25′ (m) x 13′, 2 9-pdrs., 9 24-pdr. carronades, brigantine rig. Built by Boston Navy Yard, 1836. Lost at sea in the East Indies, 1854.

Portsmouth—Pacific Squadron

First-class sloop of war. 1,022 tons, 153′1″ x 38′1″ x 17′6″, 4 8-inch shell guns, 18 32-pdrs., 210 men, ship rig, 14 kts. Built by Portsmouth Navy Yard, 1844. Sold, 12 July 1915.

Potomac—Home Squadron

First-class frigate. *See* the *Cumberland* for characteristics. Built by Washington Navy Yard, 1831. Sold at Philadelphia, 24 May 1877. Sister to the *Cumberland*, the *Raritan*, and the *Savannah*.

Preble—Pacific Squadron

Third-class sloop of war. *See* the *Dale* for characteristics. Built by Portsmouth Navy Yard, 1840. Burned at Pensacola, Fla., 27 April 1863. Sister to the *Dale* and the *Decatur*.

Princeton—Home Squadron

First-class steamer. 672 tons, 156′6″ x 30′6″ x 19′11″, 1 8-inch shell gun, 12 42-pdr. carronades, 166 men, 204 h.p. semi-cylinder engine, 1 screw, 10.5 kts. Built by Philadelphia Navy Yard, 1843. Broken up at Boston Navy Yard, 1849.

Raritan—Home Squadron

First-class frigate. *See* the *Cumberland* for characteristics. Built by Philadelphia Navy Yard, 1843. Scuttled at Norfolk Navy Yard, 20 April 1861. Sister to the *Cumberland*, the *Potomac*, and the *Savannah*.

Reefer—Home Squadron

Schooner. *See* the *Bonita* for characteristics. Built by Brown and Bell, New York, 1846. Purchased at New York, 25 May 1846. Transferred to the Coast Survey, 1850. Sister to the *Bonita* and the *Petrel*.

Relief—Home Squadron

Storeship. 467 tons, 109′ x 30′9″ x 16′6″, 4 18-pdr. gunnades, 2 12-pdr. gunnades, 44 men, ship rig, 10.5 kts. Built by Philadelphia Navy Yard, 1836. Sold at Washington, 27 Sept. 1883.

St. Mary's—Home Squadron

First-class sloop of war. 958 tons, 150′ x 37′4″ x 17′3″, 4 8-inch shell guns, 18 32-pdrs., 210 men, ship rig. Built by Washington Navy Yard, 1844. Sold at New York, 1908.

Santa Anna—Home Squadron

Revenue cutter. Schooner rig. Acquired from the Republic of Texas.

Saratoga—Home Squadron

First-class sloop of war. 882 tons, 146′4″ x 36′1″ x 16′8″, 4 8-inch shell guns, 18 32-pdrs., 275 men, ship rig, 13 kts. Built by Portsmouth Navy Yard, 1843. Sold to the State of Pennsylvania, 14 Aug. 1907.

Savannah—Pacific Squadron

First-class frigate. *See* the *Cumberland* for characteristics. 4 8-inch shell guns, 28 32-pdrs., 22 42-pdr. carronades. Built by New York Navy Yard, 1843. Sold at Norfolk, 27 Sept. 1883. Sister to the *Cumberland*, the *Potomac*, and the *Raritan*.

Scorpion—Home Squadron

Third-class steamer. 339 tons, 160′9″ x 24′6″ x 9′9″, 2 8-inch shell guns, 2 18-pdr. carronades, 61 men, 69 h.p. inclined engine, side wheels, 7.5 kts. Built in New York, 1846. Purchased at New York, 4 Jan. 1847. Sold at New York, 18 Oct. 1848. Ex-*Aurora*.

Scourge—Home Squadron

Third-class steamer. 230 tons, 120′ x 23′ (m) x 9′, 1 32-pdr., 2 24-pdr. carronades, 61 men, horizontal engines, 2 screws, iron hull, 10.5 kts. Built by Betts, Harlan and Hollingsworth, Wilmington, Del., 1844. Purchased at New York, 24 Dec. 1846. Sold at New Orleans, 7 Oct. 1848. Ex-*Bangor*.

Shark—Pacific Squadron

Schooner. 198 tons, 86′ x 24′7″ (m) x 12′4″, 2 9-pdrs., 10 24-pdr. carronades, 100 men, schooner rig. Built by Washington Navy Yard, 1821. Wrecked at the mouth of the Columbia River, 10 Sept. 1846.

Somers—Home Squadron

Brig. 259 tons, 100′ x 25′ (m) x 13′, 10 32-pdr. carronades, 80 men, brig rig, 11 kts. Built by New York Navy Yard, 1842. Capsized off Isla Verde, near Veracruz, 8 Dec. 1846.

Southampton—Pacific Squadron

Storeship. 567 tons, 152′6″ x 27′10″ (m) x 16′, 2 42-pdr. carronades, 4 18-pdr. carronades, 2 12-pdr. gunnades, 43 men, ship rig, 11 kts. Built by Norfolk Navy Yard, 1845. Sold at Boston, about 1855.

Spencer—Home Squadron

Revenue steamer. 398 tons, 160′ x 24′ x 9′3″, 4 12-pdrs., 1 18-pdr. carronade, horizontal engines, 2 screws. Built by West Point Foundry Association, Cold Spring, N.Y., 1844. Converted to a lightship, 1848.

Spitfire—Home Squadron

Third-class steamer. 241 tons, 118′ (d) x 22′6″ x 8′3″, 1 8-inch shell gun, 2 32-pdr. carronades, 50 men, 50 h.p. half-beam engine, side wheels, 9 kts. Built by Brown and Bell, New York, 1846. Purchased at New York, 21 May 1846. Sold at Norfolk, 11 Oct. 1848. Sister to the *Vixen*.

Stromboli—Home Squadron

Bomb brig. 182 tons, ? x ? x 9′8″, 1 10-inch columbiad, 47 men, brig rig. Purchased at Boston, 16 Feb. 1847. Sold at New York, 18 Oct. 1848. Ex-*Howard*.

Supply—Home Squadron

Storeship. 547 tons, ? x ? x 18′, 4 24-pdr. carronades, 37 men, ship rig, 12 kts. Built by Henry Ewell, Medford, Mass., 1846. Purchased at Boston, Dec. 1846. Sold at New York, 3 May 1884. Ex-*Supply*.

Tampico—Home Squadron

Schooner. 75 tons, ? x ? x 7′, 1 24-pdr., 40 men, schooner rig. Captured at Tampico, 14 Nov. 1846. Sold at Norfolk, 11 Oct. 1848. Ex-*Pueblano*.

Truxtun—Home Squadron

Brig. 331 tons, 100′ x 27′4″ (m) x 13′, 10 32-pdr. carronades, 80 men, brig rig. Built by Norfolk Navy Yard, 1843. Wrecked near Tuxpan, 14 Aug. 1846.

Union—Home Squadron

Schooner. 74 tons, 68′6″ (oa) x 19′ x 6′, 1 24-pdr., schooner rig. Captured at Tampico, 14 Nov. 1846. Wrecked off Veracruz, 16 Dec. 1846. Ex-*Union*. May be sister to the *Bonita*, the *Petrel*, and the *Reefer*.

Van Buren—Home Squadron

Revenue cutter. 112 tons, 73'4" x 20'6" x 7'4" (h), 4 12-pdrs., schooner rig. Built in Baltimore, 1839. Sold at New York, 1 June 1847.

Vesuvius—Home Squadron

Bomb brig. 240 tons, ? x ? x 11'4", 1 10-inch columbiad, 47 men, brig rig. Built in 1846. Purchased at New York, 14 Jan. 1847. Sold at Norfolk, 11 Oct. 1848. Ex-*St. Marys*.

Vixen—Home Squadron

Third-class steamer. *See* the *Spitfire* for characteristics. 3 32-pdr. carronades. Built by Brown and Bell, New York, 1846. Purchased at New York, 21 May 1846. Transferred to the Coast Survey, 21 July 1848. Sister to the *Spitfire*.

Warren—Pacific Squadron

Second-class sloop of war. *See* the *Lexington* for characteristics. 24 32-pdrs., 190 men. Built by Boston Navy Yard, 1827. Sold at Aspinwall, Panama, 1 Jan. 1863. Sister to the *Lexington*.

Washington—Home Squadron

Coast Survey brig. 91'2" x 22'1" (m), 1 42-pdr., brig rig. Built in Baltimore, 1837. Seized at New Orleans by the State of Louisiana, 31 Jan. 1861.

Water Witch—Home Squadron

Third-class steamer. 255 tons, 131' x 21'10" x 7'3", 1 8-inch shell gun, 2 32-pdrs., 54 men, inclined engine, side wheels, 9 kts. Built by Washington Navy Yard, 1845. Expended as a target, 1851.

Whiton—Pacific Squadron

Bark. Chartered or impressed in the Gulf of California, 1847. Probably returned to owner, 1848.

Woodbury—Home Squadron

Revenue cutter. *See* the *Van Buren* for characteristics. 4 12-pdrs., 1 6-pdr. Built by L. H. Duncan, Baltimore, 1837. Sold at New York, 1 June 1847.

VESSELS OF THE MEXICAN NAVY, 1846–48

This appendix was prepared especially for this book by Robert L. Scheina of the Division of Naval History, Department of the Navy. Mr. Scheina is probably the most knowledgeable student of the Mexican Navy of the 1840s. The list is based primarily upon Archivo General de la Nación, Mexico City, Ramo de Marina, Tomo 312, and *Memoria del secretario de estados y del despacho de guerra y marina . . . 1845* (Mexico, 1845). The form in which the information is presented is the same as that used in the list of American vessels.

Aguila
Schooner. 130 tons, 99′(oa) x 23′ x 10′, 1 32-pdr., 6 18-pdr. carronades, 40 men. Built by Brown and Bell, New York, 1842. Scuttled in the Alvarado River, April 1847.

Anahuac
Schooner. 105 tons, 1 12-pdr. Built in Mexico. Burned at Guaymas, 7 Oct. 1846.

Guadaloupe
Steamer. 775 tons, 200′ (oa) x 34′ x 10′, 2 68-pdrs., 4 12-pdrs., 180 h.p. engine, side wheels, iron hull. Built by William Laird and Sons, Birkenhead, England, 1842. Repossessed by British interests, May 1846, on default of purchase contract.

Guerrero
Schooner. 48½ tons, 64′(oa) x 19′ x 6′, 1 24-pdr., approx. 25 men. Built in the United States, 1844–45. Scuttled in the Alvarado River, April 1847. Sister to the *Victoria*.

Isabel
Schooner. 74 tons, 68′6″(oa) x 19′ x 6′, 1 24-pdr., approx. 25 men. Probably built by Brown and Bell, New York, 1845. Captured by U. S. squadron at Tampico, 14 Nov. 1846. Became USS *Falcon*. Sister to the *Pueblano* and the *Union*.

Libertad
Schooner. 89 tons, 78′(oa) x 20′ x 7′6″, 1 12-pdr. Captured from Yucatán. Scuttled in the Alvarado River, April 1847. Ex-*Campecheno*.

Mexicano
Brig. 208 tons, 108′(oa) x 27′ x 11′6″, 14 18-pdr. carronades, 2 8-pdr. howitzers. Captured from Yucatán, 9 Oct. 1842. Scuttled in the Alvarado River, April 1847. Ex-*Yucateco*.

Montezuma

Steamer. 1,111 tons, 204'(oa) x 34' x 11', 1 68-pdr., 2 32-pdrs., 4 32-pdr. carronades, 1 9-pdr., 280 h.p. engine, side wheels. Built in England, 1842. Repossessed by British interests, May 1846, on default of purchase contract.

Morelos

Schooner. 59 tons, 74'(oa) x 18' x 7', 1 12-pdr. Scuttled in the Alvarado River, April 1847.

Pueblano

Schooner. 74 tons. 68'6"(oa) x 19' x 6', 1 24-pdr. Probably built by Brown and Bell, New York, 1845. Captured by U. S. squadron at Tampico, 14 Nov. 1846. Became USS *Tampico*. Sister to the *Isabel* and the *Union*.

Queretana

Schooner. 1 24-pdr. Scuttled in the Alvarado River, April 1847.

Sonorense

Schooner. 27 tons, 1 12-pdr. Probably built in Mexico. Burned at Guaymas, 7 Oct. 1846.

Union

Schooner. 74 tons, 68'6"(oa) x 19' x 6', 1 24-pdr. Probably built by Brown and Bell, New York, 1845. Captured by U. S. squadron at Tampico, 14 Nov. 1846. Became USS *Union*. Sister to the *Pueblano* and the *Isabel*.

Veracruzano Libre

Brig. 174 tons, 103'(oa) x 24' x 10'6", 1 32-pdr., 6 18-pdr. carronades, 2 12-pdr. howitzers, approx. 70 men. Purchased in Great Britain, 1843. Scuttled in the Alvarado River, April 1847. Ex-*Santa Anna*.

Victoria

Schooner. 48½ tons, 64'(oa) x 19' x 6', 1 24-pdr. Built in New York, 1844–45. Scuttled in the Alvarado River, April 1847. Sister to the *Guerrero*.

Zempoalteca

Brig. 6 12-pdr. carronades. Captured from Yucatán. Scuttled in the Alvarado River, April 1847.

LANDING AT VERACRUZ
TABLE OF ORGANIZATION

GENERAL-IN-CHIEF: MAJOR GENERAL WINFIELD SCOTT

1st Division: Brigadier General William J. Worth

2d Artillery: Colonel James Bankhead
3d Artillery: Lieutenant Colonel F. S. Belton
4th Infantry: Lieutenant Colonel John Garland
5th Infantry[1]: Lieutenant Colonel J. S. MacIntosh
6th Infantry[2]: Colonel N. S. Clarke
8th Infantry: Major C. A. Waite
Duncan's Field Battery: Captain James Duncan
Provisional Rocket and Mountain Battery: Captain G. H. Talcott
Company of Sappers: Captain A. J. Swift
Marines of the Home Squadron: Captain Alvin Edson, U.S. Marine Corps

2d Division: Brigadier General David E. Twiggs

1st Artillery: Colonel Thomas Childs
4th Artillery: Major J. L. Gardner
1st Infantry: Colonel William Davenport
2d Infantry: Lieutenant Colonel Bennett Riley
3d Infantry: Captain E. B. Alexander
7th Infantry: Lieutenant Colonel Joseph Plymton
Regiment of Mounted Riflemen: Colonel P. F. Smith
Taylor's Field Battery: Captain Francis Taylor

3d Division: Major General Robert Patterson

Pillow's Brigade: Brigadier General Gideon J. Pillow
1st Pennsylvania: Colonel F. M. Wynkoop

[1] One company of Louisiana Volunteers attached.
[2] One company of Kentucky Volunteers attached.

2d Pennsylvania: Colonel J. W. Geary
1st Tennessee: Colonel W. B. Campbell
2d Tennessee: Colonel W. T. Haskell
Patterson's Brigade: General Patterson
South Carolina Regiment: Colonel P. M. Butler
Steptoe's Field Battery: Captain E. J. Steptoe

Headquarters Reserve:

Composite Detachment Dragoons: Colonel W. S. Harney
Tennessee Mounted Volunteers: Colonel J. E. Thomas
Siege Train

HOME SQUADRON: COMMODORE DAVID CONNER

Frigates:
Raritan (Captain French Forrest)
Potomac (Captain John H. Aulick)

Sloops of War:
St. Mary's (Commander John L. Saunders)
Albany (Captain Samuel L. Breese)

Brig:
Porpoise (Lieutenant William E. Hunt)

Steam Frigate:
Princeton (Commander Frederick Engle)

Steamers:
Petrita (Lieutenant Samuel Lockwood)
Spitfire (Commander Josiah Tattnall)
Vixen (Commander Joshua Sands)

Schooners:
Bonita (Lieutenant Timothy G. Benham)
Reefer (Lieutenant Isaac Sterrett)
Petrel (Lieutenant T. Darrah Shaw)
Tampico (Lieutenant William P. Griffin)
Falcon (Lieutenant John J. Glasson)

THIRD LOS ANGELES CAMPAIGN
TABLE OF ORGANIZATION

COMMANDER-IN-CHIEF: COMMODORE ROBERT F. STOCKTON

COMMANDING DIVISION: BRIGADIER GENERAL STEPHEN W. KEARNY

1st Division: Lieutenant Jacob Zeilin, U.S. Marine Corps
  Company C: *Portsmouth*'s musketeers
  Company E: *Cyane*'s carbineers
  Company G: *Congress*' carbineers

2d Division: Captain H. S. Turner, U.S. Army
  Company C: 1st Dragoons
  Company D: *Cyane*'s musketeers
  Company K: 1st Dragoons
  Company of Artillery

3d Division: Lieutenant William B. Renshaw, U.S. Navy
  Company A: *Congress*' musketeers
  Company B: *Savannah*'s musketeers

4th Division: Captain Archibald H. Gillespie, U.S. Marine Corps
  50 Mounted Volunteers
  30 Californians
   3 Topographical Engineers
  46 Others

BIBLIOGRAPHIC NOTES

"United States Naval Operations During the Mexican War," the author's dissertation at Indiana University, is the basis for this history. Most of the information in that fully documented study was drawn from the reports of the commanders of the Home Squadron, the commanders of the Pacific Squadron, the orders issued by the Secretary of the Navy, and the logs of the vessels involved. In the interests of space and simplicity, references to those sources have been kept to a minimum in the following notes.

ABBREVIATIONS

AF	Area File, RG–45, NA
BL	Letters from Bureaus, RG–45, NA
BLUC	Bancroft Library, University of California
CHSQ	*California Historical Society Quarterly*
CLB	Letter Books of Commodore David Conner, RG–45, NA
Conner FDR	Commodore David Conner Papers, Franklin D. Roosevelt Library
Conner LC	Papers of David Conner, LC
Conner NY	Commodore David Conner Papers, New York Public Library
ELB	Executive Letter Books, RG–45, NA
HSL	Home Squadron Letters, RG–45, NA
HSSCP	*Historical Society of Southern California Publications*
Larkin *Docs.*	Papers of Thomas O. Larkin, BLUC
Larkin *Off. Corres.*	Official Correspondence of Thos. O. Larkin, BLUC
LB	Letters to Bureaus, RG–45, NA
LC	Library of Congress
LNA	Letters to Navy Agents, RG–45, NA
LO	Letters to Officers, Ships of War, RG–45, NA
MLB	Letter Book, Capt. John B. Montgomery, RG–45, NA
NA	National Archives
NAL	Letters from Navy Agents, RG–45, NA
PSL	Pacific Squadron Letters, RG–45, NA
RCL	Record of Confidential Letters, RG–45, NA
RG	Record Group
USNIP	*United States Naval Institute Proceedings*

GENERAL

The best general study of the war is Justin Harvey Smith, *The War with Mexico* (2 vols. New York, 1919). Robert Selph Henry, *The Story of the Mexican War* (Indianapolis, 1950) is shorter and more readable. Other shorter studies include Alfred H. Bill, *Rehearsal for Conflict* (New York, 1947) and Otis A. Singletary, *The Mexican War* (Chicago, 1960).

For general accounts of naval operations alone, the following works are the most useful: James Fenimore Cooper, *The History of the Navy of the United States of America* (3 vols. in 1, New York, 1853); Louis N. Feipel, "The United States Navy in Mexico, 1821–1914," *USNIP*, XLI–XLII; Dudley W. Knox, *A History of the United States Navy* (New York, 1946); Edgar Stanton Maclay, *A History of the United States Navy* (2 vols. New York, 1894); and John R. Spears, *The History of Our Navy* (4 vols. New York, 1897). K. Jack Bauer, "United States Naval Operations During the Mexican War" (Ph.D. dissertation, Indiana University) is a fully documented study of the naval war, from which the present work is derived. Two other dissertations that deal with the subject are: J. L. Betts, "United States Navy and the Mexican War" (University of Chicago) and F. J. Manno, "History of United States Naval Operations, 1846–1848" (Georgetown University).

Earlier general works which are useful include: Nathan Covington Brooks, *A Complete History of the Mexican War* (Philadelphia, 1849); John Frost, *The Mexican War and Its Warriors* (New Haven, 1850); John S. Jenkins, *History of the War Between the United States and Mexico* (Auburn, N.Y., 1860); *Niles National Register* (76 vols. Baltimore, 1811–1849); Charles J. Peterson, *The American Navy* (Philadelphia, 1848); Edward Deering Mansfield, *The Mexican War* (New York, 1860); Roswell Sabine Ripley, *The War with Mexico* (2 vols. New York, 1849); Cadmus Marcellus Wilcox, *History of the Mexican War* (Washington, 1892).

Marine Corps operations are covered in M. Almy Aldrich, *History of the United States Marine Corps* (Boston, 1875); Charles Lee Lewis, *Famous American Marines* (Boston, 1950); Clyde H. Metcalf, *A History of the United States Marine Corps* (New York, 1939). Revenue Marine activities are described in Stephen H. Evans, *The United States Coast Guard 1790–1915* (Annapolis, 1949); Horatio Davis Smith, *Early History of the United States Revenue Marine Service or United States Revenue Cutter Service 1789–1915* (n. p., 1932); U. S. Coast Guard, *Record of Movements, Vessels of the U. S. Coast Guard* (2 vols. Washington, 1935).

The most useful sources for general discussions of the Mexican operations are Ramon Alcaraz, *et al.*, *Apuntes para la historia de la guerra entre Mexico y los Estados Unidos* (Mexico, 1848), which was translated by Albert C. Ramsey and published under the title *The Other Side* (New York, 1850); Carlos María de Bustamente, *El nuevo Bernal Diaz del Castillo* (Mexico, 1949); Vicente Riva Palacio (Ed.), *Mexico a través de los siglos* (6 vols. Mexico, 1940); Alfonso Toro, *Compendio de historia de Mexico* (Mexico, 1943). José María Roa Barcena, *Recuerdos de la invasión norteamericana* (3 vols. Mexico, 1947) has the best coverage of naval events.

Many of the important reports and orders are reprinted in the annual reports of the Secretaries of State, War, and Navy for the war years, as well as in special reports to Congress, the most useful of which is House Executive Document 60, 30th Congress, 1st Session, *Mexican War Correspondence*. The George Bancroft Papers at the Massachusetts Historical Society contain few pieces dealing with the war. There is no significant collection of the papers of John Y. Mason.

Collections of statistics related to the war, lists of officers, lists of vessels, and similar reference materials are collected in House Executive Document 24, 31st Congress, 1st Session, *Military Forces Employed in the Mexican War*; Edward W. Callahan, *List of Officers of the Navy of the United States and of the Marine Corps* (New York, 1901); George Fox Emmons, *The Navy of the United States* (Washington, 1853); Francis B. Heitman, *Historical Register and Dictionary of the United States Army* (2 vols. Washington, 1903); Forrest R. Holdcamper (Ed.), *Merchant Steam Vessels of the United States* (Mystic, 1952); Robert Weldon Neeser, *A Statistical and Chronological History of the United States Navy* (2 vols. New York, 1909).

WAR IN THE GULF OF MEXICO

HSL contains all the most important reports of both Commodore Conner and Commodore Perry, along with many of the reports of their subordinates; other reports by subordinates are to be found in Conner FDR, Conner LC, and Conner NY; copies of the reports and correspondence of the commander of the *St. Mary's* are in the John L. Saunders Papers, LC. The log books are in RG–45, NA.

RCL contains most of the orders issued by the Secretary of the Navy to the Home Squadron, but a few of them are in LO. The orders issued by Conner are in CLB, and there is an incomplete set of Perry's orders in the "Letter Book of M. C. Perry, Comdg. U. S. Frigate Cumberland, May 1, 1848—November 21, 1848," RG–45, NA.

The most useful contemporary accounts of operations in the Gulf of Mexico are *Niles National Register*; William Harwar Parker, *Recollections of a Naval Officer* (New York, 1883); Raphael Semmes, *Service Afloat and Ashore During the Mexican War* (Cincinnati, 1851); and Fitch Waterman Taylor, *The Broad Pennant* (New York, 1848). Conner's illuminating letters to his wife are in Conner FDR.

Among secondary accounts, the best are in Philip Syng Physick Conner, *The Home Squadron Under Commodore Conner* (n. p., 1896); and Hubert Howe Bancroft, *History of Mexico* (6 vols. San Francisco, 1883–88). Samuel Eliot Morison, *"Old Bruin:" Commodore Matthew Calbraith Perry* (Boston, 1967), and William Elliot Griffis, *Matthew Calbraith Perry* (Boston, 1890) both devote extensive coverage to Perry's activities. Edward M. Barrows, *The Great Commodore* (Indianapolis, 1935), is so inaccurate as to be valueless.

CHAPTER I

The prewar diplomatic relations of the United States and Mexico are covered in James M. Callahan, *American Foreign Policy in Mexican Relations* (New York, 1928); Jesse S. Reeves, *American Diplomacy Under Tyler and Polk* (Baltimore, 1907); George Lockhart Rives, *The United States and Mexico* (2 vols. New York, 1913).

Conner's reports are in HSL and the orders to him in RCL. The Cabinet discussions are summarized in Milo Milton Quaife (Ed.), *The Diary of James K. Polk* (4 vols. Chicago, 1910), I, 9–34, while H. Ex. Doc. 60, 30th Cong., 1st Sess., 13–23, 144, and H. Ex. Doc. 167, 29th Cong., 1st Sess., 5, contain most of the army documents relating to Taylor's move into Texas. Brainerd Dyer, *Zachary Taylor* (Baton Rouge, 1946), 154–163, and William Seaton Henry, *Campaign Sketches of the Mexican War* (New York, 1847), 12–52, contain descriptions of the advance.

CHAPTER II

Parker, *Recollections*, 50–56; Taylor, *Broad Pennant*, 165–6; and Metcalf, *History of the Marine Corps,* 111–12, contain accounts of the landing party at Point Isabel. Monroe's request for assistance on 8 May 1846 is in Conner NY.

CHAPTER III

The instructions issued by Conner on 14 May 1846 are in HSL; those to Captain Howard, 9 Feb. 1846, in CLB; and the Secretary's to Commodore Jones, 28 Oct. 1847, in S. Doc. 1, 30th Cong., 1st Sess., 1304.

Correspondence relating to the purchase of the small steamers and gunboats is in LNA, VII, 96–8, 106, and NAL, Jan.–June 1846, #115. The vessels are described in Howard Irving Chapelle, *The History of the American Sailing Navy* (New York, 1949), 460; Frank M. Bennett, *The Steam Navy of the United States* (Pittsburgh, 1896), 92; Charles B. Stuart, *The Naval and Mail Steamers of the United States* (New York, 1853), 40; and Parker, *Recollections,* 65.

The extensive correspondence between Conner, his subordinates, and the neutral naval and diplomatic representatives is preserved in the Saunders Papers, Conner LC, and Conner NY. Conner's over-all report in HSL is dated 10 June 1846. The description of the blockade quoted herein is from Semmes, *Service Afloat and Ashore,* 76.

Bancroft's orders of 6 June 1846 to Mackenzie in RCL; Quaife, *Diary of Polk,* III, 290; and Reeves, *American Diplomacy Under Tyler and Polk,* 299–305, all relate to Mackenzie's mission.

Saunders' reports on the *St. Mary's* attack on Tampico are in Conner NY. James D. Bruell, *Sea Memories* (Biddeford Pool, Me., 1886), 34–8, has a colorful but confused account of the attack. The Mexican side is told in Anastasio Parrodi, *Memoria sobre la evacuación militar del puerto de Tampico de Tamaulipas* (San Luis Potosí, 1848).

Many letters concerning the logistic support of the squadron appear in HSL, Conner NY, Conner FDR, and LB. Morris' letter of 8 June 1846 is in Conner FDR.

Conner's report, dated 10 Aug. 1846, of the attack on Alvarado is in HSL. Other valuable accounts are in Roa Barcena, *Recuerdos,* I, 249–52; Parker, *Recollections,* 65–6; *Niles National Register,* LXXI (1846), 34, 36, 199; and Conner's letter of 4 Sept. 1846 to his wife in Conner FDR.

The peace feelers are dealt with in Buchanan's letters of 27 July and 1 Oct. 1846 to Conner in Conner NY and in Quaife, *Diary of Polk,* II, 144–5.

CHAPTER IV

Conner's reports of 12 and 24 Aug. 1846 on the loss of the *Truxtun* are in HSL along with their enclosures; Engle's to Conner, 22 Aug. 1846, in Conner NY; and Mason's letter to the President, 27 Oct. 1846, in ELB, V, 309–10.

Saunders' letter of 15 Aug. 1846 to Conner in Conner NY and the latter's order of 14 Sept. to Saunders deal with the execution of Seaman Jackson, and John M. Ellicott, *Life of John Ancrum Winslow* (New York, 1905), 38–9, comments on it.

Morris' comments of 14 November 1846 about the appointment of Perry are in Conner NY. Philip S. P. Conner, "Griffis's Commodore Perry," *Magazine of American History,* XIV (July 1885), 96–7, attacks Perry's biographer for suggesting that the command of the squadron was split between Commodores Conner and Perry.

The basic report on the second attack on Alvarado is Conner's of 17 Oct. 1846 in HSL. Enrique Hurtado y Nuño, "Ataque y defensa del puerto de Alvarado," *Rivista general de la armada de Mexico,* III (Aug. 1963), 11–18; Parker, *Recollections,* 71–2; Roa Barcena *Recuerdos,* I, 252–3; and Semmes, *Service Afloat and Ashore,* 88–9, are useful descriptions.

CHAPTER V

Conner's letter of 5 Nov. 1846 to Mason in HSL encloses Perry's undated report of the Tabasco expedition, from which the unattributed quotations are drawn. "List of Vessels Captured and destroyed . . . Tabasco," is in Conner NY.

The Tampico reports from Conner, 5 Nov.–1 Dec. 1846, are in HSL; his letter of 17 Nov. 1846 to his wife is in Conner FDR; and those of Mrs. Chase and Lt. Hunt are in Conner LC.

Pearson's report to Conner on the loss of the *Boston*, 21 Nov. 1846, is in AF (A–8), Box 173; his report to the Secretary of the Navy is reprinted in *Niles National Register*, LXXI (1846–7), 256.

The burning of the *Criolla* is covered in Parker's report to Semmes, 28 Nov. 1846, in Conner NY; Semmes, *Service Afloat and Ashore*, 91; and Colyer Meriwether, *Raphael Semmes* (Philadelphia, 1914), 35–8. Semmes's reports on the loss of the brig are in Conner FDR and HSL; and his account of the incident is in *Service Afloat and Ashore*, 91–2. S. Doc. 43, 29th Cong., 2nd Sess. reprints the documents which led Congress to authorize, on 3 March 1847, gold and silver medals for the foreign seamen involved in the rescues.

CHAPTER VI

Scott's various plans, orders, and correspondence are in H. Ex. Docs. 56, 59, and 60, 30th Cong., 1st Sess.; and his account of the preparations in *Memoirs of Lieut-General Scott* (2 vols. New York, 1864), II, 399–402.

Erna Risch, *Quartermaster Support of the Army* (Washington, 1962), 287–8, and William G. Temple, "Memoir of the Landing of the United States Troops at Vera Cruz in 1847," in Conner, *Home Squadron*, 60–65, describe the surfboats and their construction. The largest size of surfboat is diagramed in Plan No. 107–13–17 in Dash Plan Series, RG–19, NA. Extensive correspondence concerning the acquisition and outfitting of the bomb brigs is in RCL, I, 259–61; ELB, V, 347; NAL, 1847, #17, 32, 37, 43; LNA, VII, 157; and Morris to Conner, 4 March 1847, in Conner NY.

The fortifications of Veracruz are described in detail in Bancroft, *Mexico*, V, 440–1, and in *Memoria del Ministerio de Estado y del Despacho de Guerra y Marina . . . 1846* (Mexico, 1846), carta 11. Scott's report of 29 March 1847 to Marcy is in Huntington Miscellaneous Collection, Henry E. Huntington Library and Art Gallery, #1958, inventories the guns found in the defenses after the surrender of Veracruz.

S. Doc. 94, 29th Cong., 2nd Sess. contains many of the documents related to the return of the *Mississippi*.

The Army's movements are detailed in H. Ex. Doc. 60, 30th Cong., 1st Sess., 845–900; Risch, *Quartermaster Support*, 284–90; Smith, *War with Mexico*, I, 365–8; H. Judge Moore, *Scott's Campaign in Mexico* (Charleston, 1849), 1. Commander Saunders' reports are in Conner NY and his correspondence with Army officers in the Saunders Papers; Conner's letter of 11 Jan. 1847 to Scott and those to his subordinates are in CLB.

CHAPTER VII

A great deal of Scott's correspondence is reprinted in H. Ex. Doc. 60, 30th Cong., 1st Sess., and his significant General Orders in Temple, "Memoir of a Landing." His letters to Conner are in Conner NY and the replies from the naval commander in CLB.

There are many "I was there" accounts by members of Scott's army, the most valuable being: Scott, *Memoirs*; George Ballantine, *Autobiography of an English Soldier in the United States Army* (New York, 1853); Emma Jerome Blackwood, *To Mexico with Scott* (Cambridge, 1917); J. Jacob Oswandel, *Notes on the Mexican War* (Philadelphia, 1885); Maria Clinton Collins, "Journal of Francis Collins," *Quarterly Publication of the Historical and Philosophical Society of Ohio*, X (1915); An Eyewitness, "The Capture of Vera Cruz," *The Knickerbocker*, XXX (July 1847); Ethan Allen Hitchcock, *Fifty Years in Camp and Field* (New York, 1909); J. B. Robertson, *Reminiscences of a Campaign in Mexico* (Nashville, 1849). The best for the naval aspects of the landing are Semmes, *Service Afloat and Ashore*, 125–6, and Parker, *Recollections*, 83–5.

The most useful secondary accounts are Temple, "Memoir of a Landing;" W. S. Lott, "The Landing of the Expedition Against Vera Cruz in 1847," *Military Service Institution of the United States*, XXIV (May 1899); K. Jack Bauer, "The Veracruz Expedition of 1847," *Military Affairs*, XX (Fall 1956). Charles Winslow Elliott, *Winfield Scott, the Soldier and the Man* (New York, 1937) is the only modern biography of the Commanding General.

CHAPTER VIII

Scott's reports on the siege are in S. Ex. Doc. 1, 30th Cong., 1st Sess., 217–28, 241–4. Other useful accounts are in Conner, *Home Squadron*, 20, 47; Parker *Recollections*, 85–97; Risch, *Quartermaster Support*, 290–1; George C. Furber, *Twelve Months Volunteer* (Cincinnati, 1851), 505–17; *Niles National Register*, LXXII (1847), 142; Semmes, *Service Afloat and Ashore*, 129–40; Douglas Southall Freeman, *R. E. Lee* (4 vols. New York, 1945), I, 229; William Starr Myers (Ed.), *Mexican War Diary of George B. McClellan* (Princeton, 1917), 68. Scott's message to his staff about "a long butcher's bill" is taken from Marcus Joseph Wright, *General Scott* (New York, 1847), 164–5. The exchange between Scott and Mayo is in Griffis, *Perry*, 235–6.

Upshur's comments on Perry taking command are in Griffis, *Perry*, 222–3, and Mason's offer to appoint Conner Chief of the Bureau of Construction, Equipment, and Repair is in Conner FDR. In a postscript dated 5 March and appended to his letter of 2 March 1846 to his wife, Conner FDR, Conner states he has already requested relief, but that request has apparently not survived.

The effect the opening of the bombardment had upon the crews of the warships is described by An Eyewitness in "The Capture of Vera Cruz," 3. Descriptions of the naval bombardment are in Semmes, *Service Afloat and Ashore*, 130–1; Charles Colcook Jones, Jr., *The Life and Services of Commodore Josiah Tattnall* (Savannah, 1878), 55–60; Richard S. West, Jr., *The Second Admiral: A Life of David Dixon Porter* (New York, 1937), 46–7; James Russell Soley, *Admiral Porter* (New York, 1903), 67–9. Tradition holds that Tattnall refused to recognize Perry's signal for him to abandon his attack and returned only after the latter sent Captain Mayo in an open boat with a peremptory order.

Scott's correspondence with Landero and his reports of the surrender are in S. Ex. Doc. 1, 30th Cong., 1st Sess., 234–41; a copy of the Articles of Capitulation is in HSL. Semmes, *Service Afloat and Ashore*, 141–5, and the logs of the small craft provide the best descriptions of the surrender.

CHAPTER IX

Perry's plan is in HSL.

Perry's report of 4 April 1847 on the seizure of Alvarado is in HSL; Quitman's report is in H. Ex. Doc. 56, 30th Cong., 1st Sess., 917–18, and John Francis Hamtramck Claiborne (Ed.), *Life and Correspondence of John A. Quitman* (2 vols. New York, 1860), II, 295, also contains information on the operation. *Niles National Register*, LXXII

(1847), 131–2, reprints the "Charges and Specifications Against Lieutenant Charles G. Hunter by M. C. Perry." Casper F. Goodrich, "Alvarado Hunter," *USNIP*, XLIV (March 1918) is a good account of Hunter's tempestuous career.

Perry's reports of 8 and 24 April 1847, along with their numerous enclosures, covering the attack on Tuxpan are in HSL. The detachments that made up the landing party were: *Ohio*, 16 officers, 320 men; *Mississippi*, 19 officers, 190 men, 2 guns; *Raritan*, 7 officers, 190 men; *Potomac*, 7 officers, 175 men; *Germantown*, 15 officers, 136 men; *Decatur*, 14 officers, 118 men; *John Adams*, 10 officers, 111 men; *Albany*, 7 officers, 109 men; *Hecla*, 3 officers, 22 men, 1 gun; *Vesuvius*, 3 officers, 22 men, 1 gun; *Etna*, 3 officers, 22 men.

The reports on operations east of Veracruz are in HSL but other details appear in Benjamin Franklin Sands, *From Reefer to Rear Admiral* (New York, 1899), 182, and Arthur Winslow, *Francis Winslow* (Norwood, Mass., 1935), 167–8. The question of Perry's Marines is covered in Quaife, *Diary of Polk*, III, 23–4; Mason to the President, 13, 22 May 1847, in ELB, V, 376, 381; and Perry to Mason, 29 May, 1 July 1847, in HSL.

CHAPTER X

Perry's reports on the operation at Tabasco, along with their enclosures, are in HSL. Among the most valuable personal accounts are An Officer of the Navy, "Capture of Tabasco," *The Rough and Ready Annual* (Philadelphia, 1848); Parker, *Recollections*, 108–11; Charles Lee Lewis, *Admiral Franklin Buchanan* (Baltimore, 1929), 119–20; Winslow, *Francis Winslow*, 171–3; David Dixon Porter, "Journal of David D. Porter," D. D. Porter Papers, LC. Good secondary accounts are Morison, *"Old Bruin,"* 230–3; Metcalf, *History of the Marine Corps*, 123–6; Aldrich, *History of the Marine Corps*, 100–2. The landing party consisted of the following detachments: *Mississippi*, 26 officers, 233 men; *Albany*, 9 officers, 135 men; *Raritan*, 9 officers, 233 men; *John Adams*, 8 officers, 133 men; *Germantown*, 10 officers, 120 men; *Decatur*, 8 officers, 104 men; *Washington*, 6 officers, 30 men; *Vesuvius*, 3 officers, 28 men; *Etna*, 4 officers, 26 men; *Stromboli*, 4 officers, 22 men; *Potomac*, 2 officers, 20 men.

CHAPTER XI

The orders setting up the watch for privateers in the Mediterranean are those to Commodore George C. Read, 7 April 1847, Commander Engle, 20 July 1847, and Lieutenant Charles G. Hunter, 24 Aug. 1847, in RCL; Secretary Buchanan's to Consul T. N. Carr, 28 May, 26 June 1847, are in John Bassett Moore (Ed.), *Works of James Buchanan* (12 vols. Philadelphia, 1908–11), III, 53–4; S. Ex. Doc. 1, 30th Cong., 1st Sess., 945–6; Quaife, *Diary of Polk*, III, 53–4. The anti-piracy act of March 1847 is in *U. S. Statutes at Large*, IX, 175.

Lucius W. Johnson, "Yellow Jack, Master of Strategy," *USNIP*, LXXVI (July 1950) is an excellent discussion of the impact of the disease on the operations of Perry's squadron and on other campaigns.

Material on Yucatán is in Eugene Irving McCormac, *James K. Polk* (Berkeley, 1922), 697; Quaife, *Diary of Polk*, III, 314; Perry's reports of 15, 29 Feb., 8, 13, March, and 2 April 1848, in HSL; Morison, *"Old Bruin,"* 242–9. The story of the Indian war in Yucatán is well told in Nelson Reed, *The Caste War of Yucatan* (Stanford, 1964).

Colonel Henry Wilson's report of 15 Aug. 1847 on the Paredes incident is in H. Ex. Doc. 60, 30th Cong., 1st Sess., 701; Perry's report of 18 Aug. to Mason and his General Order 11 are in HSL; Farragut's letter of 25 Jan. 1848 to Mason is in Lloyd Farragut, *The Life of David Glasgow Farragut* (New York, 1879), 163. Recent treatments of the episode are in Charles Lee Lewis, *David Glasgow Farragut: Admiral in the Making* (Annapolis, 1941), 247-8, and Morison, *"Old Bruin,"* 240.

Perry's reports on the concluding operations are in HSL, except for that of 7 July 1848, which is in AF (A-8), Box 174. His orders to his subordinates are in Perry's Letter Book.

WAR IN THE PACIFIC

PSL contains the most important reports of Commodores Sloat, Stockton, Biddle, and Jones, along with many of those made by their subordinates. Commodore Shubrick's reports are missing from PSL, but copies of many have been preserved in AF.

Most of the orders issued by the Secretary of the Navy are in RCL. A few, mainly routine ones, are in LO. The Sloat Documents at the California Historical Society include most of the orders and reports received by him. The two groups of Larkin documents, Papers of Thomas O. Larkin and Official Correspondence of Thomas O. Larkin, at BLUC, which are even more useful, have been edited by George P. Hammond and published as *The Larkin Papers* (9 vols. Berkeley, 1951–63).

BLUC contains the indispensable documents and eyewitness accounts collected by Hubert Howe Bancroft, which include Juan B. Alvarado's five-volume "Historia de California." Among the Bancroft documents, the collections of Antonio F. Coronel, Augustín Olvera, and Thomas Savage are of particular value to this study.

Many of the journals and letterbooks of officers serving in the Pacific have survived, the most valuable being: Robert Carson Duvall, "Cruise of the U. S. Frigate Savannah," photostat copy in Los Angeles Public Library; Alonzo C. Jackson, "Journal of a Cruise in the U. S. Frigate Savannah," LC; "Log of U. S. S. Cyane, Wm. Mervine Comdg.," RG–45, NA, which is more properly described as "Mervine's Journal"; "Letterbook, Captain John B. Montgomery," RG–45, NA; "Journal of Lt. [T. A. M.] Craven, . . . 1846 . . . to 1848," RG–45, NA, which has been edited by Charles Belknap and reprinted in *USNIP*, XIV (March–June 1888), and by John Haskell Kemble as "Amphibious Operations in the Gulf of California, 1847–1848," *American Neptune*, V (April 1945). Most of the log books have been preserved in RG–45, NA. More useful material is to be found in the H. H. Bancroft Collection, BLUC, and in the Facsimile Collection and Fort Sutter Papers, Henry E. Huntington Library and Art Gallery. A collection of Archibald H. Gillespie Papers is held by the Library of the University of California at Los Angeles, and a group of Stockton Papers by the Firestone Library, Princeton University. No collections of Shubrick, Biddle, or Jones papers are known to have survived.

Printed accounts by participants are numerous and of varying quality. The most useful are: George Walcott Ames, Jr., (Ed.), "Gillespie and the Conquest of California," *CHSQ*, XVII (June–December 1938), reprints of Gillespie's reports from California; Edwin Bryant, *What I Saw in California* (New York, 1848); Walter Colton, *Deck and Port* (New York, 1850) and *Three Years in California* (Cincinnati, 1851); Joseph T. Downey, *The Cruise of the Portsmouth* (New Haven, 1958).

The conquest of California is covered in many books with widely divergent points of view. Among the best are: Hubert Howe Bancroft, *History of California* (7 vols. San Francisco, 1884–90); Bernard DeVoto, *The Year of Decision, 1846* (Boston, 1943); John Adam Hussey, "California's Day-Book," *CHSQ*, XXV (June 1946), 121-31; Robert Erwin Johnson's history of the Pacific Squadron, *Thence Round Cape Horn* (Annapolis, 1963); Irving Berdine Richman, *California Under Spain and Mexico*

(Boston, 1911); Josiah Royce, *California* (New York, 1948). Although Edwin A. Sherman, *The Life of the Late Rear Admiral John Drake Sloat* (Oakland, 1902) and *A Sketch of the Life of Com. Robert F. Stockton* (New York, 1856) are outstanding examples of uncritical, laudatory biographical works, they are useful. More balanced biographies are Allan Nevins, *Frémont, Pathmaker of the West* (New York, 1955) and Werner H. Marti, *Messenger of Destiny* (San Francisco, 1960), a biography of Archibald H. Gillespie. Many of the important documents pertaining to the war in the Pacific are reprinted in A Captain of Volunteers, *Alta California* (Philadelphia, 1847) and J. Madison Cutts, *The Conquest of California and New Mexico* (Philadelphia, 1847).

CHAPTER XII

Jones's reports on the premature seizure of Monterey are in PSL and the most significant ones are reprinted in H. Doc. 166, 27th Cong., 2d Sess., and Charles Roberts Anderson (Ed.), *Journal of a Cruise in the Pacific Ocean, 1842–1844, in the Frigate United States with Notes on Herman Melville* (Durham, 1937). A good recent study is G. M. Brooke, Jr., "The Vest Pocket War of Commodore Jones," *Pacific Historical Review*, XXXI (Aug. 1962), 217–33. Royce's comment is from *California*, 40.

Material on Gillespie's mission was gathered from a number of sources: Quaife, *Diary of Polk*, I, 83–4; Larkin's letter of appointment, 17 Oct. 1845, and Gillespie's letter of 17 April 1846 to Larkin, in Larkin *Docs.*, III, 357, IV, 91; Gillespie's reports of 11 and 18 Feb. 1846 to the Secretary of the Navy in AF (A–9), Box 250, and Ames, "Gillespie and California," 130; Frémont's deposition, S. Rpt. 75, 30th Cong., 1st Sess., 12. Bancroft to W. B. Scott, 31 Nov. 1845, LNA, VII, 60; and Gillespie to Bancroft, 10 Nov. 1845, and Bancroft to Gillespie, 12 Nov. 1845, Bancroft Papers, deal with the mechanics of the trip. Other significant accounts include Raynor Wickersham Kelsey, "United States Consulate in California," *Publications of the Academy of Pacific Coast History*, I, No. 5, 218–9; John Adam Hussey, "Commander John B. Montgomery and the Bear Flag Revolt," *USNIP*, LXXV (July 1939), 974; Samuel Francis Du Pont, "The War with Mexico; the Cruise of the U. S. S. Cyane during the Years 1845–48," *USNIP*, VIII (Sept. 1882), 419. Larkin's activities are covered best in Reuben L. Underhill, *From Cowhides to Golden Fleece* (Palo Alto, 1940).

The events leading to Frémont's expulsion are discussed from differing viewpoints in: John C. Frémont, *Memoirs of My Life* (2 vols. Chicago, 1887), I, 439–91, *passim.*; Josiah Royce, "Notes of an Interview with General Frémont," BLUC; Bancroft, *History of California*, V, 3–28; Nevins, *Frémont*, 199–205. Larkin *Off. Corres.* contains extensive correspondence concerning the incident.

Similar discussions of the meeting between Frémont and Gillespie are in Royce, "Notes of an interview"; John C. Frémont, "The Conquest of California," *Century Magazine*, XLI (April 1891), 920–4; Frémont, *Memoirs*, I, 488–90; Nevins, *Frémont*, 239–50; Roa Barcena, *Recuerdos*, I, 240; Royce, *California*, 91–118; Gillespie's report of 25 July 1846 to the Secretary of the Navy in PSL; George Tays, "Frémont Had No Secret Instructions," *Pacific Historical Review*, IX (May 1940), 153–71; William N. Chambers, *Old Bullion Benton* (Boston, 1956), 265, 306, 310. Larkin's letter of 23 April 1846 to Gillespie, from which the quotation is taken, is in Larkin *Off. Corres.*, I, 95.

Sloat's reports in PSL cover his actions at Mazatlán, while William Maxwell Wood, *Wandering Sketches* (Philadelphia, 1849), 362–9, describes the dispatching of the messenger from Guadalajara. Sloat's letter of 18 May 1846 to Larkin is in Larkin

Docs., IV, 122–3, and his "upon my own responsibility" is taken from his letters to Bancroft, 31 July 1846, in PSL, and to Wood, 20 May 1855, in Sherman, *Sloat*, 65–6.

Frémont's Bear Flag activities are covered in his *Memoirs*, I, 525–6; Gillespie's report of 25 July 1846 to the Secretary of the Navy in PSL; Montgomery's letter of 3 June 1846 to Frémont in MLB, and those of 18 and 24 June 1846 to Castro in Sloat Documents; Gillespie's deposition in S. Rpt. 75, 30th Cong., 1st Sess., 27; Bancroft, *History of California*, V, 287–8; Josiah Royce, "Montgomery and Frémont," *Century Magazine*, XLI (March 1891), 780–3.

Quaife, *Diary of Polk*, III, 439, 443; Marcy to Kearny, 3 June 1846, in H. Ex. Doc. 17, 31st Cong., 1st Sess., 153–5; Scott to Capt. C. Q. Tompkins, 20 June 1846, in H. Ex. Doc. 60, 30th Cong., 1st Sess., 245–6, deal with the dispatch of land forces to California.

CHAPTER XIII

Sloat's report of 31 July 1846 in PSL, along with the logs of the vessels involved, form the basis for the account of the seizure of Monterey. Other useful accounts are Aubrey Neasham, "The Raising of the Flag at Monterey, California, July 7, 1846," *CHSQ*, XXV (June 1946), 193–203; Bancroft, *History of California*, V, 224–35; Sherman, *Sloat*, 71–8; Colton, *Three Years in California*, 63; George Walcott Ames, "Horse Marines: California, 1846," *CHSQ*, XVIII (March 1939), 72–84; "Mervine's Journal." The Sloat-Larkin correspondence is in Larkin *Docs.*, IV, 193–4; Montgomery's letter of 2 July to Mervine in MLB. Silva's reply is in PSL, as are copies of Sloat's General Order and Proclamation.

Montgomery's reports to Sloat on the seizure of San Francisco, as well as his instructions to his subordinates and a copy of his address and his proclamation, are in PSL. Other valuable accounts of the seizure are in Bancroft, *History of California*, V, 238–40; Downey, *Cruise of the Portsmouth*, 130–6; Fred Blackburn Rogers (Ed.), *Filings From An Old Saw* (San Francisco, 1956), 35–40; Joseph Warren Revere, *A Tour of Duty in California* (New York, 1849), 52. The reality of the British threat is demolished by Ephraim Douglas Adams, "English Interest in the Acquisition of California," *American Historical Review*, XIV (July 1909), 744–63.

The best accounts of the Sloat-Frémont-Stockton discussions are in *Sketch of Stockton*, 101, 110–2; Bancroft, *History of California*, V, 247–53; Frémont, *Memoirs*, I, 530–5, 543; Frémont, "Conquest of California," 935–8; William Baldridge, "The Days of 1846," BLUC; Gillespie to Secretary of the Navy, 25 July 1846, in PSL; Stockton's testimony in S. Ex. Doc. 33, 30th Cong., 1st Sess., 178–80; Nevins, *Frémont*, 288–9. Colton's quotation is from *Deck and Port*, 390–1.

Many of the claims against the California Battalion are reprinted in S. Rpt. 75, 30th Cong., 1st Sess.

CHAPTER XIV

Stockton's reports and the supporting correspondence in PSL are the primary sources for the campaign in the south. Valuable contemporary accounts are in Larkin's report to Bancroft, [29] July 1846, and one dated 23 Aug. 1846 to Buchanan, in Larkin *Off. Corres.*, II, 55, 58; Mervine's letter of 13 Aug. 1846 to Montgomery, AF (A–9), Box 250; "Mervine's Journal"; Frémont, *Memoirs*, I, 563–6; Du Pont's reports, 29 and 31 July 1846, to Stockton in *Official Despatches and Letters of Rear Admiral Du Pont* (Wilmington, 1883), 2–3, 5–6; Du Pont, "Cruise of the *Cyane*," 420. Important secondary accounts appear in *Sketch of Stockton*, 116–22; Bancroft, *History of Cali-*

fornia, V, 257–9, 267, 272–3; Duncan Gleason, "The Lost Islands of San Pedro," *Sea*, XV (May 1951), 18–9; James M. Guinn, "Siege and Capture of Los Angeles," *HSSCP*, III (1893), 47–8; James M. Guinn, *A History of California and an Extended History of Los Angeles* (3 vols. Los Angeles, 1915), I, 124; Corrine King Wright, "The Conquest of Los Angeles," *HSSCP*, XI, (1918), 18–21; Sophie Radford de Meissner, *Old Naval Days* (New York, 1920), 130.

Contemporary copies of Stockton's proclamation (carrying various dates between 27 and 31 July) are in AF (A–9), Box 250, PSL, and Clements R. Markham, "Annexation of California," BLUC. Copies of the later proclamations and correspondence establishing civil government are in PSL.

Hull's and Du Pont's reports on their operations in the Gulf of California are in PSL. Du Pont's reply to Miranda is in AF (A–9), Box 251.

Gillespie's account of the Los Angeles revolt is in his report of 16 Feb. 1847 to Bancroft, in Ames, "Gillespie," 283, from which the quotation is drawn. Other useful accounts are Bancroft, *History of California*, V, 308–17; Arthur Woodward, "Juan Flaco's Ride," *HSSCP*, XIX (Jan. 1937), 22–39; José del Carmen Lugo, "Life of a Rancher," *HSSCP*, XXXII (Sept. 1950), 199–200; Guinn, *History of California and Los Angeles*, I, 127.

CHAPTER XV

The chief accounts of Mervine's defeat are his reports to Stockton, 9 and 25 Oct. 1846, and Stockton's report of 23 Nov. 1846 to Bancroft, in PSL; "Adjutant's Report of Marine and Small Arms-men of the U. S. Ship Savannah and Captain Gillespie's Riflemen on Shore in California, October 7th and 8th 1846," in AF (A–9), Box 251; "Mervine's Journal;" Helen Hunt Jackson, "Echoes in the City of the Angels," *Century Magazine*, XXVII (Dec. 1883), 208; Flores's letter to Varela, 26 Oct. 1846, in "Olvera Documentos," BLUC. Stockton's letter of 1 Oct. 1846 to Larkin, Larkin *Docs.*, IV, 300, gives his first plan.

Stockton's reports concerning the preparations to retake Los Angeles and his orders to his subordinates are in PSL and AF (A–9), Box 251. Other contemporary material appears in *Sketch of Stockton*, 129–34; Bryant, *What I Saw in California*, 332–3; Frémont, *Memoirs*, I, 374; Colton, *Three Years in California*, 73–98; Alvarado, "Historia de California," V, 268; Enoch Greenleafe Parrott's letter of 11 Feb. 1847, BLUC.

Du Pont's report on his operations in the Gulf of California (with numerous enclosures) is in PSL. It is supplemented by his "Cruise of the *Cyane*;" Stephen Clegg Rowan, "Recollections of the Mexican War," *USNIP*, XIV (Sept. 1888), 543; Meissner, *Old Naval Days*, 128.

The material on Kearny's march and the Battle of San Pasqual is voluminous. Aside from Kearny's reports in S. Ex. Doc. 1, 30th Cong., 1st Sess., 514–6, the best is William H. Emory, *Notes of a Military Reconnaissance* (Washington, 1848), 32–113. A shortened version, edited by Ross Calvin, is *Lieutenant Emory Reports* (Albuquerque, 1951). The journal of Kearny's surgeon, Dr. John S. Griffin, is reprinted in George Walcott Ames, "A Doctor Comes to California," *CHSQ*, XXI (Sept.–Dec. 1942). Two significant recent studies are Dwight L. Clarke, *Stephen Watts Kearny* (Norman, 1961) and Arthur Woodward, "Lances at San Pascual," *CHSQ*, XXV (Dec. 1946)–XXVI (March 1947).

CHAPTER XVI

Basic sources for any study of the Third Los Angeles campaign are Stockton's reports with their enclosures in PSL; Kearny's report, 14 Jan. 1847, in S. Ex. Doc. 33,

30th Cong., 1st Sess., 6–7; Emory, *Notes of a Military Reconnaissance*, 115–21; *Sketch of Stockton*, 142–8; Clarke, *Kearny*, 233–56; Bancroft, *History of California*, V, 288–404, *passim*. Among the best accounts by less prominent participants are Downey, *Cruise of the Portsmouth*, 181–213, and Joseph Warren Revere, *Keel and Saddle* (Boston, 1872), 146–7.

Frémont, *Memoirs*, I, 568–601, describes his movement southward. There is a copy of the Treaty of Cahuenga in PSL.

Oscar Osburn Winther, *The Story of San José* (San Francisco, 1935), 25–6; Bancroft, *History of California*, V, 377–8; Ernest A. Wiltsee, "The British Vice Consul and the Events of 1846," *CHSQ*, X (June 1931), 125–6; Metcalf, *History of the U. S. Marine Corps*, 150–1; and Aldrich, *History of the U. S. Marine Corps*, 95–6 describe Sanchez' revolt.

Material relating to the settlement of the dispute over control of the government of California is in PSL, S. Ex. Doc. 33, 30th Cong., 1st Sess., and H. Ex. Doc. 17, 31st Cong., 1st Sess. Frémont's court-martial proceedings are reprinted in S. Ex. Doc. 33, 30th Cong., 1st Sess. Theodore Grivas, *Military Governments in California* (Glendale, 1963), 58–75, and Thomas Kearny, "The Mexican War and the Conquest of California," *CHSQ*, VIII (Sept. 1929), 251–61, discuss in detail the dispute between Stockton and Kearny, and both side with the General.

CHAPTER XVII

Hammond, *Larkin Papers*, V–VI, contain extensive correspondence about the supply difficulties. Colton's quotations are from *Three Years in California*, 160, 183. James Brown Scott (Ed.), *Prize Cases Decided in the United States Supreme Court* (2 vols. Oxford, 1923), II, 1393, deals with the admiralty court set up in California.

Materials relating to Montgomery's operations in the Gulf of California are in AF (A–9), Box 251, and MLB. The extensive litigation that resulted from the seizure of the *Admittance* is contained in S. Ex. Doc. 72, 30th Cong., 1st Sess.

Shubrick's and Selfridge's reports on the naval side of the occupation of Baja California and Pineda's reply are in AF (A–9), Boxes 251–2; Kearny's orders of 30 May 1847 to Burton are in H. Ex. Doc. 17, 31st Cong., 1st Sess., 310.

The operations of the New York Volunteers are covered in Francis D. Clark, *The First Regiment of New York Volunteers* (New York, 1882).

The description of the false alarm at Mazatlán caused by the *Cyane* and the *Independence* is from Henry A. Wise, *Los Gringos* (New York, 1849), 85–6.

Operations at Guaymas are described in La Vallette's report of 28 Oct. 1847 to Shubrick in H. Ex. Doc. 1, 30th Cong., 2nd Sess., 107–08; those of La Vallette, Selfridge, W. T. Smith, Stanly, and Yard in AF (A–9), Box 252; and Commodore Jones's report of 11 July 1848 is in PSL.

CHAPTER XVIII

There is a scarcity of material bearing on Shubrick's operations. Because his reports are missing from PSL, his activities have to be reconstructed from the few duplicates in AF (A–9), Boxes 251–2, and from contemporary printed copies.

The description of San José del Cabo is from Wise, *Los Gringos*, 140. Peter Gerhard, "Baja California in the Mexican War," *Pacific Historical Review*, XIV (Nov. 1945), 418–24, is basic to any understanding of the operations there. The uprising in Baja California is also treated in Henry W. Halleck, "Memorandum . . . Concerning His Expedition in Lower California," BLUC; Shubrick's, Burton's, Du Pont's, and Heywood's reports in AF (A–9), Box 252, H. Ex. Doc. 1, 30th Cong., 2nd Sess., and H. Ex. Doc. 17, 31st Cong., 1st Sess.; Clark, *New York Volunteers*; and Henry A. Du Pont, *Rear Admiral Samuel Francis Du Pont* (New York, 1926), 48–55.

Aside from the reports of Shubrick and his subordinates, the best accounts of the occupation of Mazatlán are in Susan F. Cooper, "Rear Admiral William Branford Shubrick," *Harpers New Monthly Magazine*, LIII (Aug. 1878), 404; Francis Javier Gaxiola, *La invasión norte-americana en Sinaloa* (Mexico, 1891), 168–88.

The evacuation of the posts in Mexico is covered in Jones's reports in PSL and Gaxiola, *La invasión norte-americana*, 215–7. The description of Jones is from P. Taft, "Reminiscences of the Last Cruise of the Ohio," *Nautical Gazette*, XX (6 Nov. 1884).

CHAPTER XIX

The quotations are drawn from the following sources: Alfred Thayer Mahan, *The Influence of Sea Power Upon History* (Boston, 1890), 138; Matthew Forney Steele, *American Campaigns* (2 vols. Washington, 1943), I, 120; Barrows, *Great Commodore*, 196; Knox, *History of the U. S. Navy*, 179; and Jackson, "Journal of a Cruise in the U. S. Frigate Savannah."

INDEX

Those American officers whose branch of service is not indicated were naval officers.

Edited by Mary Veronica Amoss.
Designed by Gerard A. Valerio.

Composed, printed, and bound by Kingsport Press.

Composed in eleven-point Linotype Janson, with two points of leading.

Printed offset on 60 Pericles Opaque Text

Bound in Columbia Fictionette.

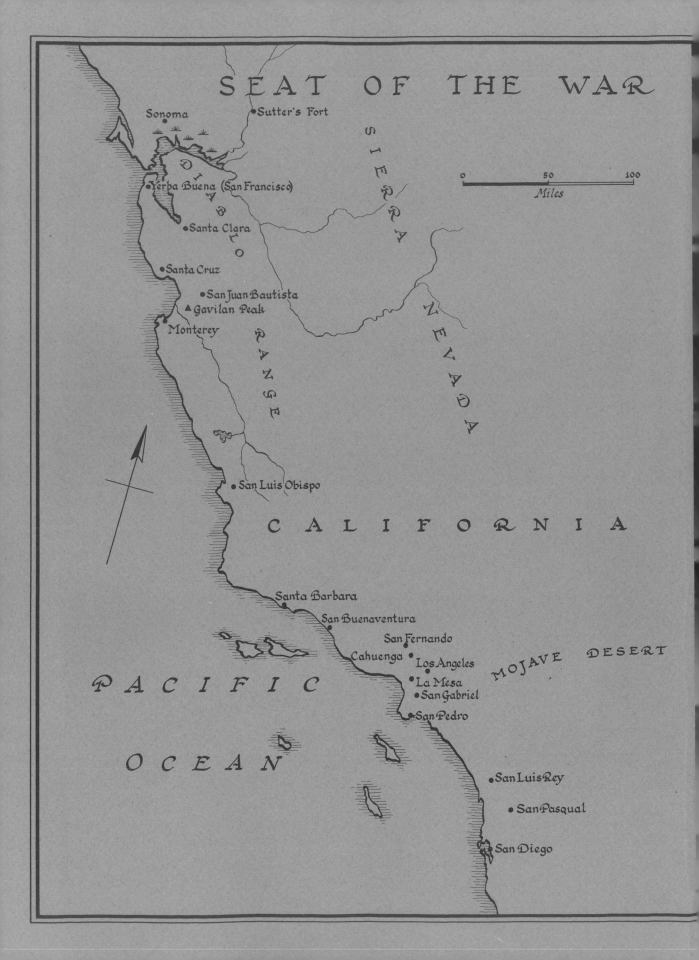